CHICKEN SOUP
FOR THE SOUL®
CHILDREN WITH
SPECIAL NEEDS

Chicken Soup for the Soul Children with Special Needs
Stories of Love and Understanding for Those Who Care for Children with Disabilities
Jack Canfield, Mark Victor Hansen, Heather McNamara, Karen Simmons

Published by Backlist, LLC,
a unit of Chicken Soup for the Soul Publishing, LLC. www.chickensoup.com

Front cover photo ©Wolfgang Weinhäupl, topimages.com
Front cover design by Lawna Patterson Oldfield
Originally published in 2007 by Health Communications, Inc.

Back cover and spine redesign by Pneuma Books, LLC

Distributed to the booktrade by Simon & Schuster. SAN: 200-2442

Publisher's Cataloging-in-Publication Data
(Prepared by The Donohue Group)

Chicken soup for the soul : children with special needs : stories of love and
   understanding for those who care for children with disabilities / [compiled
   by] Jack Canfield ... [et al.].

   p. : ill. ; cm.

   Originally published: Deerfield Beach, FL : Health Communications, c2007.
   ISBN: 978-1-62361-061-6

   1. Children with disabilities--Anecdotes. 2. Anecdotes. I. Canfield, Jack,
1944- II. Title: Children with special needs

HV888 .C475 2012
362.4083   2012944409

PRINTED IN THE UNITED STATES OF AMERICA
on acid free paper

21 20 19 18 17 16 15 14 13 12   01 02 03 04 05 06 07 08 09 10

CHICKEN SOUP FOR THE SOUL® CHILDREN WITH SPECIAL NEEDS

Stories of Love and Understanding for Those Who Care for Children with Disabilities

Jack Canfield
Mark Victor Hansen
Heather McNamara
Karen Simmons

Backlist, LLC, a unit of
Chicken Soup for the Soul Publishing, LLC
Cos Cob, CT
www.chickensoup.com

Contents

Introduction xiii

See Me *Melissa Riggio as told to Rachel Buchholz* xvi

1. ADJUSTING

Welcome to Holland *Emily Perl Kingsley* 2

In the Game *Reverend Johnny Wray*
    as told to Stephanie Welcher Thompson 5

A Message from John *Jo Clancy* 10

The Miracle of Jay-Jay *Louise Tucker Jones* 14

Out of the Mouths of Babes *Sarah and MMC John S. Smigal* 18

Tomorrow *Jill Presson* 19

No Words *Stacey Flood* 23

Seeing Through Josh's Eyes *Deborah Rose* 26

The Voice of Reason Wears SpongeBob Underpants
    Shari Youngblood 28

One Mother to Another *Donna Turenne* 33

Reaching Back *Pam Wilson* 35

A Reason to Celebrate *Janet Lynn Mitchell* 38

My Finest Teachers *Gina Johnson* 42

Out of the Mouths of Babes *Cheryl Kremer* 45

The Vacation *Michelle M. Guppy* 46

What They Forgot to Mention *Sandy Sotzen* 51

2. GRATITUDE

Is That All? *PeggySue Wells* 54

The Little Boy Who Waves *Michelle M. Guppy* 57

All She Has *Connie Ellison* 60

One Brief Hour *Suzanne Woods Fisher* 63

The Gift *Jeffrey J. Cain, M.D.* 67

I Won't Do It *Nanette Whitman-Holmes* 70

Out of the Mouths of Babes *Jimmy Hinkley* 73

McBuns! *Trisha Kay Kayden* 75

Challenges *Mary Mooney* 78

What's the Truth About Thomas?
   Laura Dean as told to Jeanne Pallos 81

Kids Amaze Me *Chynna Laird* 85

A Whale of a Time *Michelle Ward* 89

Talking to Strangers *Jennifer Lawler* 92

On the Inside *Susan Farr-Fahncke* 95

Broken-Down Signs *Scott Newport* 99

Broken Shells *Debbie Jaskot* 104

3. MILESTONES

Dancing with Myself *Stephanie Welcher Thompson* 108

Sunday Morning *Hillary Key* 112

Speech Therapy *Karen Brill* 116

Toss of a Coin *Ted Kuntz* 119

Miniature Angels *Susan Farr-Fahncke* 122

Milestones *Gina Morgan* 126

Baby Steps Came in Her Own Time *Beverly Beckham* 130

The Race *Lisa J. Schlitt* 133

In Life and in Death, Always Faithful *Sarah Smiley*............................137

Perspectives *Dick Sobsey*..140

4. BREAKING BARRIERS

Music to My Ears *Jacqui Kess-Gardner*...144

I Am *Dillon York*..149

The Spirit of Travis *Teresa D. Huggins*..150

Amanda's Triumphant March *Carol Willoughby*...............................152

The Need for Speed *Linda Muzzey*...157

The Most Famous Kid at School
      Rachel Ezekiel-Fishbein and Joel I. Fishbein............................161

Trials and Tribulations *Ellis Rubin as told to Dary Matera*....................166

You Didn't Give Me a Turn *Mary Henderson*....................................171

I'm a Dancer *Briana Hobbs*...174

One Special Olympian *Dominick Castellano*......................................176

5. COMMUNITY

An Appalachian Miracle *Cookie Bakke*...180

Out of the Mouths of Babes *Rosita Ferro*..184

A Classy Kind of Love *Patricia Gillule*...185

Swimming with John *Michele Iallonardi*...189

Miracle Field *Scott Newport*..194

The Dance *Kristy Barnes*..199

Silent Grace *Ashley Carroll*...202

The Goal *Susan McMullan*..206

What I Learned in Middle School *Donna Larkin*...............................210

Motherhood *Donna Judge Malarsky*..214

An Angel Among Us *Margaret Prator*...217

6. SIBLING REVELRY

Something about Benny *Kimberly Jensen* 222

Believe *Jennifer M. Graham* 226

Silent No More *Jordan* 231

Teaching by Example *Jeanne Moran* 233

Just Tori *Katherine Schroeder* 236

Switching Roles *Gina Favazza-Rowland* 239

Big Brother Time-Off *Kimberly Jensen* 241

Out of the Mouths of Babes *Deana Newberry* 245

7. EARLY LEARNING

The Slide *Corinne Hill* 248

Three Houses Down on the Left *Deborah McIntire* 252

Illumination *Jeanne Schmidlin* 256

One Egg at a Time *Dawn Morrison* 260

Out of the Mouths of Babes *Karen Simmons* 264

The Case of the Silent Kindergartner *Amanda Green* 266

Out of the Mouths of Babes *Ava Crowell* 270

Ace of Hearts *Lynn Skotnitsky* 271

Labels *Lisa Scott Macdonough* 274

8. FOSTERING INDEPENDENCE

Joey's Gold Medal *Perry P. Perkins* 278

A Simple Question *Bonnie Mintun* 282

Step by Step *Amy Baskin* 286

Independence Day *Daniel Wray* 290

The Class Trip *Debra Behnke* 295

Good Night, Faith *Paulette Beurrier* 299

My Dad Made the Difference *Pam Johnson* 302

The Most Important Words *Daria J. Skibington-Roffel* 307

Something in Football *Lauri Khodabandehloo*..309

A Revelation *Lisa Logsdon*..312

Bearing Gifts *Mimi Greenwood Knight*..316

The Freed Bird *Dillon York*..320

Who Is Jack Canfield?..323

Who Is Mark Victor Hansen? 324

Who Is Heather McNamara?...325

Who Is Karen Simmons?..326

Permissions 327

Introduction

If we had a nickel for every time we heard, "Love the book idea, but I'm uncomfortable with the term 'special needs,'" we'd all be chaise-lounging while counting our riches in five-cent increments.

Choosing the right title has been a difficult and delicate task. In all of our years of compiling Chicken Soup books, we have never had such a reaction to any of our other titles. Since it is our mission to make this book accessible to anyone who might receive comfort or be empowered from it, we needed to go with a title that most people will recognize. So, it is with great pleasure that we present *Chicken Soup for the Soul: Children with Special Needs.*

If you've picked up this book, you most likely know a child who has "special needs" or a disability. This book is for moms, dads, grandparents, foster parents, teachers, doctors, social workers, friends of the family, and everyone else who is participating in the raising of a child or children with a disability on a day-to-day basis.

Perhaps we should warn you that there is one thing you won't read: a pat answer for the challenges of life. Throughout this book, families of children with disabilities will meet other families "who have been there," identify with their struggles, and read of their victories along the way.

You'll read how one mother overcame her fear when her

eight-year-old daughter with Down syndrome was asked to her first slumber party. And what one father said to the dentist who scolded him after learning he allowed his daughter with limited vision to roller-skate. Plus, read what one teacher did to help her students grieve and commemorate one of their classmates.

Parenting is challenging. Parenting a child with a disability has its own set of challenges. Recent statistics show that more than 20 million families in the United States have a child with a disability—that's nearly one in three families.

After reading the more than 5,000 submissions received for this book, we have come to the realization that we don't have a monopoly on the world's problems. Others have their share, often far bigger than any of ours. This has helped us to see our own tribulations in truer perspective. And by learning how others have faced their challenges, we've been given fresh ideas about how to tackle our own.

It is our hope that through reading *Chicken Soup for the Soul: Children with Special Needs*, your heart will be lifted and your journey made lighter as you come to know you are not alone. If this book does either of these for you, we can finally put all those nickels to good use.

"Do you have just a plain Happy Birthday?
I don't want her 'specialness' to go to her head."

Reprinted by permission of Martha Campbell. ©1992 Martha Campbell.

See Me

I still have to remind myself all the time that it really is okay to just be myself. Sometimes all I see—all I think other people see—is the outside of me, not the inside. And I really want people to go in there and see what I'm all about.

Maybe that's why I write poetry—so people can find out who I really am. My poems are all about my feelings: when I hope, when I hurt. I'm not sure where the ideas come from—I just look them up in my head. It's like I have this gut feeling that comes out of me and onto the paper.

I can't change that I have Down syndrome, but one thing I would change is how people think of me. I'd tell them: Judge me as a whole person, not just the person you see. Treat me with respect, and accept me for who I am. Most important, just be my friend.

After all, I would do the same for you.

> Love is everything
> Love is all around
> Love is not hopeless
> Love is passion
> Love will not stop
> Love is an ocean

Melissa Riggio as told to Rachel Buchholz

Melissa Riggio is a nineteen-year-old woman who happens to have Down syndrome. She is the recipient of the Self-Advocate Award from the National Down Syndrome Society. She enjoys swimming, singing, and writing. She has cowritten two songs with British singer-songwriter Rachel Fuller. To learn more about Melissa, please visit her website at www.riggio.net. Rachel Buchholz is the senior editor for National Geographic Kids.

1

ADJUSTING

If apples were pears,
and peaches were plums,
and the rose had a different name.

If tigers were bears,
and fingers were thumbs,
I'd love you just the same.

Anonymous

Welcome to Holland

[EDITORS' NOTE: *Despite, or perhaps because of, its familiarity, we decided the best choice to kick off this book and this chapter is with the well-known, well-loved, and oft-reprinted "Welcome to Holland" by Emily Perl Kingsley.*]

Emily writes to Chicken Soup readers: I had no idea, in the beginning, how wide "Welcome to Holland's" applicability would turn out to be. Although originally written in the framework of adjusting to the birth of a child with Down syndrome, "Welcome to Holland" has been reprinted in brochures and flyers for many different associations and conditions. It has been published all over the world in dozens of formats and languages. It's been sewn into patchwork quilts and pillows. It's been made into a stained-glass wall hanging. It's been printed in beautiful calligraphy, illustrated with gorgeous tulips, and distributed as posters, note cards, and bookmarks. The response to "Welcome to Holland" has been incredibly gratifying. I'm always so touched when people write or tell me how much it helped or comforted them. Perhaps the most overwhelming tribute of all was to learn that two children have actually been named in recognition of the hope and support the parents received through "Welcome to Holland": a little girl named

Holland Abigail and a little boy named Daniel Holland. Holly's sweet, smiling photo sits in a central place on my own refrigerator. It keeps me humble and grateful.

* * *

I am often asked to describe the experience of raising a child with a disability—to try to help people who have not shared that unique experience to understand it, to imagine how it would feel. It's like this . . .

When you're going to have a baby, it's like planning a fabulous vacation trip—to Italy. You buy a bunch of guidebooks and make your wonderful plans. The Coliseum. The Michelangelo *David*. The gondolas in Venice. You may learn some handy phrases in Italian. It's all very exciting.

After months of eager anticipation, the day finally arrives. You pack your bags, and off you go. Several hours later, the plane lands. The stewardess comes in and says, "Welcome to Holland."

"*Holland*?!?" you say. "What do you mean 'Holland'? I signed up for Italy! I'm supposed to be in Italy. All my life I've dreamed of going to Italy."

But there's been a change in the flight plan. They've landed in Holland, and there you must stay.

The important thing is that they haven't taken you to a horrible, disgusting, filthy place, full of pestilence, famine, and disease. It's just a different place.

So you must go out and buy new guidebooks. And you must learn a whole new language. And you will meet a whole new group of people you would never have met.

It's just a *different* place. It's slower-paced than Italy, less flashy than Italy. But after you've been there for a while and you catch your breath, you look around . . . and you begin to notice that Holland has windmills . . . and

Holland has tulips. Holland even has Rembrandts.

But everyone you know is busy coming and going from Italy . . . and they're all bragging about what a wonderful time they had there. And for the rest of your life, you will say, "Yes, that's where I was supposed to go. That's what I had planned."

And the pain of that will never, ever, ever, *ever* go away . . . because the loss of that dream is a very, very significant loss.

But . . . if you spend your life mourning the fact that you didn't get to Italy, you may never be free to enjoy the very special, the very lovely things . . . about Holland.

Emily Perl Kingsley

Emily Perl Kingsley is a mother, lecturer, and professional writer who has received seventeen Emmy awards for writing scripts and songs for *Sesame Street*. A frequent speaker on the subject of disability rights, she serves on a committee to improve the way people with disabilities are portrayed in the media. She and her son, Jason, who has Down syndrome, have appeared on *Today*, *Good Morning America*, and *All My Children*. Jason and his friend, Mitchell Levitz, are coauthors of *Count Us In: Growing Up with Down Syndrome*, just published in an updated edition by Harcourt, Inc.

In the Game

The time to be happy is now. The place to be happy is here. The way to be happy is to make others so.

Robert Green Ingersoll

High-school sports. It's about the biggest thing that happens in our town of Verden, population six hundred. And sports are important in our family. Both of our sons were high-school athletes. So I shouldn't have been surprised when Lauren announced she was going out for the girls' basketball team. But I was. At just five feet, one inch tall, our daughter's lack of height wasn't my worry.

She has Down syndrome.

My wife and I never told Lauren that she was different. We treated her like our other children. Same school. Same church camp. Same chores around the house. We didn't want her to feel disabled or different because she had Down syndrome.

"I'm gonna play basketball, Daddy." Lauren ran to meet me when I came in from work. She flew into my arms and lingered long in my embrace, her brown curls tickling my chin. Unlike some sixteen-year-olds, Lauren was outwardly affectionate.

"That's nice, honey," I replied automatically, and patted her shoulder. I figured she meant outside—on the driveway.

Walking into the kitchen, I kissed my wife Laura on the cheek. She looked up from slicing tomatoes and studied me hard. We'd been married more than twenty years, so I usually could tell what she was thinking, but her furrowed brow indicated I'd missed something. Laura spoke slowly, her tone steady. "What Lauren's trying to tell you is that she's joining the girls' high-school basketball team."

Just as my wife's words sunk in, I heard Lauren behind me.

"I'm gonna be a Lady Tiger," she whooped, skipping into the room and throwing her arms in the air. She raced out of the kitchen to one of her favorite activities, watching cartoons on television.

Everything that could happen flashed through my mind. Lauren's reflexes were slow. *What if she got injured during practice or trying to keep up with the other players? What if the other girls on the team failed to accept her? What if an insensitive spectator made fun of her? Or what if Lauren's feelings got hurt because she spent most of her time on the bench?*

I was eager to discuss Lauren's announcement with my wife that evening, but with four kids popping in and out, the time was never right. *What should we do?* Parenting seldom had clear-cut answers, and bringing up a child with a disability was an additional challenge.

Hours later, with the kids in bed, I shanghaied Laura at the bathroom sink. "Maybe she won't make the team," I offered.

"Everybody makes the team, Johnny," she whispered, patting her face with a towel. "It's Verden. There are only eleven sophomore girls, and not all of them want to play."

The next afternoon, I parked in front of the school gymnasium. *What would I say to the coach?* I jingled change in my pocket as I walked through the double doors.

Ponytails flopped as teenaged girls clad in T-shirts and shorts ran across the hardwood floor. Coach Forsythe stood on the other side of the gym.

"Hey, Johnny," Coach called. Before I could speak, he continued, "We're glad Lauren came out for the team."

Whew. "Well, you know we don't expect you to play her in a game, just include her when you can."

I was thankful for the coach's sportsmanlike attitude, but worry rebounded in my stomach. I moved up into the bleachers. Lauren stood alone at the other end of the court, shooting free throws. Short legs and a stout torso hampered her running and jumping ability. And where was her competitive drive? No other girl on the court grinned like Lauren did during a layup. After every shot, Lauren approvingly hollered, "Woo hoo!" She didn't seem to care if she made the basket or not.

Mid-November, the season's first basketball game arrived. I settled into a seat on the second row with the rest of my family.

"Nervous?" Laura whispered as she quieted my fingers from drumming beside her on the bench.

Just then, a low roar erupted. Cheerleaders sprinted on the court, rooting, jumping, and flipping. Their excitement wafted up into the stands. I stood along with the crowd and clapped. Moments later, a train of girls wearing white uniforms with burgundy and gold accents chugged out of the locker room. Last in line was Lauren. Following her teammates, she grabbed a practice ball. Serious game-faces seemed determined to conquer this new season as the Lady Tigers passed balls from player to player. But before Lauren took her warm-up shot, she searched the stands. Spotting us, she tucked the ball under her arm and waved broadly.

The game got off to a good start, but soon Verden was behind. Even after a rally in the second half, I knew the Lady Tigers were destined to lose. I gazed at Lauren's profile from her seat on the bench. She intently followed the movement on the court and reacted to every play. By far the most animated on the team, she slapped her knee when the opponents scored. Her arms flailed in the air each time Verden shot. I even recognized her voice shout "No way!" when a referee made a call against a teammate. Even though she wasn't playing, she looked as if she were having the time of her life.

As the father of a child with special needs, I'd experienced many emotions. But now, I felt admiration for my daughter. Some players might sulk or react negatively to sitting on the sidelines, but not Lauren. Plus, her team was getting beat, yet she still enjoyed the action.

Just less than two minutes were left, and Verden was down by seventeen points. Coach called a time-out. I bent over to ask if the kids wanted anything from the concessions. The announcer's voice boomed over the public-address system. "Number thirty-three, Lauren Wray, in for the Lady Tigers."

I quickly looked to the last seat on the bench. Lauren wasn't there. She stood next to Coach Forsythe at the scorer's table. With a slap on her back, he sent Lauren running onto the court. My heart quadrupled its beat, and I watched wide-eyed. Lauren was in the game.

My wife tugged at my sleeve. "Get up, Johnny."

As I stood, I noticed what was happening. All across the stands, fans were on their feet clapping for Lauren. Our Lauren!

Play resumed. Lauren kept pace with the others fairly well. The visitors scored again. With less than a minute left, the Lady Tigers were near their goal. I saw the point guard shout and flash a signal to her teammates. Then something I consider sacred happened on the hardwood. They passed Lauren the ball. She caught it and dribbled toward the goal. Lauren went in for a layup. Amazingly, the opposing team did not block her. She shot. She scored!

Applause exploded, and the thunderous sounds reverberated off the metal walls of the building. "Laur-en, Laur-en, Laur-en," chanted the cheerleaders.

Instead of reacting to the noisy crowd, my daughter kept her head in the game. The final buzzer sounded. Verden lost by seventeen points.

A few minutes later, Lauren joined us in the stands.

"Did you see? I scored!" Her brown eyes shone as she wiped a bead of sweat from her forehead. "I made a basket!"

For sixteen years, I'd tried hard to shield Lauren and prevent her from feeling like she was different. But watching Lauren in the game, I saw that she really was different—not physically or emotionally, but spiritually. I, nor probably anyone else in that gymnasium, had ever seen a player with so much heart.

My daughter wasn't like everyone else. I wrapped my arms around her and hugged her tight. Lauren was different. And I was glad.

Reverend Johnny Wray
As told to Stephanie Welcher Thompson

Stephanie Welcher Thompson is a wife and stay-at-home mom who writes when she is apart from daughter, Micah, age four, and husband, Michael. Her stories have appeared in *Guideposts, Angels on Earth, Positive Thinking, Sweet 16,* and ten Chicken Soup books. Reach Stephanie at P.O. Box 1502, Edmond, OK 73083 or stephanie@stateofchange.net.

A Message from John

If you judge people, you have no time to love them.
                                        Mother Teresa

Early in my career as a social worker, my boss came into my office and said, "Jo, I have a student who wants to do a rotation with you in the substance-abuse program. He's quadriplegic, but very capable and eager to learn." My first reaction was to say no. This student's disability was one of my greatest fears. I fought off the impulse to protest, however, and replied, "Send him over for an interview so we can get acquainted." John rolled into my office about twenty minutes later.

John and I began our conversation with the usual exchange of information about past experiences and career goals. Then I took a risk. I said, "John, my greatest fear in life is being in an accident that leaves me a quadriplegic. I'm ready for some personal growth if you are willing to teach me. In exchange, I can teach you a lot about working with addicts and alcoholics." John thought about my comment and replied, "No sweat! Most people are very uncomfortable with my physical condition until they get to know me. That's part of what comes with having a physical challenge."

John began his rotation on my unit one week after our initial interview. He amazed me with his creative adaptation to his disability. He typed up assessments and progress notes with a mouth stick, and was active and engaging in group therapy sessions. One day, a new member appeared for his first therapy session. He had paraplegia and was still very angry about his disability. He looked around the room for a scapegoat and quickly targeted John. He began with disparaging comments about John's "obvious" challenges. He taunted John by stating, "You're only half a man. What business do you have leading therapy groups?"

John remained calm during this verbal assault. When the new patient finally fell silent, John said, "When I was first injured, I was very angry, too. I was mad at God, my parents, and myself. Becoming a quadriplegic cost me a football scholarship, my girlfriend, and my ability to meet my own needs without help. As I adjusted to my challenges and worked through my grief and anger, I began to realize I still have a lot going for me . . . if I have the courage to take risks. I'm a pretty good therapist, and I hope you will give me a chance to help you." The patient remained sullen, but stayed for the remainder of the session without making any further negative comments.

This angry new patient returned to group week after week, and with John's encouragement and guidance, he began to share his fear, pain, and frustration. John was a powerful role model for this patient. He extended hope and encouragement that he, too, might move forward with life plans by learning to live with his disability.

John was on my rotation for eight weeks. During that time, we worked closely together and began to develop what would later become a lasting friendship. He told me that, at age seventeen, he and a group of friends went swimming at a local rock quarry. He dove in and hit the bottom, breaking his neck. John talked about his struggles to cope with his family's reactions and the drastic changes this single event made in his young life.

When I voiced my own fears about becoming disabled, he made a profound comment. He said, "Jo, a person can be more disabled by their fears than I will ever be by my physical challenges. The most important lesson I learned during my recovery is the difference between a disability and a handicap. A disability means the loss of part or all functional ability of certain parts of one's body. Handicaps are the roadblocks other people, and in some cases our own minds, put in the way of people with disabilities who are trying to live normal lives."

John went on to say, "I can't get out of bed or even roll over without the help of my attendant. Once I am in my chair, I can do almost everything for myself. My life is more challenging, and I have to be creative in solving life's problems. But, as long as I remain hopeful, anything is possible."

John went on to receive a master's degree in social work. He used his talents by working at the Center for Independent Living, counseling others with significant physical disabilities.

John taught me a lot during the course of our affiliation. The true significance of his gift was not realized until the birth of my youngest son, born thirteen weeks premature. Soon after his birth, Vincent was diagnosed with an eye condition called retinopathy of prematurity. This condition can result in total blindness. Four eye surgeries later, the doctor told us, "We were able to save some of Vincent's central vision, but he is still legally blind." This was a devastating blow to our family.

When Vincent was two, we noticed that he didn't seem

to respond when we spoke to him. A trip to the audiologist revealed that he had severe hearing loss in both ears. Vincent also has a chronic lung disease, a reflux disorder, and several other physical conditions that greatly delayed his development. With the discovery of each disability, I grieved as any parent would. Then I thought about John and what he taught me about the difference between being disabled and handicapped. I vowed not to become a handicap to my son.

Vincent has limitations, but compensates well. He can run, ride a bicycle, and swim like a fish. He is a high-spirited child with a wonderful sense of humor. His love of life gives him the determination to laugh at himself and keep on trying. The hope John instilled in me the day he shared his own experience has been a source of strength for me each time Vincent faces new challenges. This hope keeps me focused on Vincent's "other abilities" rather than his disabilities. I am constantly amazed by his tenacity and determination, but, then, I had John for a teacher, and he taught me well.

Jo Clancy

Jo Clancy, LCSW, received a bachelor's degree in psychology in 1985. She completed a master's degree in social work in 1987. Jo is employed full-time in the Trauma Recovery Program at the Houston Veterans Affairs Medical Center. Her specialty areas include anger management, relapse prevention, and psychiatric trauma. She dedicates her story to the memory of John Parker, her teacher and friend.

The Miracle of Jay-Jay

Age does not protect you from love. But love, to some extent, protects you from age.

Jeanne Moreau

"He doesn't look like the other boys," Grandpa said as he viewed the blanketed bundle I held in my arms. He was right. James Ryan, whom we called Jay-Jay, with his skinny little legs, almost bald head, and tiny, slanted eyes, bore little resemblance to my other chubby babies with their full heads of hair. But I knew the comment went far beyond looks. Grandpa couldn't accept the fact that Jay-Jay had Down syndrome and mental retardation.

On subsequent visits, Pa-Pa, the name the other children used for their grandpa, ignored Jay-Jay. He picked him up once at a family reunion when it seemed to be expected for a family picture. Other than that, he never touched him, and looked upon him with something between pity and displeasure.

Then, one day, a miracle began. We were once again at a family reunion, and Jay-Jay, being the outgoing little boy he was at three years old, walked over to his grandpa and crawled onto his lap. Pa-Pa was a little shocked, but what could he do in front of all these people? This was his grandson. How could they understand that he hardly knew Jay-Jay?

Jay-Jay took his grandpa's glasses out of his shirt pocket and placed them on his own face, upside down, precariously perched on his short, pudgy nose. He looked at Pa-Pa and giggled, making Pa-Pa laugh, too. Soon they were walking around the room, Jay-Jay leading Pa-Pa, a little smile on the older one's face.

Their next encounter came months later when Pa-Pa decided to visit. Jay-Jay played the clown, making his grandpa laugh and pick him up and throw him into the air.

Pa-Pa turned to my husband and said, "Why, he's just like any other kid."

We had tried to tell him, but Pa-Pa's preconceived ideas and fears of the disabled had kept him out of his grandson's life. But Jay-Jay, being an effervescent little boy, would not let him remain in darkness. With his love and actions, he showed Pa-Pa and others that they were missing out on some of God's greatest blessings by not loving and caring for him.

After that day, a strong bond began to form. Pa-Pa found that Jay-Jay loved balloons and would have one waiting for him each time we came to visit—visits he now welcomed. Then he discovered that Jay-Jay was not only sweet, but ornery, and he loved pillow fights. So each visit would end up with pillows flying across the room. I never figured out which of the two enjoyed it most. Soon Pa-Pa began to telephone—supposedly to talk to my husband, who was now glowing in the new relationship between his father and son—but always insisting on speaking to his youngest grandson.

Although Jay-Jay has a severe speech articulation disorder, he can understand most of what is said to him. Yet he finds it difficult to form the words he wants to say, making communication difficult. Nevertheless, Pa-Pa always wanted to speak to him by phone, and Jay-Jay would laugh and talk in words that neither his dad nor I understood. Pa-Pa swore he understood every word.

The phone chats became a weekly ritual. Every Saturday morning, Jay-Jay knew it was the day to talk to Pa-Pa. Since it was long distance, they took turns calling. One week, Pa-Pa would call. The next week, all excited, Jay-Jay would make the call and talk until we made him hang up.

Through the years, Jay, as he is called today, and Pa-Pa continued those weekly phone calls, along with letters, cards, fishing trips, and frequent trips to Wal-Mart. They became "best buddies."

When Jay was nineteen, his beloved Pa-Pa died unexpectedly. One of the hardest days of my life was watching Jay stand at his Pa-Pa's graveside as he was presented the American flag that draped the casket. But one of the things I cherish most is knowing that Jay's unconditional love built a bridge to his grandfather's heart and changed both of their worlds forever.

Louise Tucker Jones

Louise Tucker Jones is a vibrant speaker and award-winning author of *Extraordinary Kids* (coauthor, Cheri Fuller). Her son Jay has participated in Special Olympics Art for most of his thirty-one years and has won numerous ribbons and trophies for his photography. Louise resides in Edmond, Oklahoma, with her husband, Carl, and son Jay, the youngest of their four children. Contact Louise at LouiseTJ@cox.net or www.LouiseTuckerJones.com.

"My grandkids keep me young alright. I don't know
whether to throw a tantrum or take a nap."

✈ Out of the Mouths of Babes ✈

Our boys, Devon and Kaleb, had been with their Nana and Grandpa all day long while I was at work. When I arrived to pick them up, Devon immediately started to recant the list of the day's events in his usual manner, basically telling me everything for which he had gotten into trouble all day long. When Grandpa got down on his knees to give Devon his good-bye kiss, Devon stopped him with a little outstretched hand and simply stated, "What happened to Grandpa's hair?"

I quickly muttered, "He lost it."

Devon started looking around to find it, when he found his answer. "Mommy, it's okay. Look! It's all on his back!"

Sarah and MMC John S. Smigal

John and Sarah Smigal, along with Devon and Kaleb, are stationed in Groton, Connecticut, where John is a chief aboard the USS *Hawaii*. Devon was diagnosed with autism in 2006. Devon has conquered a great many things since his premature birth, and he is destined for greatness.

Tomorrow

To love is to receive a glimpse of heaven.
                                                    Karen Sunde

"What doing tomorrow?" asked my son, Jeff, whose speech lacked some of the necessities required to form grammatically correct sentences.

Lately, these were the first words from his mouth almost every morning. Jeff had already known what we would be doing that day because he had asked yesterday. I soon realized that he understood much more than I had imagined.

Jeff was born with Down syndrome. At age eleven, he was diagnosed with acute lymphatic leukemia (ALL). This disease required a specific regime of treatment every day. Sometimes it required a hospital admission for chemotherapy. On other days, it required an outpatient visit to the hospital for IVs, spinal taps, or blood tests, and other days would involve frequent administrations of medications that tasted like aluminum foil. Sometimes, unexpected complications required further tests, procedures, or medications. I did not think that Jeff would understand the reasoning for so many things that only made him feel worse, but he did. Asking about tomorrow was his way of preparing for what lay ahead, and I always felt that I owed him complete honesty. We both clung to the hope of tomorrow—not like the tomorrows of the past or the present, but the hope of a new tomorrow that would allow for living without sickness or pain.

Jeff had changed, not only physically, but in his whole personality. The light that had always twinkled in his eyes was gone. Our interactions seemed always to reflect our caregiver and patient relationship. This disease saturated his spirit. He knew what I would not allow in my deepest thoughts.

We were once in a waiting room waiting to be called in for a blood test. The nurse came out and called Jeff's name.

He responded, "No, no Jeff, I Jack."

It was heart-wrenching to see my little boy trying to assume a new identity. How I longed to press rewind to take us back to our lives behind the white picket fence— back to the days of laughter when Jeff would get off the school bus and come running up our driveway.

"Wilma, I'm home," he would shout as he walked into our front door, borrowing the line from Fred Flintstone.

Jeff also liked to pretend that he was the scarecrow from *The Wizard of Oz*.

"'Over the Rainbow,' Mom, sing it," he often requested.

He watched the video so many times I think I knew the entire script by heart. Through Jeff, I was able to see the Land of Oz. He opened my eyes to the vibrant colors of a majestic land where trees could talk, scarecrows could walk, and horses were of many colors. Everyone was different, yet no one noticed. My heart would tingle with what I can only describe as a surge of joy each time I saw Jeff perform this song.

But my favorite performance was "Tomorrow" from the

musical *Annie*. With his arms stretched out wide, and a simultaneous jerk of his head and hands, Jeff would sing out loudly, "Tomorrow, tomorrow, the sun tomorrow." He was quite a performer and always willing to entertain.

When Jeff was first diagnosed with leukemia, I had no idea how to explain to him that he would not get well for a long time. What the doctors called "Phase One" of treatment, an intensive phase to say the least, was to last six months, before progressing to the next less-intensive phase. *How could I explain that to my little boy?* It soon occurred to me, once again, that I did not have to. Jeff would be my teacher. My challenged little boy was also my most influential mentor.

Jeff had been feeling sick since the beginning of his treatments. As the days wore on, I tried desperately to raise his spirits and give him hope. At this point, I had to carry him into the bathroom because he was too weak to walk.

"I very sick, Mom," Jeff said, while standing in the shower with my support.

I replied, "Tomorrow, we will see the doctor, and he will make you feel better."

With his head hung down, Jeff replied, "No, I die."

In desperation, I grabbed his chin and raised his head to meet my eyes. My body trembled. I struggled to speak with confidence. I needed to reassure not only Jeff, but myself as well. "You are not going to die! Do you hear me? Do you understand? You are not going to die!" Jeff did not reply.

He knew and accepted what I could not.

After ten weeks of chemotherapy, my son developed an infection. He was hospitalized for six days before the infection became worse, and he had to be moved to the intensive-care unit. Despite his pain and suffering, Jeff began to teach me new lessons. He had taught me

countless lessons about living, and now he was teaching
me about dying.

The doctors were getting ready to intubate Jeff to help
him breathe. I think on some level we both knew that once
they placed that tube in his throat, the end was near. With
all of the strength he could muster, Jeff looked at me and
said, "Tomorrow, tomorrow, you and me go shopping.
Okay? You and me. Okay?" This was his way of telling me
that he could no longer deal with "his today," and that he
was going to "his tomorrow." He wanted the pain to end.
I contracted every muscle in my body and demanded
myself to stop the trembling. I prayed for one last moment
of peace so that I could answer my son with the respect
that he so deserved.

"Yes, Jeff," I said. "Tomorrow, just you and me, tomorrow."

The doctors paralyzed him and placed the tube in his
throat. I watched the numbers on the machine gradually
decrease as it measured his heartbeats. With one finger, I
gently swept Jeff's hair back across his forehead as I sang
softly. This was the usual routine, one that he was so fond
of, that I had used to get him to go to sleep when he was
younger. Knowing that these would be my final moments
with my son, I told him that if he needed to go, it would
be all right. And with my cheek against his, I whispered in
his ear, "I'll meet you just over the rainbow, tomorrow."

Jill Presson

Jill Presson has worked in occupational therapy for over ten years. She is the
proud parent of four children, two biological and two through the gift of adoption.
Three of Jill's children have Down syndrome. She is an active advocate for Down
syndrome, special-needs adoption, and grieving parents. Jill can be reached at
bus665@sbcglobal.net.

No Words

T.J. struggles with the pencil in his left hand, pushing it carefully up and down on the notepad that sits in his lap. My middle sister, Kellie, has asked him to write the word "Mommy" on the paper to show my younger sister and me what he has recently learned in school. The pencil stops moving. T.J. yells "Mommy!" and turns the notepad around to show us the scribbled letters M-O-M on the paper. We all clap and cheer at his accomplishment, and we watch as a proud smile spreads across his face. This may seem like an insignificant feat, but for T.J., it is a milestone. He has just learned how to spell "Mom," and he is ten years old.

My little brother, T.J., was born on my first day of high school. My parents were in their early forties at the time, and it was a surprising situation for all of us to have a new baby in the house. My dad, Tom, was the most excited of all, since he finally had a boy to balance out his houseful of women.

When he was three, my family discovered that T.J. was not developing language skills at a normal rate. The doctors did not have any answers as to what could be causing the delay.

T.J.'s disorder put a strain on my family, and our household could be a tense place to live during some of the years that followed. As my brother got older, it became more apparent that his disabilities reached beyond simple language skills.

My mom spent a lot of her time trying to find a solution. My dad reacted in a very different way. He embraced his chance to be a father to his son. They would go for haircuts, hang out at the mall, or just drive around listening to sports radio in the car. T.J. loves these outings with our dad, and the minute he returns from work, my brother pulls on his shoes and waits by the door. He and my dad have developed a bond that goes beyond my brother's "problem," and have become buddies who struggle every day to maintain a semblance of normalcy.

There was one day in particular when I realized that my father had fully accepted T.J. for who he is, and it was this same moment in which I saw the true depth of my father's love for my brother. We were sitting on a bench by the lake—the three of us—and my dad was making funny faces to make my brother laugh. In the midst of the laughter, T.J. stopped and reached up to softly touch our father's face. My dad looked down at him and said almost so softly that I couldn't hear, "Well, kiddo, it looks like it's you and me for the rest of my life." There wasn't a sense of sadness or burden in my father's voice, only acceptance and unconditional love for the little boy who sat beside him. It seemed that T. J. understood this, too, in his own way, and he smiled and touched our father's face again.

T.J.'s condition has yet to be fully diagnosed. My parents continue to help T.J. express himself with words, pictures, and sounds. My dad and T.J., however, have become a duo, and when it's time for them to go "cruising" in Dad's car, we all know that it is strictly boys' night out. The women in our house know that T.J. loves all of us, each in a different way, but the love he has for his dad is written in a language only he understands. All of us have the privilege of speech, but only the two of them speak *their* language, and it requires no words.

Stacey Flood

Stacey Flood received her B.A. in English from DePaul University in 2003. She lives in Chicago with her boyfriend and their three dogs. She is currently attending culinary school, and she loves to cook for her friends and family. T.J. continues to learn new things every day with the help of his extraordinary speech therapists, and he and his dad are still "partners in crime." The two of them have developed a new passion—anytime you ask T.J. where he wants to go, all he will say is "Monster trucks." Contact Stacey at jgar54@aol.com.

"My sister has special needs—
and my dad has special *knees*."

Reprinted by permission of Jonny Hawkins. ©2007 Jonny Hawkins.

Seeing Through Josh's Eyes

Forget past mistakes. Forget failures. Forget everything except what you're going to do now and do it.

William Durant

After years of doctors, counselors, and visits to the school, the word "bipolar" should have been a relief. My thirteen-year-old son had always been different and unusual, but the problems had escalated. Even if it was my fault, as one doctor told me, our family and my son needed help, and we weren't getting it. Not until now. The words hung in the air, and I swear I could touch them—they were so heavy and dense.

Josh sat with my husband and me as the doctor told us what bipolar disorder is, described the symptoms, and outlined the line of treatment that was needed. But all I remember hearing were two words—bipolar disorder.

After our meeting, my son and husband were picking up some literature and filling out paperwork, so I offered to go warm up the car. There was snow on the ground. I remember feeling like my whole life was in a frozen picture. I couldn't think; I couldn't breathe; I couldn't cry. I was numb.

At that very moment, my husband and son jumped into the car, and I remember looking into the rearview mirror and seeing my son grinning from ear to ear. He jumped into the seat and said, "Mom, let's go celebrate."

At that very moment, I knew that my son was in the middle of what the doctor had described as a "manic episode." *Why else would he say something so ludicrous?*

As calmly as I could, I turned to him and said, "Son, I'd love to go celebrate, but what exactly are we celebrating?"

And with the most sincere voice I have ever heard, he looked me in the eye and said, "Don't you get it, Mom? We're celebrating because I am sick. I'm not evil."

It was in that moment that I realized it was time for me to start seeing things the way my son did. I thought we had been striving for normality, but all along he had been fighting for his soul.

Deborah Rose

Deborah Rose is a private investigator, spending her free time advocating for people with mental illness. She is heavily involved with the NAMI (National Alliance on Mental Illness) Texas as an educator and stigma buster. Deborah enjoys reading, writing, debating, and eBaying. Full-time writing is next on her agenda. Joshua is now a twenty-two-year-old college graduate with a degree in business management and marketing, working as a case manager for the Salvation Army while working toward his master's degree in business. He is also working on a documentary that focuses on the shared problems of teens and young adults, whether they have mental illness or not. Please e-mail Deborah at dcr@isgu.com.

The Voice of Reason Wears SpongeBob Underpants

In the book of life, the answers are not in the back.

Charlie Brown

"Oh, my child will never behave like that in public," I remember smugly telling a friend over lunch one day. "I simply won't allow it." Seven months pregnant with my first baby, I watched in horror as a preschool-aged girl screamed, kicked, and flailed while her humiliated mother tried to drag her away from the play area and out the door.

"I tell you, I'll never let a three-year-old run my life!" I smirked as we got back to our discussion of nursery themes.

Looking back, I seemed to have all the answers regarding child rearing before I ever had one of my own: when and what they should eat, the proper cartoons to watch, which toys they should be playing with, the best way to potty-train. If it concerned children, this expectant mother had an opinion about all the "right" ways to do things, and shame on anyone who disagreed!

So sure was I that badly behaved children were the direct result of bad parenting that nothing short of a whack over the head could have convinced me otherwise. And, as karma would have it, that whack occurred late one night in June 2003 in the form of a four-pound, nine-ounce screeching baby boy.

Difficult from the beginning, little Antoine was determined to put our fledgling parenting skills to the test. I was committed to nursing him, but he refused to latch on. Gastrointestinal problems meant that the milk I spent so much time pumping almost always came back up. He screamed, sometimes for hours on end, for no apparent reason. He stared, not at us, but at a bright light on the ceiling. And the child never *ever* slept, which meant, of course, that neither did we.

As time went on, his behavior became even more challenging, and sometime around his first birthday we stopped taking him to public places altogether unless we simply had no other choice. His unpredictability and his "nuclear meltdowns" in the supermarket, for example, more often than not had me terrified that one of my fellow shoppers would summon the police.

Gone were the days of enjoying restaurant meals as a family, as even a fast-food experience with Antoine was likely to deteriorate into a chaotic scene. In fact, a trip outside our home for any reason typically meant enduring finger-pointing, cold stares, and rude comments from perfect strangers as Antoine, oblivious to his surroundings, carried on as though he were being prodded with hot pokers.

"Can't you control your child?" "Ma'am, if he doesn't quiet down, I'm going to have to ask you to leave," "Spoiled brat," or "Give him to me for a few days, I'll straighten him out!" came my way so often that I began to categorize my days by the number of insults I received from people who knew absolutely nothing about me or my child.

Worst of all was the "advice" we received from friends and family whenever we attempted to voice our concerns that something wasn't quite right with our little boy. Some tried to reassure us, claiming that perhaps the "terrible twos" had set in a bit early, that tantrums were *normal,* and that he'd settle down once he got older. "He's just all boy," some said. Others gently pointed out that he would behave better if we could simply learn to show him "who's boss," while still others were competitive: "Oh, you think he's bad, you should see my Brian."

How on Earth could we possibly explain what it was like to live with this whirling dervish, this Tasmanian devil of a boy to people who clearly thought that children came in a one-size-fits-all model? And who was to say that they weren't right? As first-time parents, what did we know? After all, no one had ever told us that raising kids was easy.

What we did know was that the level of stress in our household (already at an incomprehensible high from trying to meet the day-to-day needs of a child who alternated between ramming his head into the armoire and spending hours at a time lining his toy cars into neat little rows) was made even higher by the large amount of seemingly thoughtless commentary we received, no matter which way we turned. Indeed, it was commentary of the very type I had made myself once upon a time.

When Antoine's diagnosis of autism was eventually confirmed, we—like most parents confronted with the disorder—were devastated. At the same time, the sense of relief was profound. Knowing that there was a reason behind our child's erratic behavior and that we weren't crazy after all gave us the strength to go on when it seemed like our whole world was falling apart.

These days, Antoine has more good days than bad. At three and a half, he is the light of my life and has taught me more about myself than I could have imagined possible. He still does not make transitions well, and, though fewer and farther between, his meltdowns can still be considered "nuclear" by anyone's standards. That much has not changed.

What has changed is my own ability to empathize, to put myself into the shoes of another. Never again will I be so quick to make judgments. These days, thanks to knowing and loving my amazing little boy, if I say anything at all, it is this: How can I help?

Shari Youngblood

Shari Youngblood received her B.A. in cultural anthropology and M.A. in sociology from the University of Florida. Proceeds from her ASD-centered merchandise (www.cafepress.com/madwhirl) go toward autism research, and her forthcoming book, *Imbecile*, concerns raising an autistic child in France. Currently, Antoine can usually be found keeping his mother in line, as happened recently at the local supermarket. Upon sensing that Shari wanted to ram a rude customer's shopping cart with her own, a slow shaking of Antoine's head and a solemn "No, Mama" nipped her recalcitrant behavior in the bud. E-mail her at shari.youngblood@gmail.com.

"I feel a tantrum coming on.
You better start thinking up some excuses for it."

One Mother to Another

*O*ur *lives begin to end the day we become silent about things that matter.*

Martin Luther King, Jr.

See the little girl, who stands out most
and has troubles following suit,
who forgets a lot, and talks out of turn
and to others doesn't seem very cute.

"She's disruptive" . . . "Doesn't listen,"
"Shouldn't be with all the rest,"
You see it . . . we hear it,
"She holds your son back from his best."

We see your looks of disapproval
through eyes that have never seen,
the struggles that we face each day,
the place where she has been.

We hear you talk . . . those things you say,
though you fail to really listen,
to the voice whose words seem disregarded
"Our star," who to us, does glisten.

She comes home after school, to laugh and play
with her sister and baby brother,
she's tucked in at night, with a hug and a kiss
just the same as any other.

She wakes each morn, with a yawn and a stretch
and wonders of each new day,
what things she'll see, what things she'll do
in her world . . . in her own way.

She puts her shoes on, one at a time
and kisses me good-bye,
to stand in "the group" next to your little one,
Who draws away, her wondering why.

She's young right now, and sees the "good"
although in time, that's bound to change,
she may hear those words and see those looks
that will make her "feel"—but strange.

If I could make a wish tonight,
I'd wish to make it right,
not for a different or shinier star,
just that ours would forever "feel" bright.

To that little girl, who stands out most
and has troubles following suit,
who forgets a lot, and talks out of turn
"We love you . . . you are you . . . and you are cute!"

Donna Turenne

Donna Turenne is, first and foremost, a mother of three beautiful children (Camille, Caslyn, and Landon). Married to the love of her life, Donald, she is a practicing registered nurse in Chilliwack, British Columbia. Her stories are inspired by her family's strength and God's love expressed in living with a child who has special needs. Donna dedicates her story to Caslyn and Landon, Camille's true guardian angels on Earth. Please e-mail Donna at dturenne@telus.net.

Reaching Back

Some luck lies in not getting what you thought you wanted but getting what you have, which once you have got it you may be smart enough to see it is what you would have wanted had you known.

Garrison Keillor

When my son Evan was born, and I was told he had Down syndrome, I did not cry for a long time. But when I saw a girl walking hand in hand with her little brother to the viewing window of the hospital nursery, I could not hold back my tears. I knew my daughter would never walk with her little brother that way. I knew he would never experience the small pleasures of life I always took for granted. In those minutes, my heart was broken, and I was overcome with sadness for both my children.

Now, almost six years later, I am filled with pity for the misinformed, heartbroken woman who sat crying in that cold hospital corridor, without hopes, dreams, or fight in her. She was wrong about so many things. That part of me continues to be reeducated: I am grateful for every new lesson I learn. I am thankful to that woman. She found she did have some fight in her. She was not the first mother to fall in love with her newly diagnosed child. She learned of brave and stubborn mothers who put themselves forward in the media to spread a message of hope. She let the memories of those mothers stir her into action. I will always revere the mothers and fathers who reached out a hand, and who built a foundation of support, information, and resources for women like me to draw upon. What they did for their children transformed my son's life. They continue, still looking forward, always reaching back to help others.

I still reach back to the woman I was. I hold her gently and wish that in her grief she could hear me. "It's not like that. Please don't lose yourself in that sadness. Hold on, wait and see. So much of that grief is over things that are just not true." I know she has to sit there crying, and I don't know how long. I will wait with her and be a friend.

Evan will be six years old in a month. His sister, Zoë, is seven and a half. When they are not arguing ferociously or ignoring one another, as siblings do, they are the best of friends. They help one another scheme, and protect each other from harm. Both have argued seriously about how life for the whole family would be better if the other disappeared, leaving an "only child." Each misses the other when they are separated overnight. I rarely think about the sister and brother walking toward the nursery viewing window, but sometimes when I see my two walking hand in hand down the beach or up a hiking trail, I think of the poor, sad woman I was that day.

I can't imagine life without my son. Sometimes, when he barrels into my bedroom early Saturday morning to tell me a great cartoon is on, I wonder what life would be like without little boys. But I get up and find he has quite good taste in cartoons. I think of him in his preschool days, chin raised in pride over some fabulous work of art, like the turkey he pasted up when he was three. I remember him seeing his good buddy from class, Terrell, at a school carnival, and how their eyes met. They squealed in unison and ran to each other like sweethearts in a perfume commercial. I enjoy the story his teacher relayed to me about how, during a cookie-baking class, he slyly nibbled his chocolate chips instead of saving them for the cookie. I am glad every day to have this son. The world is a better place with him in it.

Evan is not a Down syndrome "superstar," but I wanted him to have the experience of a regular kindergarten. He loves school and has a wonderful teacher. His classmates are charming and funny and bright. But I was afraid of their parents. Evan has missed some fine opportunities because many people are as inexperienced and uninformed as I was six years ago.

I believe Evan needs an edge before he can participate successfully in mainstream activities, and that edge is casual acceptance. Last night was parent night at my son's kindergarten class. I was overwhelmed by the relaxed but purposeful way different parents let me know that they accept my son simply as a child in the kindergarten class. Their hands reach back to comfort the heartbroken woman in the hospital corridor. They comfort her in ways that I cannot. I thank every person who has brought us all this far. Thank you so much.

Pam Wilson

Pamela Wilson graduated from UC Berkeley in preparation for work and starting a family. Her children and those she met through special programs and mainstream activities continue to inspire her to advocate for opportunities, support, and encouragement for every child and family. Visit her website or contact her through www.specialneedschildren.bellaonline.com.

A Reason to Celebrate

The soul would have no rainbow if the eyes had no tears.

Native American Proverb

Numbly, I left my husband, Marty, at the hospital where I had been visiting two of my children and headed for the grocery store. Since it was 11:00 PM, I drove to the only store I knew was open twenty-four hours a day. I turned my car motor off and rested my head against the seat.

What a day, I thought to myself. With two of my young children in the hospital, and a third waiting at Grandma's, I was truly spread thin. Today I had actually passed the infant CPR exam required before I could take eight-week-old Joel home from the hospital. *Would I remember how to perform CPR in a moment of crisis?* A cold chill ran down my spine as I debated my answer.

Exhausted, I reached for my grocery list, which resembled a scientific equation rather than the food for the week. For the past several days, I'd been learning the facts about juvenile diabetes and trying to accept Jenna, my six-year-old daughter's, diagnosis. In addition to the CPR exam, I'd spent the day reviewing how to test Jenna's blood and give her insulin shots. Now I was buying the needed food to balance the insulin that would sustain Jenna's life.

"Let's go, Janet," I mumbled to myself while sliding out of the car. "Tomorrow is the big day! Both kids are coming home from the hospital." It didn't take long before my mumbling turned into a prayer.

God, I am soooo scared! What if I make a mistake and give Jenna too much insulin, or what if I measure her food wrong, or what if she does the unmentionable—and sneaks a treat? And what about Joel's apnea monitor? What if it goes off? What if he turns blue and I panic? What if? Oh, the consequences are certain to be great!

With a shiver, my own thoughts startled me. Quickly, I tried to redirect my mind away from the *what ifs.*

Like a child doing an errand she wasn't up for, I grabbed my purse, locked the car, and found my way inside the store. The layout of the store was different from what I was used to. Uncertain where to find what I needed, I decided to walk up and down each aisle.

Soon I was holding a box of cereal, reading the label, trying to figure out the carbohydrate count and sugar content. *Would three-fourths of a cup of cereal fill Jenna up?* Not finding any "sugar free" cereal, I grabbed a box of Kellogg's Corn Flakes and continued shopping. Pausing, I turned back. *Do I still buy Fruit Loops for Jason?* I hadn't even thought how Jenna's diagnosis might affect Jason, my typical four-year-old. *Is it okay if he has a box of Fruit Loops while Jenna eats Kellogg's Corn Flakes?*

Eventually I walked down the canned fruit and juice aisle. *Yes, I need apple juice, but how much? Just how often will Jenna's sugar "go low" so she will need this lifesaving can of juice? Will a six-year-old actually know when her blood sugar is dropping? What if . . . ?* I began to ask myself again.

I held the can of apple juice and began to read the label.

Jenna will need fifteen carbohydrates of juice when her sugar drops. But this can has thirty-two. Immediately I could see my hand begin to tremble. I tried to steady the can and reread the label when I felt tears leave my eyes and make their way down the sides of my face. Not knowing what to do, I grabbed a couple six-packs of apple juice and placed them in my cart. Frustrated by feelings of total inadequacy, I crumpled up my grocery list, covered my face in my hands, and cried.

"Honey, are you all right?" I heard a gentle voice ask. I had been so engrossed in my own thoughts that I hadn't even noticed the woman who was shopping alongside of me. Suddenly I felt her hand as she reached towards me and rested it upon my shoulder. "Are you all right? Honey, are you a little short of cash? Why don't you just let me . . . ?"

I slowly dropped my hands from my face and looked into the eyes of the silvery haired woman who waited for my answer. "Oh, no, thank you, ma'am," I said while wiping my tears, trying to gather my composure. "I have enough money."

"Well, honey, what is it then?" she persisted.

"It's just that I'm kind of overwhelmed. I'm here shopping for groceries so that I can bring my children home from the hospital tomorrow."

"Home from the hospital! What a celebration that will be. Why, you should have a party!"

Within minutes this stranger had befriended me. She took my crumpled-up grocery list, smoothed it out, and became my personal shopper. She stayed by my side until each item on my list was checked off. She even walked me to my car, helping me as I placed the groceries in my trunk. Then with a hug and a smile, she sent me on my way.

It was shortly after midnight, while lugging the groceries into my house, that I realized the lesson this woman had taught me. "My kids are coming home from the hospital!" I shouted with joy. "Joel is off life support and functioning on a monitor. Jenna and I can learn how to manage her diabetes and give her shots properly. And just as God met my needs in a grocery store, He will meet each and every need we have. What a reason to celebrate." I giggled to myself. "I have a reason to celebrate!" I shouted to my empty house.

"Why, you should have a party," the woman had exclaimed.

And a party there would be!

Janet Lynn Mitchell

Janet Lynn Mitchell is a wife and mother of three incredible kids. She is also an inspirational speaker and author of numerous articles and stories in compilations. Janet's latest book, *Taking a Stand*, has just been released. Through it all, Janet and her family have learned that together they can face mountains and reach new heights. Janet can be reached at JanetLM@prodigy.net.

My Finest Teachers

I was five years old when I first learned how cruel kids could be. My friend and I were riding the bus to school, and a little girl with blonde hair was sitting behind us. We didn't know her, but we knew her name was Sue.

As Sue sat there, my friend and I began to hurt her. We pushed her and scratched at her arm. We said mean things to her. *What had prompted this most hurtful and cruel behavior? What had she done?* Nothing.

Her only "crime" was that she looked different. Her mouth was different than ours, and when she spoke, it sounded different. She sat silently and endured our cruelty. She could have called to the bus driver or told us to stop, but she chose not to.

After arriving at school, I was called to the principal's office. I can still remember the look on Mrs. Barto's face and the sadness in her eyes as she asked me why I had done this. I hung my head and said I didn't know, and I honestly didn't. That was the sad part. That was the last day Sue ever came to our school.

Years later, in high school, I met Sue again. She was nice to me. Although she didn't recognize me, I knew it was Sue. I could still see the mild trace of a scar on her upper lip. I wanted to tell her how sorry I was, that I was the mean little kid who had taunted her that day, but instead I hid in the anonymity of being a teenager. She never knew it was me, and I never had the courage to tell her.

In a hospital room some twenty-six years after kindergarten, my fifth baby was born. The words they used to describe him were hard for me to hear, "Down syndrome."

As I looked at my newborn son, my heart ached. All I could think about was Sue. *Had her mother held her and loved her, just as I did with my David?* Of course, she had. Though David looked different to the doctors, he looked beautiful to me. All of a sudden, I realized that, someday, others might be as cruel to David as I had been to Sue—all because he was different.

It felt like my life was shattering. I felt like God had made a mistake in sending David to me. I was sure some other mother could love him more and be a better mom. I knew I didn't have what it took to be the mother of a child with a disability. This was more than I could bear.

Then a phone call came to the hospital. It was my friend Kris. With her usual enthusiasm, she greeted me with, "I heard you have a beautiful baby boy!" My mind raced. Surely, no one had told her about my baby because they didn't want to hurt her. They knew that her daughter Kari was profoundly mentally and physically disabled and was not expected to live very long.

I never quite understood Kris. She treated Kari as you would any baby. I never once saw that look of disappointment that I thought the mother of a child with a severe disability should have. Secretly, I wondered if she really understood how bad off Kari was.

I didn't know the words to say, but I knew I had to tell her the truth. Through my tears, I replied, "I do, Kris, but he's handicapped."

Immediately, and with excitement in her voice, she said, "I know. Isn't that wonderful?"

I was so taken aback. When she said that, it was almost as if she were sharing a delightful secret that only she and I knew. *How could she, of all people, be happy for me?* Something in her voice gave me hope.

Yet, even with that hope, I struggled. I have never grieved so much for anything or anyone as I did for my David.

Are there still unkind children left in this world? Perhaps, but my experience has been that most kids are good and kind.

Sue taught me forgiveness. It is because of her that I can forgive myself for how I once treated her, as well as for my uninformed thoughts regarding my son.

Kris taught me acceptance. She taught me to be able to see what others could not—the worth of a child.

I remembered how Kris had told me that when Kari was born, the doctors had told her to take her baby home and just love her because she would not live through the weekend. Kris told me that when she got home, she made a list of the things she wanted to do before her baby died. She wanted to kiss her and sing to her. She wanted to rub baby lotion on her and put a pink bow in her hair. She wanted to cut a locket of her hair and tell her how much she loved her. Kris told me she considered each day after completing the items on that list a Bonus Day. God gave Kris 3,779 bonus days.

But it has been my son, David, who has become my finest teacher. He has taught me that the only sadness I should feel at the birth of a child with a disability is for those who have not learned how to love him yet.

Gina Johnson

Gina Johnson is the proud mother of seven beautiful children, including a son, David, who has Down syndrome. She is the founder of the nonprofit Sharing Down Syndrome Arizona, (www.sharingds.org), and an outspoken disability advocate who loves her faith, her family, and all children, but especially those who have Down syndrome. Reach her at gina@sharingds.org.

✎ Out of the Mouths of Babes ✎

One of my six-year-old daughter's favorite kids in school is a nine-year-old boy named Sammy. According to Nikki, Sammy is in a wheelchair and has a feeding tube.

One day, during one of our after-school chats, I asked, "Nikki, can Sammy talk?"

"Oh, yes," she assured me. "He can talk."

"Are you sure?" I asked her. "I thought the kids in his class couldn't talk."

"Yes, he can," insisted Nikki, her voice growing louder. "Sammy talked to me today."

"What did he say?" I asked her.

Nikki responded, "When I said 'hi' to him, he smiled at me."

Cheryl Kremer

Cheryl Kremer lives with her husband, Jack, and children, Nikki (now fifteen) and Cobi (twelve), in Lancaster, Pennsylvania. She has been published in several Chicken Soup books and is thrilled every time she sees her work in print. She spends her time working in preschool and watching her kids play soccer, basketball, and field hockey. She can be reached at j_kremer@verizon.net.

The Vacation

Sometimes adversity impels a person to greater heights, and sometimes it provides the opportunity for that person to be a blessing in the lives of others.

Norma H. Hill

One summer, my entire family planned a family reunion. When I was talking to my best friend about this, she offered to watch Brandon for the week, but I declined. We were going on a family vacation, and Brandon is part of our family. "It's all for one and one for all," I told her. It would be much later that I would learn the hard way the true meaning of those words I so lightly spoke.

My husband had reservations. We had never even taken a vacation since Brandon was diagnosed with autism, except for those "safe" trips to Grandma's house for respite and reprieve. But I'm Italian, and I'm stubborn, not to mention sentimental.

I grew up on Long Island Sound in New Jersey, and have many, many wonderful memories of the beach, "Ole Barney" the lighthouse, fishing, and being around a bunch of loud, hearty Italians. I wanted to bring Brandon with the hope that maybe, just maybe, something from my world would touch his. Maybe something about the ocean atmosphere would reach him. There are so many things that I want to share with him, and I wanted this vacation to be the picture that painted, for him, a thousand words. I suppose some part of me was still picturing myself as a typical mom taking her typical son on a typical family vacation, like other typical families do. But I'm not a typical mom, and I don't have a typical son, and so began our vacation.

We boarded a plane, nonstop to New Jersey. We were ushered onto the plane quickly and with no delays. I had specifically requested the last rows in the back of the plane, where the engines are the loudest, in case of shrieks, shouts, or humming from my son. The flight attendant announced we would be taking off, and my husband and I looked at each other in bewilderment as the plane was half-empty. *Could it be?* we thought. *Would we have the whole back half of the plane to ourselves?* There was no one in front of us for at least five rows. Brandon was free to wiggle, stand up, move around, and have a grand old time. He was happy. I looked over at my husband with that "I told you so" expression, and started to relax, thinking that this was too good to be true. Indeed, it was.

The moment we arrived at our destination and walked into the tiny house full of smoke and boisterous Italians, Brandon changed. Within thirty minutes, he fell off an unfamiliar porch trying to escape the mayhem, busted his knee open, and was smacked in the face with the back of a porch swing because the relatives didn't know that he didn't know to not go behind a swinging porch swing. Within one hour, it took my holding his top half and my husband holding his bottom half to calm him down from an overstimulated sensory dysfunction rage. Within two hours, I was begging my husband to send Brandon and me back home. My husband had the good grace not to give me that "I told you so" expression.

After our poor child finally fell asleep from sheer exhaustion, leaving us both disgruntled and exhausted from the ordeal, my husband looked at me and said, "We can do this." I have never felt so much love for him as I did at that moment. There was as much pain and heartache in his eyes as I felt in my heart. They say that having a child with a disability either makes or breaks a marriage. For us, that moment was our test, determining how we would handle things for years to come. I'll never forget what my husband said next: "I may not have been put on this Earth to be a great athlete, or a Wall Street wizard, or to be famous. Instead, I think God put me on this Earth to be a good daddy to Brandon, and a good husband to you."

That was the defining moment of our vacation, our marriage, and of our lives with Brandon. The rest of the week was no different. We couldn't take him on the boat because he kept trying to climb out. Seeing the lighthouse was no thrill; in fact, I'm not sure he ever quit flapping his shirt long enough to notice it. He dealt with things better in the quiet of his room at the shore house, playing with his familiar toys. And so it was there that I learned acceptance. Not defeat, but acceptance.

I learned to accept that it's okay that he didn't enjoy everything. To accept that it would be okay to bring someone along next time to stay with him in the shore house, or better yet for him to stay at home in his familiar surroundings, doing the things he likes to do. To accept that I don't have to include him, just for the sake of including him. I felt such peace when I came to terms with the fact that I can't always do typical things with a child who is not typical.

Finally, the week was over, and it was time to get on the airplane to go home. We planned carefully and paid extra money to book another nonstop flight. Unfortunately, Murphy's

Law came into effect: if anything can go wrong, it will. Our predicted two-and-a-half-hour flight was packed. I knew Brandon had had a hard week, so I gave him some Benadryl to allow him to sleep on the plane ride home, timing it perfectly so that he would be asleep about the time we were in the air. Brandon did sleep, but it's too bad it was while we were stuck on the runway with one delay after another. When he woke up, I had a wide-awake, energetic, can't-sit-still, overstimulated child. I faintly remember begging the flight attendant to let us off the plane after sitting on the runway with the engines off for two and a half hours. I faintly remember standing in the aisle so Brandon could have more room once we finally took off. I faintly remember lying on the galley floor, trying to hold down a child with autism in the middle of a meltdown, while crying almost hysterically myself because it was now too late to even jump off the plane.

When we finally arrived home—with no one in the house but us—my husband did a little "Yeah, we're home" dance and clapped his hands. Brandon looked straight at him, smiling and laughing for the first time in a week. He clapped his hands for the first time ever. That week, I learned that with my family, it is indeed, "All for one, and one for all." Autism did not, and will not, ever defeat us. It may slow us down and change the way we do things, certainly how we travel, but defeat us? Never.

Michelle M. Guppy

Michelle M. Guppy is a wife, mother, and autism advocate. While Brandon has adapted to traveling by car for family vacations to Grandma's, their family has yet to brave tackling another vacation where they have to travel by airplane! They have decided that the best vacation with their son is simply jumping on the trampoline and swimming in the pool in the comfort and safety of their own backyard. Michelle often uses humor in writing inspirational stories for parents who have children with autism. She can be reached at MichelleMGuppy@yahoo.com or through her website at www.TexasAutismAdvocacy.org. Michelle is creator of the Autism Awareness Calendar for Texas.

"It's been a tough day, Al,
you better make mine a double."

What They Forgot to Mention

The strongest and sweetest song remains to be sung.

Walt Whitman

I remember the day of my son's diagnosis of autism as if it were yesterday. The tone of the doctor's voice, the silence in the room, the words "lifelong disability, no cure, I'm sorry" still sting when I allow myself to reflect on that day.

But I have paused on occasions too numerous to count and thought, *Someone should've mentioned that* this *would be part of the package* when my child was diagnosed with autism.

Someone forgot to mention that I would listen to my child's simple utterances or attempted approximations as if he were a world leader giving the speech of a lifetime. I could never have imagined the worth of a single word despite the fact that I may never hear it again.

Someone forgot to mention that when my son was finally potty-trained at age nine, there would be few people who could understand the significance of such an accomplishment, and even fewer with whom I could actually share it. Accomplishments of any size, their true worth known only to me, would bring quiet celebrations between my son and me.

Someone should've mentioned that autism is messy! Wallpaper's meant to be shredded, bathrooms are designed to be flooded, walls are bare in order to smear stuff on them, washable paint really isn't, and more food will actually be crushed and dropped than eaten.

I wish someone would've mentioned that autism is extremely expensive! Doctors, therapists, medications, supplements, conferences, and sensory equipment are only the tip of the iceberg. I could not have guessed that my child's disability would allow people to cross our path in life who otherwise would not have, and that such people would willingly respond to a child in need.

Someone should have mentioned that each time a child with autism initiates or engages in a reciprocal hug, that feeling that you had when you held him for the first time comes back time and time again.

And they forgot to mention the day my son was diagnosed with autism that the triumphs over this disability would far outweigh the tears, that laughter would eventually ease the sense of loss, and that sheer faith would allow me and millions of other parents to fall into bed exhausted each night, only to get up the next day eager to discover what else they forgot to mention.

Sandy Sotzen

Sandy Sotzen holds a master's degree in education and has been a special-education teacher for twenty-one years. Sandy is the proud mom of two boys, ages fifteen and twelve, the youngest of which is identified with autism. She can be reached at sandysotzen@comcast.net.

2

GRATITUDE

The greatest gift you can give a child is the essence of your true self.

Fred Rogers

Is That All?

*It is only with the heart that one can see rightly;
what is essential is invisible to the eye.*

Antoine de Saint-Exupéry, *The Little Prince*

Immediately upon giving birth to her fifth child, Nelma's arms were empty. The hospital staff whisked away the baby before she could see him.

"I want to see my son," Nelma insisted.

"You need to understand that there are problems with the baby." The doctor explained that perhaps Nelma and her husband should consider an institution for their newborn.

"I want to see my son," Nelma demanded.

So the new bundle of babe was brought and placed in his mother's arms. Nelma smelled the sweet new baby smell of him. She cooed to the little boy and cradled him to her heart. Then, ever so carefully, she unwrapped his blanket. There lay her infant, born without legs, his hands and arms not fully developed. Nelma took it all in, caressed his soft new skin, and smiled into his trusting eyes.

"Oh," she smiled softly, "is that all?"

And so Jerry went home with his mother to the welcoming arms of his family. There were struggles along the way as there are for all families, yet Nelma continued to love her children and cover them with prayer. One of seven children, Jerry was treated just like everyone else in the family with the exception that there was no chair at Jerry's place at the dinner table, to allow for his wheelchair. When it was Jerry's turn to wash the dishes, he washed the dishes.

When a man from the circus came to ask if Jerry could be part of their freak show, Nelma and her husband took the man by the scruff of his neck and threw him out of their home. "Jerry is not a freak," Nelma informed the visitor. "Jerry is our son."

Years later, Jerry prepared to move away to college. A friend from church, Barbara, was overjoyed that Jerry would attend the same college where her daughter, Kathi, was enrolled. "Be sure to look her up when you get there," Barbara said.

Nearly a year later, Kathi made an impulsive trip home. In the familiar surroundings of her mother's living room, Kathi's confused emotions exploded into tears. "Mom, Jerry wants to marry me. I know he loves me, and I love him. But, Mom, Jerry doesn't have any legs. Can you marry someone without legs?"

Barbara's arms and calm voice encircled her grown daughter. "Honey, since you were young I have prayed for just the right husband for you. I prayed he would be a thoughtful, compassionate man. I prayed your husband would be strong in character and integrity, that he would be a leader in his home, that he would provide well for you and your children. I prayed your future husband would know God, that he would be an honest, hard worker, and that he would love you and be a tender life partner. I prayed you would be best friends, as well as husband and wife."

Barbara paused to lift Kathi's chin so their eyes met. "But, Kathi, I never prayed he would have legs."

With the blessing of their parents, Jerry and Kathi were married. They have five beautiful children, and every other one has red hair like their mother.

One day, Jerry and Kathi's oldest daughter invited her school-age friend to come for dinner. Partway through her hot dog, the guest turned to her young hostess. "Your dad doesn't have any legs," she reported.

Anna paused, and then peered under the dining table to study her dad parked in his wheelchair. Returning upright, she regarded her friend. "Your dad doesn't have a wheelchair," she replied.

All too soon, Jerry escorted his eldest daughter down a long church aisle to meet her groom, a young man she had grown up with in church. Next, Jerry and Kathi welcomed a daughter-in-law and the joyous arrival of grandchildren.

A lot of credit for the success of Jerry and Kathi's family is directly attributed to Jerry and Kathi's mothers. Nelma saw not her son's disabilities, but his potential. And Barbara saw not the wheelchair that held the man, but the answered prayers within the man.

PeggySue Wells

PeggySue Wells is the author of several books, including *What to Do When You Don't Know What to Say*, and *What to Do When You Don't Want to Go to Church*. She is an award-winning writer and speaker. Her articles appear nationally in newspapers and magazines. Today, Jerry is a teacher. As a public school resource specialist, he works with seventh-graders with learning disabilities. Jerry serves as an elder at Open Door Christian Church in American Canyon, California. As vice president of the Institute of Abundant Living, Jerry is a popular guest speaker, sharing his story and the stories of others who have overcome great challenges. Contact PeggySue at www.peggysuewells.com.

The Little Boy Who Waves

"Hope" is the thing with feathers
That perches on the soul
And sings the tune without the words
And never stops at all.

Emily Dickinson

On the first day of school, the yellow bus with the squeaky brakes stopped in front of our house. The attendant took my child's hand as he made his way up the steps into the bus. She told him, "Good morning ... this is your seat." I stepped away from the door and went to the window where he was sitting. I tapped on the window, trying to get my son to look at me. He wouldn't. The fan on the dashboard had caught his attention, and there was no distracting him from that. I waved good-bye to him anyway.

Time went on. We had our routine down, Brandon and me. I would guide him up the stairs of the bus, and then go to the window to try and get my son to look at me. He never would. I simply could not compete with the fan on the dashboard that fascinated him so. But I kept waving.

One day, I noticed the other children sitting behind my child. One child would stare out the window as he rocked back and forth. I wondered what he was thinking. He had such a serious, far-off expression on his face. One morning, I noticed another child a couple rows behind him. As I was waving to my son as the bus left, this particular child was waving back at me and smiling. And so it became our new routine. Each morning after I would tap on the window and wave to my son, I would then turn and wave to this little boy. He actually appeared to be anticipating his turn to be waved at. I admit I am very jealous of this boy's mom. Every morning she gets a wave and smile from her son, and my son doesn't even know I am there waving at him. Once my son gets on the bus, his focus turns to the fan on the dashboard. Yet this little boy I now wave at gives me hope that someday my child might notice me, and wave to me with a smile. It is a very bittersweet moment each morning, but hopeful, as well.

Many mornings I have walked back into my house in tears, pleading with God to make my child be more like that child. One morning, I woke up on the wrong side of the bed. After I grumpily handed my child off to the attendant, I turned to go back inside. I didn't tap on the window to wave good-bye to my child—or anyone else's. As I got to my front door and was about to open it, something made me turn and look at the bus. There it was—a panic-stricken face pressed against the school-bus window with a little hand waving frantically at me. A wave of guilt spread over me. I hastily stepped back and put my hand up to wave—but it was too late. I don't think the little boy who waves saw me. Never again did I forget to wave to him. And I truly miss that little boy when he's not there to wave at me.

I was sick one morning, and my husband had to do the bus routine for me. As I was giving him instructions as to what to put in the backpack and so on, I told him about the little boy who waves in the sixth row and made him promise me he wouldn't forget to wave at him. "Why do you want me to wave at someone else's kid?" he asked me. I didn't have the energy to explain my feelings to him right then—that the little boy was my hope, my inspiration, my prayer for my own son. That I do it because, for that one moment, I imagine my son being the little boy who smiles and waves good-bye to me each morning. Instead, I merely replied, "Just please . . ." My husband promised he would.

I would never trade my son for anyone else's. I thank God every day for my child and what he *can* do. But inside of me, I do long for the day that the "little boy who waves" will be mine.

Another school year came and went. The little boy in the sixth row is no longer on the bus, but still I wave at my son in the hope that he will wave to me. One day, out of the blue, the attendant said to me, "You know, it's the cutest thing—whenever the bus starts moving, and your son is humming and watching the fan, he will hold his hand beside his leg and start opening and closing his fist like he is waving."

Never give up hope. Have faith that what may seem impossible may just become possible someday . . . because you never know when the little boy who waves could be yours.

Michelle M. Guppy

Michelle M. Guppy is a wife, mother, and autism advocate. But more than that, she is constantly amazed at the inspiration received from watching her son grow and learn and do things that she was told, or that she thought, would never be possible for him! Brandon inspires her to give faith and hope to other parents through her writings. Michelle can be reached at MichelleMGuppy@yahoo.com or through her website at www.TexasAutismAdvocacy.org.

All She Has

We don't see things as they are. We see them as we are.

Anaïs Nin

"Hey, honey!" I said, hugging my seven-year-old, Jean Prince, as she got off the bus. "How was school?"

"Well, not so real good," she replied, looking glum. "Everyone has their pictures on the Reading Bulletin Board but me. I never get my picture up, not for math or reading or anything." Her shoulders slumped, and her chin began a definite quiver.

I'd like to believe that, with enough educational therapists, visits to the doctor, experimenting with different medications for ADHD, and drill, practice, and patience at home, I can turn my Jean into a valedictorian, a teacher's "dream child," the whiz kid who gets everything right and never colors outside the lines.

But I can't. And every failure is yet another blow to me, as well as to Jean. Taking a deep breath, I turned on the "building self-esteem" mode. "Well, hon, I'm sorry. But I'll bet something good happened in school today, didn't it?

What was the best thing that you did today?" Jean took
her own sweet time, thinking things through. She wasn't,
however, on the verge of tears anymore.

Finally, she brightened a bit and said, "I gave my bunny
from the prize box to Jeffrey when he fell down and cried
'cause his knee bled. Mrs. Lawrence said she was proud of
me, and she put my name on the 'Character Counts' tree."

"Sweetie, that's great!" I blessed Mrs. Lawrence in my
mind yet again.

The next day, we were reading the weather report in
the paper, ever mindful of the science curriculum, which
this month was focusing on weather. As I was trying to
help Jean sound out "partly cloudy," she grabbed the
paper and shrieked, "Mommy! Mommy! Why is that lady
crying, Mommy? She's holding those two little kitties,
and she's crying! Why?" I sighed. We were distracted
from the task at hand yet again—something that happens
with Jean on a minute-by-minute basis.

"Well, let's read the story," I replied, hoping to turn the
task into yet another school lesson. "It says here that the
lady is Mrs. Hamilton, and she lost her home yesterday
when lightning struck it." I read on, and the story was
indeed a heartbreaking one. The poor woman from the
small town of Monroe had lost everything—even her pet
dog—and had no insurance.

"Hmm, Jean," I concluded. "It says here that Pastor Barry
(our minister) is taking donations for Mrs. Hamilton. We'll
make sure to give him a check tomorrow at church to help
her out, okay?" Then I went off to locate Jean's elusive
three-year-old brother, James Moses, and begin dinner.

The next day, as I was trying to herd the crew out the
door for Sunday school, Jean suddenly wheeled around.
"Wait, I've got to get my stuff!" She came back with her
special heart-shaped box and a homemade card. I
strapped James Moses in the car seat and took off down

the drive. When we got to church, Jean didn't head straight to her Sunday school classroom. "I've got to find Pastor Barry!" she exclaimed. "Where is he?" It wasn't until then that I bothered to check out Jean's special box and card.

The card read, "Mrs Hamitlon, I am saveng mony for yuo. I pray for yuo. I love yuo. Jean." Inside the box was $8.54—every penny the child had saved from her allowance for the past month. The fifty cents she saved by not getting ice cream one day at school. The dollar she got for picking up all her toys and putting them away. The dollar her Meme sent her in the mail. The change from her last big purchase, a Barbie doll. The dollar and some change she'd been allowed to keep when she helped me clean out the car.

The pure magnitude of the gesture literally took my breath away. This was truly the widow's mite—every coin the child had in the world, wrapped up in her most special keepsake box, and accompanied with a card decorated with rainbows, a happy sun face, two smiling kitties, and every happy image the child could draw, along with as many words of encouragement as she could get down on paper. This was so much more important than reading or math. Her future? The sky's the limit.

Connie Ellison

Connie Ellison has taught English in Virginia's public schools for twenty-eight years. She is the author of the memoir, *Any Road: The Story of a Virginia Tobacco Farm.* Connie lives in Elon, Virginia, with her husband, Andrew, and two children, Jean Prince and James Moses. Jean is now a third-grader and an active member of Elon Presbyterian Church. This past year, Jean raised over $300 for her school's Jump Rope for Heart for the American Heart Association, in memory of her best friend, Ian Mapes, who died of heart complications last August.

One Brief Hour

*There is no better way to thank God for your
sight than by giving a helping hand to someone
in the dark.*

Helen Keller

For one brief hour on a sunny June afternoon, my life
intersected with a nineteen-year-old young man. He
walked away from that hour with his life changed forever.
I walked away with an empty leash and a full heart. Two
years before, my family and I had just returned from living
overseas in Hong Kong. We had lived in a forty-four-story
high-rise for four years, and were now back to our
American lifestyle, backyard included. All that was missing was a dog for my eight-year-old son.

My husband, not a dog lover, thought he had found a
way to table this discussion indefinitely. "Find a purpose
to having a dog, son, and then we'll talk." That very week,
Tad brought home a permission slip for a field trip to
travel to Guide Dogs for the Blind (GDB) in San Rafael,
California. Being a dog lover, I volunteered to chaperone.
Voilà! We had found a purpose. Tad and I attended the

weekly puppy meetings, filled out paperwork, studied the manual we were given by GDB, and within a month or so, we were on our way to pick up a little eight-week-old yellow Lab male puppy named Arbor.

About that same time, in Olathe, Kansas, nineteen-year-old Jonathan Hill began to fill out his paperwork to apply for a guide dog. Nearly blind from a rare syndrome called Bardet-Biedl, a genetic disease that results in progressive blindness, Jonathan didn't let his poor vision limit his life. Not by a long shot. An Eagle Scout, avid hiker and camper, and a college student, Jonathan had big plans for life with his future guide. After completing the lengthy application, Jonathan had to wait for Guide Dogs for the Blind to contact him, meet him, and see if he met their qualifications. He was selected, so now his job was to wait until a spot opened up for him in class.

Meanwhile, back in California, our first objective was to help Arbor discover the joys of using the great outdoors for his potty. The next objective was to start basic training: sitting, laying down, waiting, and not chewing up everything that got close to his tiny, razor-sharp teeth. And, of course, we gave him lots of love. Every Tuesday night, we packed Arbor into the car and zoomed off to our weekly puppy-training classes.

In his official little green jacket, he was proudly welcomed at supermarkets, church, and restaurants. More often than not, outings to socialize Arbor were very successful. Once or twice, our cheeks burning, we cleaned up after an unfortunate miscalculation of his need to relieve himself. And Arbor grew, and grew, and grew.

By the age of one year, he was well over eighty pounds. And just a few months later, we received word that Arbor had been recalled to Guide Dogs for formal training. When we dropped off our gentle giant at the facility, I thought I heard someone mutter, "Sheesh ... the Schmaltz family is here." It was true. We were bawling. Even my stoic husband shed a few tears. So now our job was to wait.

Every few weeks, we received a new report of how Arbor was progressing during the ten-phase, four-to-six-month training program. As he neared phase eight, I let myself start thinking that he might really do it. He might just graduate! Jonathan was now allowed to pack and arrive at Guide Dogs for his one-month training program. Throughout the month, from 6:00 AM to 6:00 PM, Jonathan and Arbor, who had been matched together based on personality type and need, worked on becoming an unstoppable team.

Twenty-eight days after Jonathan arrived at Guide Dogs, he and I met for the first time, right before the graduation ceremony. Immediately, I sensed why they had been paired. Jonathan, too, was a gentle giant. We had the honor of formally presenting Arbor to Jonathan at the ceremony. Afterward, we said good-bye. The car ride home was a solemn one. We knew that, very likely, we wouldn't see Arbor again.

The very next evening, I received an e-mail from Jonathan's mother, letting me know that the flight went well and they were back in Kansas. "Jonathan took Arbor on a walk to see his friend, and I realized something," she wrote. "He hadn't felt the confidence to walk to his friend's house in years."

In just twenty-four hours, Arbor had already started changing Jonathan's life. And since then, those two have done more than most sighted people ever do. They've hiked the Oregon Trail all the way to the Pacific Ocean. They've gone deep-sea fishing off the Florida Keys. And they always send me e-mails and postcards. Last year, I received the family's Christmas card with Arbor's name included in the imprint. Since that first e-mail from Jonathan's mother, I haven't felt any tinge of loss. Only gain. And, by the way, we're now raising our fifth guide-dog puppy.

Suzanne Woods Fisher

Suzanne Woods Fisher is an author, a wife and mother, and a puppy raiser for Guide Dogs for the Blind. The best thing about being a writer, she feels, is that everything in life ends up being material. It's all grit for the oyster. Check out her website at www.suzannewoodsfisher.com.

The Gift

I am only one; but still I am one. I cannot do everything, but still I can do something. I will not refuse to do the something I can do.

Edward Everett Hale

Battered crutches leaning in the corner, Fatuma sits, head down, eyes averted. Sixteen years old, she lost her leg above the knee to a land mine a year ago in Somalia, and is now in the refugee clinic. In her culture, because of her amputation, she has become family baggage, and her father stays in the waiting room, ashamed, as her twelve-year-old sister happily translates.

The medical student hadn't asked why she did not wear a prosthesis, so as the teaching physician in the clinic, I accompany him back to the room to fill in the holes in her story.

Eyes remain downturned; hope has gone from the room. Her prosthesis was lost in their flight from Somalia and never fit well.

There is a national organization for amputees, the Amputee Coalition of America (ACA). Perhaps she would benefit from speaking with them, I suggest.

The prosthesis was painful, she replies, words barely murmured. She has yet to walk again, yet to make eye contact in the room, and clearly feels herself a burden. She is ashamed.

How much of our own story is appropriate to share with our patients? In Western medicine, the line seems very clear, separating patient and physician. We teach and are taught that as physicians we are there for the patient, and our stories can get in the way of theirs.

But for the first time with a patient, I consciously step across the line between physician and patient. Raising the leg of my pants reveals the titanium of my prosthetic ankles, for both of my legs have been amputated below the knees due to an accident six years prior.

There is a burst of words in excited Somali between the sisters.

"But you are the doctor. How can you have artificial legs?"

The message translates beyond any words that I had tried to offer.

Hope enters the room as the disbelieving father is brought in. Now the offer to connect them with the ACA is heard. There is a round of stories, handshakes, and thanks, now accompanied by smiles and laughter. I leave the family with the medical resident.

Later, as the story is replayed with our clinic's psychologist, my eyes fill with tears. Though my life is full and blessed, it is not every day that I can see my prostheses as gifts.

Perhaps there are times when it is appropriate to offer our stories to our patients. Today, as I look back on the visit, it is clear that this encounter was not just a gift to my patient, but one to me, too. Revealing my story that day was healing for both patient and physician.

Thank you, Fatuma.

Jeffrey J. Cain, M.D.

[POSTSCRIPT: *Two years later, another medical student came to review the case of an eighteen-year-old amputee from Somalia. Returning to the room, we found a smiling Fatuma, who now speaks English, goes to school, and wears a prosthesis. Now quite animated, Fatuma was still struggling a bit with her prosthetic fit and other war wounds, but she clearly has new energy and a joy for life.*]

Dr. Jeffrey J. Cain is a family physician in Denver, Colorado, where he serves as chief of Family Medicine at the Children's Hospital. Dr. Cain has bilateral below-knee amputations since an accident a decade ago. Dr. Cain enjoys bicycling, flying, teaching medical residents, and adaptive skiing. He can be reached at cain.jeffrey@tchden.org.

I Won't Do It

Like many kids with autism, Byron has a hard time believing things that are seemingly illogical or abstract. Religion, in general, is a difficult concept for him to understand and study because it asks him to have faith in things he can't use his senses to confirm.

"Mom," he whispered to me on Easter morning, "you do realize that people don't come back from the dead?"

"Yes, you're right, but Jesus was special. He was God's son. You just have to believe he rose from the dead and know in your heart it's true," was my answer.

He quickly replied, "But, Mom, you know, your heart is just a muscle."

Hmmmm, okay . . .

One morning after his Sunday school class, his teacher came to me with the news that Byron had been acting out during the lesson and said some totally inappropriate things. This wasn't the first time he had behaved in such a way, but my husband and I decided that instead of the usual punishment of no computer or television or video games, we would try a new tactic. We told him he needed to talk to God a little more, so it would be his job to say our family's grace at the dinner table for the next week.

You would have thought we were torturing him with instruments from the Inquisition! He spent the rest of the day informing me and everyone else that there was no way he would talk to God.

"You can't make me say grace" became the mantra of the afternoon. "I won't do it," he would mutter under his breath every few minutes. "Mom, that's not fair" was shouted out at regular intervals.

As luck would have it, my in-laws were visiting, and we had planned a dinner that just happened to be one of Byron's favorites. The smell of ham, au gratin potatoes, and crescent rolls in the oven had all of us anticipating the food, but not necessarily the moments that would precede our meal. Soon, I announced that everything was almost ready, so it was time to wash up and sit down.

Byron stomped into the dining room and sat slouched in his seat while the rest of us found our chairs. It was with a sinking feeling that I asked Byron to bless our table.

Nothing happened for a moment. Then another moment passed, and the hush stretched even longer. Just as I opened my mouth to speak, we heard a loud noise.

"Bbbrrrrriiing!"

Puzzled silence filled the room.

"BBBbbbrrrriing!"

This telephonelike noise was coming from Byron, whose eyes were closed tight and whose face was scrunched up!

"BBBBBBbbbbrrrrrriiiing!"

I peeked questioningly at my husband and my confused in-laws. Suddenly, Byron began speaking in a deep, formal, monotone voice.

"Hello. You have reached God's answering machine. He is not available to listen to your prayers right now, but leave a message, and he will get back to you later." This was followed by a long pause.

"BEEP."

"BEEP."

"BEEEEEEEEP."

Another moment of silence filled the room as I saw my mother-in-law's shoulders begin to shake with silent laughter and my husband's eyes roll toward the ceiling.

"God," said Byron, "bless all this food, and bless my family, too. Amen and good-bye."

He quickly opened his eyes and looked up at me. "Mom," he said, "I didn't talk to God."

We looked at each other for a moment. I saw that he was looking less angry and a little wary, but definitely relieved to have this moment over.

"I'm sure he'll get the message," I said, "and maybe you can catch him tomorrow."

"Okay," he said, glad to finally proceed with eating.

Before bed that night, I let him know that God would be there for him whenever he was ready to talk. The rest of the week, Byron's graces were wonderfully reflective and inspiring, as well as thankful and semiconventional! Byron might not have been ready to talk to God on that Sunday evening, but hopefully he knew God would get the message and appreciate that some kids need a little extra time and understanding when it comes to prayer and all the mysteries of faith.

Nanette Whitman-Holmes

Nanette Whitman-Holmes is a graduate of the University of Utah. She is a stay-at-home mother to her three sons, keeps busy with volunteer work, and plans to continue writing for pleasure. Her husband's career with the U.S. government brought the family to Concord, New Hampshire, in 2001. Byron is a fifth-grader who enjoys reading, computer art and graphics, and classic cartoons. His frequent pithy comments and quirky sense of humor keep life interesting for the whole family! E-mail them at 5holmes@comcast.net.

❧ Out of the Mouths of Babes ❧

My cousin worked as a secretary at my son Brent's old elementary school. She would fill me in on how Brent behaved at school when I would come to pick him up in the evenings.

One day, she told me Brent got into trouble for talking during silent lunch. As Brent and I were walking to the car, I thought I would check to see if he would be honest enough to tell me what had happened. I said, "Brent, how was your day?"

"Okay," he said.

"Did you get into trouble?"

"No ... umm ... let me think ... yes."

"Well, what happened?"

"Umm, we were in the cafeteria, and there were these kids at the far table near the stage. They were talking and being really loud and disrespectful, and I was one of them."

Jimmy Hinkley

Jimmy Hinkley, a para-educator for Pulaski County, Virginia schools, has dedicated his life to working with children with disabilities and finding new ways to teach those who learn differently. He's certified for sign language interpreting, and an active volunteer and mentor to children in the community. Brent was diagnosed with Asperger's syndrome in fourth grade. He is now a thirteen-year-old honor-roll student in seventh grade, and enjoys wrestling, swimming, computers, and video games. Jimmy can be reached at jimmyhinkley@hotmail.com.

"I know the difference between right and wrong.
It's the similarities that mix me up."

Reprinted by permission of Patrick Hardin and Cartoon Resources. ©2005 Cartoon Resources.

McBuns!

I not only use all the brains that I have, but all that I can borrow.

Woodrow Wilson

The sign read: *All children must wear socks while playing in McDonald's Playland. If you do not have socks, you can purchase a pair at the register.*

My daughter, Hollie, who has autism, is pretty strong-willed about not wearing socks. But we were with our friends, and they wanted to be sure to follow the rules. They chose to go to Kmart instead of buying the over-priced socks at McDonald's. I chose to carry my kicking and screaming five-year-old out the door. I got her back in the car with little resistance and drove home, explaining all the way why we needed socks. "We can't play in McDonald's without socks. It's a rule. You must wear your socks." Maybe I could pound it into her head by the time we got back. I explained to my other daughter, Taryn, that even if Hollie takes her socks off, she (Taryn) *must* leave hers on. "We need to teach Hollie that these are the rules. Please, please help Mommy do this," I begged.

We arrived back at McDonald's, and Hollie tried at once to take off her socks. "No socks, no play," I stated firmly.

She left on her socks. She entered the Playland with a huge grin on her face, climbing up and through the tunnels, and when she got to the net tunnel in the far corner, she proceeded to remove her socks and shove them down the net.

"Hmph!" I imagined her saying, as she seemed quite satisfied that she had won this battle. After stripping off her socks, Hollie exited the Playland. We hadn't had a chance to order any of our meals yet, so Hollie proceeded to find random French fries at different tables. I apologized repeatedly to puzzled parents as they watched my daughter dancing around the room, eating fries, and smiling. When we were close to the door, I shouted out our order. A baffled employee returned promptly with Hollie's favorite four-piece Chicken McNuggets with fries. I took the meal back to the table and began to set it up—nuggets on one side of the container, fries on the other, and ketchup with the fries.

Just then I heard someone say, "Ma'am, your daughter is sitting at someone else's table eating their meal!" I looked over and saw a young father politely removing his child's drink from Hollie's lips.

I ran over to nab Hollie, and we finally got situated with our own meal at our own table. My friend watched Hollie as I got the rest of our meals. Things were finally going smoothly. Just then, Mrs. Prout, Hollie's future kindergarten teacher, came to the table to say hi. She had recognized Hollie running around and wanted to greet her. I was tickled, but Hollie was unaffected by this show of affection. Mrs. Prout soon moved on to her own table.

After the kids ate, they all went back to the Playland. I watched with great pride as Hollie played right along with the other children.

And then, in an instant, I could see that things were about to take a turn for the worse. I watched Hollie through the Plexiglas high above my head as she removed her shirt. I shouted, "HOLLIE, NO GET NAKED!" and then

I heard Taryn say, "Oh, boy, she's getting naked!" A parent behind me let out a laugh. When I turned to look, she said, "Don't worry, honey, we've all been there before!" Hollie turned to face me with a smile, bunched up her shirt, and shoved it through the tennis-ball-sized hole in the yellow octagon dome. My friend caught the shirt, tossed it to me, and said, "Now she's removing her shorts." Again, Hollie shoved her shorts through the hole, and they fell right into my friend's hands. She tossed them to me as well.

I scanned the room, and all eyes were on Hollie. Parents, children, and even her future kindergarten teacher were looking up to see just how far this junior exhibitionist would go. As she removed her underpants, I began to feel mortified. *How am I going to get her down?* My friend caught the undies and tossed them to me. We searched for our other children to go up and get Hollie, but we couldn't find them. My dear friend headed up the climber, and as she rose to this occasion, I yelled, "Just say, 'Let's go potty'!" Then I came back out within viewing distance to find Hollie not there! A parent pointed to the net tunnel and said, "She's up there!" A few minutes later, Hollie came down on the green slide with a huge smile on her face.

"Let's go potty!" I said, grabbing her hand and pulling her to privacy. After the excitement had settled, I wandered over to Mrs. Prout's table to see just what this future kindergarten teacher thought of her new student. She offered up an explanation, "I guess she got hot!"

I replied, "And they were worried about her keeping her socks on!"

Trisha Kay Kayden

Trisha Kayden is a mother of two very active daughters. Her oldest child has autism. Trisha devotes much of her time to helping her daughter. Today, at the age of seven, Hollie enjoys being fully included in first grade. She loves swimming, gymnastics, and Brownie Girl Scouts. Ironically, she does not like the newly remodeled McDonald's Playland. Trisha enjoys spending time with her family, bike riding, camping, and reading. She is a strong advocate for families of children with disabilities. Please e-mail her at tkkayden@charter.net.

Challenges

It's good to have money and the things money can buy, but it's good, too, to check up once in a while and make sure that you haven't lost the things money can't buy.

George Horace Lormier

"I don't know how you can stand being in that classroom all day," people say to me when I tell them that, after two years of substituting in my local school district, I like being in the elementary emotional support classroom more than all others. I've substituted at all levels: elementary, middle, and high school; for secretaries, learning support aides, library assistants, and receptionists. Each position offers a certain amount of responsibility, but most of them leave me feeling as though I only put in my time. I'm the warm replacement body for a day. I'm a parking space filled. Some days, those positions are dull, with little to accomplish, and so few challenges that I feel as though I lose brain cells by the second. Sure, I still get paid, but it is demoralizing to watch the clock ticking hour-long seconds. But as an aide in an emotional support classroom, I never stop moving. Never. And even if my body does stop for a brief period of time, my brain is still racing. I'm watching, no, more than watching . . . observing . . . ready to intercept, redirect, call for reinforcements if one of the students becomes overwhelmed and needs more help.

I might spend hours with a group of boys who struggle to read and balk at writing anything, including their name. Getting them to sit still and stay focused is an energy-draining job most days, virtually impossible on others. There might be a few girls who only want to lay their heads on the desk all day long. How many times can you say, "You need to sit up . . . you are in school now"? Hundreds? Millions? Yes. For these children, life is tough. We only see their outside behavior. We don't see what is happening in their heads, their hearts, their souls. We repeat and repeat and repeat the same direction dozens of times, only to be faced with vacant looks when we ask why they are not following directions.

Parenting five kids full-time for eighteen years is nothing compared to working for twenty minutes on math with three of these struggling kids. Setting the bar high enough to stretch them and low enough so that they are not instantly discouraged is a constant challenge. Watching a child struggle every day of his life to spell two words correctly is disheartening.

Then one day, almost out of the blue, after you work with one of them over and over, he gets his very first 100 percent on a spelling test. And you fly right along with him, higher than you or he ever thought possible. Emotional support classrooms present the greatest challenges—and the greatest rewards. The final bell rings. The day is over, but you can't imagine how it's possible because you never once looked at the clock.

Mary Mooney

While living in Jakarta, Indonesia, for three years, **Mary Mooney** conducted team-building workshops throughout Asia and edited the American Women's Association of Indonesia magazine. She is a certified multicultural diversity trainer, a professional actress, public speaker, and a playwright. She has worked in emotional and learning support classrooms in her Pennsylvania school district, and has produced a theatrical musical addressing the needs of people with mental illness and their families. Please contact her at mooneym@verizon.net.

What's the Truth About Thomas?

Put love first. Entertain thoughts that give life, and when a thought or resentment, or hurt, or fear comes your way, have another thought that is more powerful—a thought that is love.

Mary Manin Morrissey

Nothing in my ten years of teaching children from low-income, non-English-speaking families had prepared me for the day Thomas arrived in my second-grade classroom. I had dealt with tantrums, medicated children, disabilities, and poverty, but never had I dealt with such an emotionally disturbed child as Thomas. I knew from his school files that he'd been taken away from his mother, who had exposed him to pornography, among other things. Now he lived with a couple who were one step away from being homeless, living in a cramped, dingy hotel and often lacking food.

Deep in my heart, where the sun doesn't shine, I sometimes hoped this child would not return to my classroom. Each morning, Thomas showed up ready to destroy my last thread of patience and sanity. *How do you tell a child that it's not acceptable to expose his private parts to other classmates?* I tried to get Thomas to sit in his seat, follow instructions, and do his work. But most days, he'd scream, refuse to sit in his seat, and run off to a corner.

Trying to maintain order and teach the other children left me drained. I developed chest pains and high blood pressure. I pleaded for help from the principal, the vice principal, and the school psychologist. No one had an answer. When we sent notes home, Thomas was severely punished by his guardians. I stopped sending notes home.

After Christmas vacation, Thomas didn't return. As much as I had wanted to ask God to remove this child from my classroom, I could never pray those words. Now, it seemed my problems were over. Each morning, I cautiously drove to school, wondering if this would be the day that Thomas came back.

After two weeks of bliss, Thomas walked back into my life. A few days later, I became so ill that I missed a week of school. *It's Thomas,* I told myself. *That child is ruining my health.* Stuck flat on my back in bed, I began to pray. "God, I can't take this anymore. No one can help me. I need your wisdom. I need your love for this child."

A week later, I forced myself back to school. Nothing had changed. Thomas began to throw his usual fit when I asked him to do his work. Speaking in a gentle, yet firm voice, I said, "Thomas, come here." I walked to the side of the classroom and motioned for him to come over.

With head down and eyes on the floor, he came to me. I squatted down to eye level and said, "Tell me your name."

No response. Again, "Tell me your name."

Refusing to look at me, he said, "Thomas."

"That's right," I said. "Your name is Thomas."

Still looking at his downcast eyes, I said, "Tell me what is true about you." He didn't answer.

"Then I will tell you what is true about you. Your name

is Thomas, and you are a good boy. Now tell me what is true about you."

He did not answer. I continued, "You are Thomas, and you are a very smart boy. Now repeat that to me."

He said in a whisper, "I am Thomas, and I am a very smart boy."

"What else is true about you?" I coached. "I am Thomas, and I can make good choices."

His eyes lifted to my face. "I am Thomas, and I can make good choices."

I took a breath and said, "I am Thomas, and God gave me a good mind."

By now, his body had relaxed, and he said, "I am Thomas, and God gave me a good mind."

Looking into his eyes, I said, "Thomas, I want you to use your good mind. Now go back to your desk and finish your work." To my amazement, Thomas completed his work without any disruption to the class.

Every day, I'd take him aside and say, "Thomas, what is the truth about you?"

He'd answer, "I am Thomas, and I can make good choices. I am Thomas, and I have a good mind."

One day, as I was working with some students, I noticed Thomas hiding behind a pocket chart near our group. In a voice hardly loud enough to hear, he kept repeating, "I am a bad boy. I am dumb."

I listened for a few minutes, and then said to the children I was working with, "Boys and girls, what is the truth about Thomas?"

One little girl piped up, "Thomas is smart."

Another child said, "Thomas can make good choices."

One boy raised his hand. "Thomas has a good mind."

"That's right," I said. "Thomas is smart, and he can make good choices. Thomas is a good boy." Out of the corner of my eye, I could see Thomas taking in every word.

Now, I'd like to tell you that all my problems with Thomas disappeared overnight, but they didn't. But, ever so slowly, his behavior did begin to change. One day in the teachers' lounge, the vice principal said to me, "You never send Thomas to my office anymore. What happened?" The school psychologist was grabbing a cup of coffee and turned to listen.

"Well," I said, "let me tell you the truth about Thomas." And I told them the story.

When the children were leaving my classroom later that afternoon, I stood at the door saying good-bye. Thomas managed to be the last child out and turned to give me a quick hug. As I watched him race down the hallway, unexpected words tumbled from my lips, "Luv ya!" I doubt that he heard me, but it didn't matter. I walked back to my desk, sat down, and sobbed. I had no idea when I had started to love Thomas, but I did.

Laura Dean
As told to Jeanne Pallos

Jeanne Pallos is a published author for adults and children. A resident of Orange County, California, Jeanne is a member of the Christian Writers Fellowship and a key producer of their annual conference. She and her husband, Andrew, are parents of two adult children. You may reach her at jlpallos@cox.net.

Kids Amaze Me

My daughter, Jaimie, was my miracle girl. She reminded me of one of those little babies you see in photos from the early 1900s—big, wondering, blue eyes, poker-straight strawberry-blonde hair, and creamy porcelain-doll skin.

Looking down on her each night as I watched her sleep, my heart filled with pure love I didn't know existed before she did. She was perfect. But as she grew, she became increasingly more introverted and scared of her surroundings. Something was terribly wrong. After two and a half years of her behavior getting worse, she was diagnosed with sensory integration dysfunction (SID).

Although not a life-threatening disorder, it causes her tremendous anxiety and frustration. Essentially, SID is a dysfunction of the nervous system, where information received from the environment isn't processed properly in Jaimie's brain. She has no "filtering-out" capability, causing her to get smells, sights, noises, or tactile (touch) signals all at the same time. It would be comparable to a crowd of people coming at you all at once, each demanding a different sort of attention. It can be both scary and overwhelming.

Needless to say, Jaimie's condition can alienate her from

other children, as they're unsure how to approach her. We live in a townhouse complex where the homes are lined up around a winding road. It's nice because the homes block out sound from the street, but noise within the complex is quite audible.

One day, Jaimie was in the front yard running and spinning in circles—two things she finds comfort in doing. As Jaimie spun, her strawberry-blonde hair spread out around her like a parachute coming in for a landing. She stopped only when things were spinning without her, and she fell into a pile of giggles on the prickly grass. As I laughed with Jaimie, I heard a young, but husky voice from my right ask, "What's wrong with her?" Surprised by the sudden intrusion, I turned to see a young blonde girl, her pigtails sticking out Pippi Longstocking–style from under her bike helmet.

"What do you mean?" I asked calmly. I knew what she meant. I'd heard her comment about Jaimie when we'd seen her at the park.

"She's always spinning around, talkin' to herself. I tried to talk to her at the park, but she just ran away screamin'. I didn't even do anything to her. She's always got a soother in her mouth and she's not even a baby. Her bike has three wheels, but she's big. Why is she so weird?"

Ahh, the honesty of little ones. She wasn't asking to be mean. She simply wanted to know why this other girl was . . . different . . . different from her and her friends. I crouched down and put my hand on Jaimie's chest while she stared up at the clouds. She seemed oblivious to the other girl beside me. The inquisitive girl stood astride her bike, staring down at me and waiting for her answer.

I struggled to find the right words to help her understand. "Tell me something. Have you ever tried really hard to do something, but it was really hard for you?"

"Oh, yeah, lotsa times," she nodded.

"And what happened when you tried to do something hard, and you couldn't do it right away? How did it make you feel?"

She scrunched up her face, as though it helped her to remember. "I remember learning to ride this bike with no extra wheels, and I kept falling off. I hurt myself a lot. I didn't want to do it anymore because every time I tried I fell. It made me very mad, and I cried," she said all in one breath. "My dad and mom told me to keep trying and that I could do it. Then one day, I did!"

"That's wonderful," I smiled. "Those mad feelings you felt... where you cried... didn't feel very good, did they?"

"No. I didn't like that." She looked down.

"That's how Jaimie feels every single day. The hard part is that what hurts her isn't always something we can see."

"You mean something invisible is making her like that?" she asked, her emerald eyes widening.

"I guess you could say that," I laughed. "You see, Jaimie feels things differently than you or I do. Hey! Have you ever been at the park when it's really busy and loud?"

"Oh, yes. It's like that every day at recess," she said.

"Right! Okay, well, it can get pretty busy there, right? So busy you can't always concentrate on one thing."

"Yeah, like if I'm trying to talk to my friends, but everyone is running around and screaming."

"Exactly. That's how Jaimie feels all the time. Like there are lots of sounds, things to see, smells, or people trying to touch her, and she gets scared. She doesn't know how to ignore stuff so she can listen to one noise or see one thing. She gets very scared, and she runs, or she stands there and screams."

The little girl stared at me for a good minute, then looked down at Jaimie. Her eyes rimmed with tears. "Is that why she ran away from us at the playground?" she asked.

"Yes. It wasn't because she didn't want to play with you. There was just too much going on for her to feel comfortable enough to talk to you. That's all. She's a wonderful girl to know. You just have to be patient with her until she feels safe enough with you."

The young girl wiped her nose on her arm, then got back on her bike. "I get scared, too, sometimes. That's not so weird."

"No, that's not so weird." Jaimie got up and started spinning again. The young girl rode back over to her friends, who asked her why she was talking to "the weird girl."

As I walked back to the stairs to sit down, I heard the young girl's voice echo around our complex: "Hey! She's not weird. Her name is Jaimie, and she's special. And I'm going to be friends with her." With that, she dropped her bike, ran back over to our front lawn, and began to spin with Jaimie. "See, Jaimie? There's nothing wrong with being scared. I'll spin with you until you want a friend."

Kids amaze me.

Chynna Laird

Chynna Tamara Laird lives in Edmonton, Alberta, with her partner, Steve, and three children—Jaimie (four), Jordhan (two), and new baby boy, Xander. She's a freelance writer, completing a B.A. in psychology. She eventually wants to specialize in developmental neuropsychology to help children and families with special needs. Jaimie has made excellent progress since her diagnosis. Her verbal skills are strong, she loves music and art, and she's slowly building up her courage to venture out of the boundaries of her strict routine to try new things. She'll even be attending a special preschool class with her sister, Jordhan, very soon. Please e-mail Chynna at lilywolf@telus.net.

A Whale of a Time

Last year, we went to Niagara Falls and found out that nearby Marineland had orcas. Our son, Sam, has loved killer whales since he was about a year old. The walls in his room are covered in posters and picture calendars of orcas, and we have dozens of orca toys: plastic, plush, large and small, plus magnets, stickers, and pillowcases. And did I mention books? We have countless books on whales and dolphins, but mostly orcas. *Free Willy?* He's a friend we watch nearly every day.

So off we went to Marineland on Thursday, August 16, 2005. Once in the park, we headed straight for Friendship Cove, home of four orcas. I can't tell you how excited we all were to watch Sam's face as he saw, for the first time in his life, a real killer whale. It was a moment to remember, followed by many more that weekend. We purchased tickets to stand with the trainer, and feed and pet an orca.

After a full day of fun with the family at the park, Sam and I returned for a second day—nine hours just standing at the tanks, watching the whales. Sam was in heaven. As we left, he said, "Good-bye, whales. See you next year."

From the day we departed Canada, Sam started talking about returning on Thursday, August 17, 2006. If you know a child with autism, you know that you have to talk about the upcoming trip daily, like twenty times a day. Fast-forward to this past August. Sam was ready, wearing the same shirt as last year so the whales would recognize him. We got to Friendship Cove, and there were no more ticket sales for feeding the whales! The activity had been replaced with a new Splash Show. Sure, the Splash Show was fantastic and fascinating, but I could see the despair and confusion on my sweet boy's face. We stayed for two shows, took lots of photos and video, saw the rest of the park, went on rides, and returned to say good-bye to the whales. Sam and I came back again for a second day.

We planted ourselves into position, as we had been last year, to spend the day watching the whales swim around their wide-open tanks. We were literally two feet away from those beautiful mammals. The Splash Show took place every hour and a half. People would start filing into the area ten minutes before showtime, then disperse twenty minutes later, soaking wet.

The trainers noticed we were there—and still there, and again, still there. We started up a conversation with one of the attendants, who asked Sam about the pile of books he was carrying. This young man, Nicholas, recognized that Sam was no ordinary child, and tried to keep him engaged in conversation. One thing became obvious to Nicholas— Sam adored the whales! Then, just prior to the next Splash Show, the "host" of the event, Sean, came over to talk with Sam. I could feel myself leaving my body—you know, that kind of moment you have when something really good is happening. Time stands still, you can barely speak, and tears flood down your face. Sean told Sam, "I could really use a helper for the show. Do you think you could help me?" *What did he just say? Dear God, thank you.* If I could have felt my legs at that moment, I would have dropped to my knees.

The show began. Mike and Kendra, the whale trainers,

introduced themselves to this hysterical mom with winks and smiles. Sean went up to the microphone and introduced Sam Ward from New Jersey. Sam, who had memorized the show, mimicked the trainers. He knew what to do, and he knew the act. The trainers got such a kick out of it! Sam was not afraid in the least to be in front of a huge crowd, and directed the whales to do their tricks. I will be eternally grateful to Nicholas, who had the insight, and to Sean, Mike, and Kendra, who had the hearts, to give this special boy a very special day.

Michelle Ward

Michelle Ward began her career in architecture, but has been a working artist for ten years. She is a regular contributor to *Somerset Studio* magazine and serves on their editorial advisory board. Michelle and her husband, Graham, live in New Jersey with their three children. And Thursday, August 16, 2007? You know where they'll be!

Sam enjoying a good read with a new friend.

Talking to Strangers

Better keep yourself clean and bright; you are the window through which you must see the world.
George Bernard Shaw

My nine-year-old daughter, Jessica, is a friendly soul. From the time she was tiny, she would march right up to strangers on the street and say, "Hello!" Her brown eyes would twinkle, and she'd be sporting a big grin on her face. I wish she weren't so gregarious, because she's vulnerable. Not only is she young and female, but she also has a disability: she has a cognitive disability, with a debilitating brain disorder that causes autistic and obsessive-compulsive behavior. But that's also why I've done my best to curb my nervousness. Children with autism don't relate well to others, and I don't want to discourage her attempts. I worry, though, that people will snub her or be cruel to her, or that she will trust the wrong person.

Happily, in our small town, when Jessica strikes up a conversation with someone, that person almost always responds kindly to her. She never expects to be rebuffed, but I am always waiting, tense, and ready to collect the pieces if it happens. "What's your name?" she asks total strangers. "Do you have a dog? How old are you?" It always surprises me that people patiently answer her queries. They must sense something about Jessica, that she's a little bit different. They never seem to expect me to stop her, although I've tried.

"We don't ask adults that," I say. "That's a rude question, sweetie," I tell her, to no avail. She asks anyway, and people tell her. When she is done with her inquisition, she will turn to me and say, "We know Michelle now," or "That was Mrs. Crawford." She moves them easily from one category to another: people we don't know, people we do know. Strangers are merely people she hasn't yet asked for their names. I'm less sure that finding out their names means we know them. But it's a small, easygoing town, and I don't fret too much. It's not as if she goes about unsupervised or that she tells them anything too personal.

But talking to strangers in our small town is one thing. In New York City, where we visited last year, it's another. I wasn't surprised to hear her saying "Hello!" to every single person we saw as we walked the streets of midtown Manhattan, but I certainly wasn't comfortable. On the first day, I decided not to try to stop her. *This will be a good lesson for her,* I thought. *People will snub her—these are New Yorkers, after all—and then when we get back to the hotel room tonight, she and I will talk about the difference between people in big cities and small towns. And maybe she will learn not to talk to strangers.*

But I never got a chance to have my discussion with Jessica. Every single person she said "hello" to said "hello" right back—the businessmen in their somber suits, scurrying from one place to the other; the gawking tourists with their cameras at the ready; the doormen standing at attention in their uniforms. She even said "hello" to the homeless people. She asked what they were doing there, and they told her. I've never asked because I don't talk to strangers. One man on his cell phone stopped in his tracks and told her not only his name and age, but also his occupation and what he was going to do with his girlfriend over the weekend. As he strode off after Jessica's grilling, I heard him say into the cell phone, "I have no idea who that was. Just a little kid." *Just a little kid . . . who doesn't know better than to talk to strangers.*

Later, we were at a corner waiting for the light to change, and Jessica greeted everyone there. Over the top of Jessica's head, I met the glance of a casually dressed man with curly brown hair. "She's autistic, isn't she?" he said to me, with a directness that took my breath away. After all, he was a perfect stranger. I put my hand protectively on Jessica's shoulder. "Yes," I said. This is the kind of encounter I dislike, but I wasn't telling him anything he didn't already know.

His face smoothed into a look of compassion. "I work with children who have autism," he explained. "It's a challenge, isn't it?" I felt something inside me weaken: a wall, perhaps, I never even knew I had built. Because I expected people to be indifferent to me, or to be judgmental, I never expected kindness. Not like Jessica, who always does.

The light changed. "She has a good mom," the brown-haired man said simply, and walked away. I caught my breath. If he had thrust a bouquet of gardenias into my hands, I would not have been as surprised. His words were like an offering, a gift, for which he wanted nothing in return.

"That was Mark," Jessica said. "We know Mark now."

"We sure do," I said, and smiled.

Jennifer Lawler

Jennifer Lawler is a writer who lives in the Midwest with her adorable daughter, Jessica, and their lazy mutt, Jazmine. Visit Jennifer's website at www.jennifer lawler.com.

On the Inside

What we see depends mainly on what we look for.

John Lubbock

I look like a monster. During a routine root canal last week, the dentist accidentally tore a blood vessel in my face, and the result is that the left side of my face is black and purple and swollen from eyebrow to throat.

While painful, the worst part of this mishap is the deep embarrassment at having my face look so monstrous. I hadn't realized the shock of my bruises until my neighbor dropped by and literally jumped off my porch at the sight of my face, clutching at her heart and shrieking involuntarily.

"It's not even a good story," I told her, and explained about the dentist and the torn blood vessel. After a brief visit, I said good-bye to her, knowing she had never paid attention to our conversation because my face was so distracting. I was disheartened and embarrassed.

The embarrassment grew more deeply rooted when I took my son to kindergarten the next day. Upon seeing my face (which I thought was cleverly concealed by my hair swept over my face and the sunglasses I wore indoors), Noah's teacher gasped. Expletives spewed forth, causing me to laugh, and she to slap a hand over her mouth. "I'm sorry," she apologized for her involuntary cursing. "You look like someone beat the life out of you!" I explained what had happened and literally ran to my car, heading home to hide from all human contact.

For several days, I avoided contact with people other than my family, and my first foray into public in search of a video led to new humiliation and had me determined not to leave home again.

"Mommy, look at that lady's face!" I heard the little boy's voice behind me, and the heat rose in my cheeks as I instantly knew I was the freak show he pointed at. "Don't stare," I heard the mother whisper as she yanked the boy out of the video store so he wouldn't have to see the scary-faced woman. I drove home, crawled into bed, and pulled the covers over my head, intending to stay there until I looked human again.

A couple of days later, I looked in the mirror and tried to view my face from a stranger's perspective. The perfect circle of purple around my eye lent me the look of that dog on *Little Rascals*. The huge, swollen black and purple splotches along my cheek and jaw, and the streaks of blue and green down my throat, were colorful and distracted from the fact that I wore no makeup, which was too painful to apply. I couldn't have felt more insecure.

Sighing, I told myself, *If my own children accepted this temporary ugliness, then what did I care what strangers thought. It's just my face, after all—not who I am. It's what's on the inside that matters.* I put on my sunglasses and headed to the bookstore in search of more boredom busters.

As I locked up my car and shook my hair down to cover my cheek, I realized my hands were shaking. *This is ridiculous!* I scolded myself. *It's just a bunch of bruises!*

Trying to be invisible, I headed to the kids' section to look for something my kids might like.

"Mommy, look at that lady's face!" The words again brought the blush of embarrassment, and I wished the floor would magically swallow me up. I wasn't prepared for the mother's reaction.

"I know, honey. She looks like Shaley!" The woman actually sounded happy about this, almost like I did when I saw another deaf child like my youngest.

I turned to see who was so excited about my disfigurement and saw a woman, a little girl, and another little girl in a wheelchair, all staring at me. The little girl in the wheelchair had a facial deformity that made my heart ache for her. I don't know what it's called, but I knew she had a disease that made her life expectancy uncertain. I knew she was Shaley, and I also knew there was a lesson for me here.

"Hi!" I bent down and touched the side of Shaley's face gently, fingers shaking. She had huge, sparkly brown eyes, and they shined with inner beauty that made me forget the face so obvious at first glance.

She reached a tiny hand up to me, past my bruises, and up to grab a handful of my red hair in her gnarled hand. Her touch was gentle, sweet, and careful.

"Pretty," she said simply.

Tears stung my eyes as all at once I felt shame at myself and admiration for this brave little angel. She could see beauty in a place where others saw ugliness.

I grinned at her and said, "Thank you, Shaley."

"Pretty," she said again and touched my cheeks. By now, I was fighting to keep the tears from spilling. I looked at this tiny doll and knew she was freer than most people ever were. She knew what really mattered, and she had the courage to speak up and say it. She made me feel special, as if she looked into my soul with those huge brown eyes and deemed me pretty on the inside.

We said our good-byes, and I watched her mother wheel her away. I wanted to thank her, but stood rooted in silence and tears. I watched until they were gone, and then headed to my car and home. Shaley touched a complete stranger and put things neatly in perspective. My battered outside would eventually heal. Hers would not. But she showed me that what is true, what is really important, has nothing to do with our outside packaging. It's on the inside.

Susan Farr-Fahncke

Dedicated to making a difference, **Susan Farr-Fahncke** is the creator of 2the heart.com, founder of the amazing volunteer group, Angels2TheHeart, and a busy author. With stories featured in several Chicken Soup books, she is also the author of the beloved *Angel's Legacy*. She teaches online writing workshops, and you can sign up for a workshop and see more of her writing at 2theheart.com.

Broken-Down Signs

*I am one of the last of a small tribe of trouba-
dours who still believe that life is a beautiful and
exciting journey with a purpose and grace, which
are well worth singing about.*

Yip Harburg

Signs are all around us. Signs point the way. They tell us
what we're allowed to do. They tell us where we're not
allowed to go. They keep us from getting lost.

This is a story about signs—all kinds of signs.

The story begins at the home of my folks, near the Lake
Michigan shore. It's not where I grew up, but it's where
my parents have decided to retire, and we've visited them
often enough over the years that I guess it's a bit of a
"home away from home" for our family.

We used to visit quite often. These days, we don't make
it up there as often as we'd like. It hasn't been easy to travel
ever since our son, Evan—now four years old—was born
with a terminal heart disease called hypertrophic cardiomyopathy and a variety of other complications brought
about by a genetic condition called Noonan syndrome.

This year, the family—my wife Penni, our seven-year-old son Noah, Evan, and Evan's nurse—traveled to Lake Michigan to visit my folks and get some much-needed rest and relaxation.

One afternoon just a few days into our vacation, my sons and I walked to a large community swimming pool. Since it'd been a while for all of us, we weren't exactly sure which roads led to the pool.

Noah said, "Hey, Dad, I think we're supposed to turn here."

"The street sign looks like it's been run down by a car," I replied. "How do you know this is the right place, Noah?"

"Trust me, Dad."

Well, he was right. The pool was just around the corner. That broken-down sign didn't keep us from finding the pool, or from making a new friend that day—a little girl named Renee.

Actually, we met Renee's dad first; my brother-in-law introduced us. He was about my age, wearing a T-shirt about Down syndrome. As other parents around us sunbathed and caught up on the latest gossip, I told him that I had a child with a syndrome, too.

In truth, I'd already noticed Renee, though I didn't know that was her name. She was hard to miss; even though there were close to 100 kids in the pool that day, she sparkled. I liked that about her.

Her dad called her over to us, but she flew past. "Renee," he said again. "Come here, sweetie. I want you to meet someone." Renee's fine hair framed her face, which had typical Down syndrome features. Her brown eyes glittered with life and intensity. When she spoke to her dad, her speech was a bit broken and monotonic, though he didn't seem to have any trouble understanding her. He introduced her to Evan and me.

"Hi, Renee," I said, as I got down on one knee. "Would

you like to sing the Bumblebee song with Evan and me?"

We all three sat down, and I started singing the little tune. To my surprise, she jumped right in as though she had been rehearsing for weeks! As we sang, Evan—who doesn't speak—let out an occasional happy squawk. When the song ended, Renee babbled excitedly. Because I had a hard time understanding her, I asked what she was trying to say. She amazed me by signing with her tiny fingers, "More." My heart melted.

I signed back. "More music?"

She again signed with her fingers. This time she signed "please" by placing her hand over her heart and moving it in a circular motion.

When we left the pool that day, we'd made a new friend. As I started to push Evan's stroller toward the exit, Renee ran up to me, tapped me on the back, and gave me a big hug and a kiss on the cheek. No words were spoken as we embraced, but the message was mutually clear. I turned away with a smile that matched the one on her father's face. He didn't wave as we left; he just nodded his head. I knew what he meant.

There'd been many a head turned that day around the pool . . . not toward us, but away from us. And I don't know how many times I overheard kids asking their parents, "What's wrong with them?" I guess people don't understand sign language. Or maybe they just don't like to look at people who seem to be broken.

As Noah, Evan, and I walked home from the pool, we ran into a woman we hadn't seen in a year or two. Noticing our "language" of hand signals and obnoxious grunts, she squinted her face and asked, "Does he even understand what you are saying?"

"Yes," I replied, just slightly offended.

I wanted to say, "I know he doesn't speak . . . and I know he can only sign one or two words . . . and I know those signs aren't done perfectly . . . but he does like to listen to singing . . . and he does like to go to the pool!" Hmmmppphhh.

Back at home, Evan and I sat on the front porch, swinging in the creaking wooden porch swing. We let the warm lake breeze put our souls to rest. As we rocked together, I wondered about how we communicate our wants and needs, and about how sometimes things just seem to come out of our mouths.

And I thought about some of the things that have come out of people's mouths upon meeting Evan for the first time:

"How do you know what he's saying?"
"Does he love you?"
"Does he like to play?"
"How do you know if he's crying?"
"Does he even know he's sick?"
"Is he broken?"

For each question asked, I could write so many heartwarming stories about Evan that the book would never end. Does Evan speak? Yeah, I think so. When a wife looks at her husband, puts one hand on her hip, taps one foot, and slightly cocks her head, what does it mean? Ahhh, any guy knows! She's mad about another dumb thing he's done. You see, all communication is not verbal.

Renee and Evan speak a language made up of imperfect and incomplete signing, verbalizations that are unintelligible to most people, facial expressions, and body language. Very few actual words, if any, are required. I guess Renee's dad and I have the gift of being able to look past the broken signs to the heart of the message. Along the way, I've met a number of people—mostly parents of kids with special needs—who have this same gift.

I'll end this story by telling you about one more sign.

There's a church in my hometown with a roadside sign that says: "Sign broken, message inside." I think that says it all.

Scott Newport

Scott Newport is the father of Evan, who was diagnosed with Noonan syndrome and hypertrophic cardiomyopathy as an infant. Evan spent the first 252 days of his life in the hospital, only to leave with a death notice. Now five years old, Evan uses a ventilator to breathe and has various developmental delays. The Newport family endures happily in Royal Oak, Michigan. Visit Scott's blog with Exceptional Parenting at www.eparent.com/resources—blogs/index.asp.

Broken Shells

We love because it's the only true adventure.

Nikki Giovanni

It was a warm summer afternoon in mid-July at the Jersey shore. My four-year-old son and I just loved venturing off to the beach just before dinner when the rest of the vacationers seemed to be leaving for the day. The sun was still hot and shining bright. With bucket in hand, we'd hit the sand and start our adventure. Will would run so quickly to the edge of the water and be soaked before I got there, laughing as the waves crashed and nearly knocked him down. I remember the days not so long ago when a trip to the beach was just unbearable for my little boy. His sensitivities to sights, sounds, and touches would prevent us from enjoying everyday activities, such as a walk by the shore. My son, Will, was diagnosed with autism spectrum disorder (ASD), and despite the fact that he is high-functioning, he has spent many hours in therapy, helping him to overcome the many challenges he faces. The beach is now one of his favorite places to visit. I am thrilled, because it is a place where I feel at home and filled with peace, and I wanted to be able to share that with Will.

Presently, we are able to walk along the edge of the water almost daily in the summer months, looking for seashells to fill our red sandcastle-shaped bucket. Some days, the bucket is full, and other days just a few shells make it into the bucket. On this particular day, there didn't seem to be too many shells washed up on the shore. Will began picking up whatever shells he saw lying in the sand. After a while, I peered into the bucket and saw nothing but broken shells. "Will," I said, "all of these shells are broken and no good. You need to find shells like this," I continued, as I held up a perfectly shaped clamshell. Will gave me a puzzled look and continued on his way, gathering whatever shells he came upon and dropping them into the bucket.

I continued my search for some time, and then stopped to watch him drop more broken shells into the bucket. Again I stopped, but this time I asked in a more stern voice, "Will, why do you insist on filling our bucket with shells that are broken?" He looked up at me through his glasses with his big blue eyes and replied, "Mom, there are way more shells on the beach that are broken than there are perfect ones that you are searching for. We'll get the bucket filled faster with the broken ones." *True*, I thought, *but who wants a bucketful of broken shells?* Will stared at me as if he knew what I was thinking. "Mom, these shells are broken, but they are still beautiful," he chimed. Just then he reached his little hand into the bucket and began pulling out the different shells and commenting on their uniqueness. "This one is broken, but look, it has the color purple on it. Mom, none of yours have purple on them," he said with such pride.

"You're right, Will," I agreed.

"And, Mom, this one looks like a smile when you hold it this way," he said as he reached for another broken shell.

"It reminds me of a clown. This one is round like the sun, and these ones are stuck together like butterfly wings."

My eyes filled with tears as I realized my son was teaching me a most valuable lesson. I reached my hand into the bucket and began to take out the few perfect shells I had collected and placed them back on the beach. Will and I walked along the beach, collecting only broken shells in our bucket and admiring their beauty.

When we arrived back at our beach home, we rinsed off our bucket of shells and proudly displayed our "broken shell garden" next to our patio. It is a constant reminder of how none of us are perfect. We are all broken in some way, but we still possess beauty and uniqueness beyond belief. Now, whenever we go to the beach, we gather only broken shells. Yes, it's true, while the perfect shells are few and far between, there are many more broken shells left lying on the beach that go unnoticed. If we take the time to look more closely at the broken shells, we can find beauty in their imperfections, and maybe even learn something about ourselves.

Debbie Jaskot

Deborah Hickey Jaskot received her master's of education from Cabrini College. She resides in Garnet Valley, Pennsylvania, with her husband and their five-year-old son. Debbie is currently devoting her time at home to her son, from whom she learns every day, and who inspired her to write the first of many stories to come. Please e-mail her at debjaskot@comcast.net.

3

MILESTONES

*There are only two ways to live your life.
One is as though nothing is a miracle.
The other is as though everything is a mira-
cle.*

Albert Einstein

Dancing with Myself

It's always the rug you've been sweeping things under that gets pulled out from under you.

Jim Bannerman

The e-mail popped onto my screen. "Because you lack volunteer service hours, you're invited to help at a sock hop for the Oklahoma Foundation for the Disabled this Saturday night. In order to become a Junior Hospitality Club member, you must attend this final event of the season." *A dance for people with disabilities?* I'd not been around many people with disabilities, and I didn't know how comfortable I'd feel helping out. Besides, I'd be going alone, which was sure to make me feel awkward.

I'd pledged Junior Hospitality (JH), a women's social and philanthropic organization, at the beginning of the year with the hope of meeting "couple friends" for my husband and me. What I didn't count on is that we'd be divorcing seven months after I signed up. Despite the divorce, I wanted to become a member. I tapped out a reply that I'd go. Getting to know the women of JH was fun, and I liked the idea of being part of a group that

helped the community. Unfortunately, members sometimes brought their husbands to activities. Certainly, at a
sock hop, that would be the case. I'd feel more alone than
ever. I sighed. Getting dressed up and going to a party
was the last thing I felt like doing. But it was only four
hours, then I'd be done with my requirements. After this,
all that was left was a written test.

On Saturday afternoon, I rooted around in the closet
for fifties-style clothes. I rolled up my jeans to midcalf,
slid into a white shirt, turned down the cuffs of a white
pair of socks, and slipped on a pair of retro-looking
sneakers. I even found an old bandana and tied it around
my neck. I pushed a headband over my hair and stared
at my reflection. Tears welled up in the corners of my
eyes. *Please, God, help me get through this.* I hated feeling so
alone.

A deejay was setting up his equipment as I walked into
the large gymnasium. Several club members laughed as
they filled helium balloons with their husbands. The volunteer service coordinator, who directed me to come, suggested I join a group moving tables and chairs. "This area
will be the dance floor," said a woman in saddle oxfords
and a yellow polka-dot skirt as we lifted a folding table. I
remembered her from a JH meeting. She seemed nice, and
I looked forward to getting to know her. "Let me do that."
A man with greased-back hair gave the woman on the
other end of the table a peck on the cheek. "You gals get
the chairs." I smiled, but inside I felt a pang of loneliness.
Everyone had a date except me.

At seven o'clock sharp, busloads of revelers arrived.
Some came in wheelchairs. Some walked with limps.
Others looked like they had Down syndrome or other
cognitive disabilities. The fluorescent lights shut off
abruptly, and the music blared. Most people made their
way straight to the dance floor, while others stood

around in a circle. "This is just like a high-school mixer," I commented to another JH member wearing red pedal pushers. Before she could reply, her husband grabbed her hand. It looked like they'd taken swing-dance lessons at one time. I was thankful for the darkness and hoped it covered my sadness. I edged closer to the wall and watched others wiggle and twist to the music. Not only did the rejection of my ex-husband hurt, but memories of high-school dances more than twenty years earlier returned to my mind.

That familiar sinking feeling that no one would choose me churned in the pit of my stomach. I remembered times as a young woman when I waited for a partner—dances, dinners, movies, marriage. Being alone made me feel unworthy, unloved.

Then, in the center of the dance floor, I saw something radiant. It was a young woman wearing a poodle skirt, checked shirt, bobby socks, and saddle oxfords. Her long, blonde hair was pulled into a ponytail, and a pale pink scarf flowed around her neck. Maybe it was the light reflecting off the disco ball above her, but she seemed to have an aura about her, a glow. Although a stranger, she waved at me from the dance floor. Barely five feet tall, with a stout body and thick neck, she smiled broadly. In the middle of the crowd, her skirt swished as she moved to the music—alone. She twirled around and around. She seemed so free, so at ease. Again, she waved, but this time, she motioned me out to the dance floor. I felt inhibited, and everything within me wanted to resist. I forced myself to walk toward the center of the room. Pushing my way through dancers, I made it under the disco ball. But the woman wasn't there. My first instinct was to run.

Then I noticed those surrounding me. Most of the dancers were without partners. Costumes varied, but each wore a big smile. Adults with disabilities, some even in wheelchairs, all seemed to be enjoying themselves more than me.

As I stood in the center of the floor, it hit me: in a roomful of people whom the world labeled as disabled, I was the one too afraid to dance. I really didn't need to find the woman who waved me onto the floor. What I needed was to learn how to dance by myself. Right here, right now. I closed my eyes and swayed side to side. Moving to the music, I felt more joyful than I had in a long time. When I opened my eyes, I realized I wasn't alone. True, I didn't have a partner, but I was surrounded by people—not just JH members, but a group of people who seemed to embrace life despite their limitations.

Later that month, I took the final test to become a member of JH. I giggled as I wrote the answer to the first question that asked the motto of Junior Hospitality: Help yourself while helping others. Indeed, I already had.

Stephanie Welcher Thompson

Stephanie Welcher Thompson is a wife and stay-at-home mom who writes when she is apart from daughter, Micah, four, and husband, Michael. Her stories have appeared in *Guideposts, Angels on Earth, Positive Thinking, Sweet 16,* and ten Chicken Soup books. Reach her at P.O. Box 1502, Edmond, OK 73083 or stephanie@state ofchange.net.

Sunday Morning

My little man, so handsome today, so grown-up, is sitting up tall next to me in "big church." He keeps shooting me that signature smile of his.

The music begins, and his entire body comes alive with unrestrained enthusiasm. With all the strength of his six-year-old body and the support of Mom's stronger arms, he comes to a wobbly stand. I hold tight as he sings with abandon. He does not miss a word. Neither does anyone else within earshot. He has worked very hard for every sound he makes. Full of praise (and full of himself), he sings every word in his time—and in tune, apparently, or so I've been told by people who would know.

Bennett's heart beats for music. Since he was a toddler, he has been able to recognize songs by hearing only the first few notes, as well as naming the artists of familiar tunes. At age four, he requested to hear some "oprah mulik" (opera music). He has come a long way from crying at the sound of the music therapist's guitar to strumming one of his own. Amazing, considering he cannot yet control an eating utensil enough to feed himself independently. He has come a long way. We have come a long way. . . .

Today, he is singing for God. I ask him every now and
then just to check. He will, at any given moment in the
day, break into an impromptu "ladies and dentamen
(ladies and gentlemen) presenting" . . . usually himself. In
his unlimited imagination, Bennett is not only a rock star,
but also a doctor, chef, teacher, and talk-show host. He
spends much of his time with a real or makeshift microphone in hand (occupational therapy at its best). Simple
tasks of the day are announced and presented to the imaginary studio audience that lives at our house. Pouring a
cup of milk or helping him to sit up is frequently followed
by "Mama, ladies and dentamen." Most anything is reason
for applause and accolade. Homework is usually done as a
special segment on Live with Regis and Kelly. He's Regis. I'm
Kelly. An American Idol expert extraordinaire and future
idol himself, Bennett has entertained nurses live from his
hospital bed.

I treasure these moments. I treasure every word. I treasure every breath.

He shoots that smile at me again. Minutes into the ser-
mon, he whispers, "Mama, more music." He didn't always
have the breath support to whisper.

We were told Bennett would not walk or talk, along
with an overwhelming list of neurological and medical
challenges. In addition, due to respiratory issues, there is
a high infant mortality rate for children with Joubert syndrome. When the doctor was finished, his words had not
only ripped through us, but through the dream of what
we thought was to be.

I shoot a smile down at my squirming virtuoso as I
think of how this six-year-old, thirty years my junior, has
been my teacher.

After we were given the news, my husband and I
excused ourselves to the hospital chapel. Later in the
neonatal intensive care unit, Jeff looked down at our tiny

gift, camouflaged by tubes and wires, and said, "I just want him to know I am his daddy, and I love him."

Bennett is nearly seven years old. He gives us more love than we can hold. He is our dream come true. We have walked hand in hand with sorrow and with joy, many times simultaneously. There have been many nights when I greeted the moon and the sun without a closed lid in between, some by a hospital bed, some through prayerful tears as I cry out on behalf of our suffering son. And we have seen miracles.

We have seen Bennett in the emergency room go from nonresponsive and pneumonia blue to pink and shooting that smile at a surprised ER doctor who had minutes earlier prepared us for the worst. We have seen mystery spasms that caused great struggle brought under control. We have seen provision for Bennett's care financially and through gifted specialists. We have also experienced comfort and support from friends who go above and beyond. We have heard Bennett put his first sentence together, an ironic "I luh lou (I love you)" for Daddy. Nearly every day, I watch as he is wheeled into first grade, where he is doing well. And recently, we watched with great pride as he took his first steps in a walker. (He might as well be standing on a podium, gold medal lighting up his chest with the American anthem blaring overhead. He has put in as much effort and accomplished as much by pushing himself down our hallway.) We have watched him grow into an amazing little person who shows love to others freely. It was once thought he may never lift his arms over his head. These are the same arms that wrap around my neck and pull me in close every day.

Bennett's body may never catch up with his mind and heart. Perhaps the biggest miracle is knowing it does not have to.

Our life is different from many, full of doctors' appointments, therapies, hospital stays, and advocacy. Everything takes great effort, sometimes painstaking effort. The privilege of caring for Bennett is a large part of our daily lives, but a small part of who he is.

Teacher Bennett has shown me that hope does not disappoint, that love never fails, and to take nothing for granted. I've learned there is a difference between completely relying on God's strength and relying on my own strength to hold on to him. I now know the greatest calling we have is to love and be loved. Bennett has more than enough ability to fulfill this calling. In six years, he has touched more lives than many do in sixty.

"Bennett, listen." I lean down in a whisper. "The pastor is talking about loving others." Sweet pea looks up, with arms raised to hug, and says, "I luh lou, Mama."

After the service, a lady approaches me. She had been watching us. I think she called me remarkable, encouraging words from someone kind enough to not keep them to herself. I thank her, and think, *I am a mom who loves her son.* I'd like to think there is nothing significantly remarkable about that, but I appreciated the encouragement nonetheless.

As I carefully carry Bennett down the stairs from the balcony, I tell him he is remarkable. He smiles and squeezes me a little tighter.

Bennett, ladies and dentamen.

Hillary Key

Hillary Key is a full-time mom, and lives with her husband, Jeff, and son, Bennett, in Roswell, Georgia. She received her bachelor's degree in graphic arts from the University of South Carolina in 1992. Hillary had two short stories published in 2006 in *Special Strength for Special Parents*. She enjoys painting, reading, and being a daily guest star on *The Bennett Show*, broadcast "live" from her living room, produced by the imagination of her son. Bennett, the host and creator, is doing extraordinarily well. He is enjoying good health, sweet friendships, and a new stage built into the corner of his room by special fans.

Speech Therapy

Every survival kit should include a sense of humor.

Anonymous

When my son was five years old, he displayed a variety of autistic behaviors and was classified as "speech and language impaired" by the school district. The school staff and I worked hard to achieve a comfortable and collaborative relationship.

One day, I received a telephone call from my son's speech therapist with whom I had a good relationship. She was very upset because my son appeared, for the first time, to be agitated and frustrated to the point of insubordination. She explained to me that she was trying to work with him, but he kept saying, "I don't want this sh-t anymore!" It only got worse when the therapist tried to keep him focused on the task at hand. He kept repeating, "I don't want this sh-t anymore!" Finally, in a display of exasperation, she said my son picked up his papers and threw them down, screaming, "I don't want this sh-t anymore!" The therapist apologized and said she had to bring my boy to the principal's office to be written up for his behavior.

I was quiet for a moment, trying to discern what might have caused my son to become so uncharacteristically disagreeable.

Suddenly, I realized what must have happened. I asked the therapist where my son was at that moment.

The therapist replied that he was outside playing in the courtyard where she could see him from the phone.

I asked her if he was doing anything else or if she noticed him pulling at the collar of his shirt.

"Yes, he's been pulling at his shirt all day," replied the therapist.

I could not help but laugh. I told the therapist what happened earlier that morning when he was getting ready for school.

I explained that one of his autisticlike behaviors was a sensitivity to clothing labels. In response, I had been cutting the labels out of his shirts, but sometimes the remaining pieces still irritated him.

The shirt he was wearing that particular day was bothering him, but because we were late for the bus stop, I told him he had to leave it on.

Apparently, my son was not saying, "I don't want this sh-t anymore!" He was saying, "I don't want this shirt anymore!" And then he got very frustrated when nobody understood.

The speech therapist felt awful, and said she would go outside right away and apologize to him.

Before we hung up, we both had a good laugh when I said, "I guess he still needs some help with his articulation!"

Karen Brill

Karen Brill's son is now seventeen years old and will be graduating from high school next year with a standard diploma. He plans to work as a paraprofessional with elementary-school students who have special needs, and to start his own business, "Big Matt's Auto Detailing." Contact them at Palm1010@aol.com.

Reprinted by permission of Off the Mark and Mark Parisi. ©1999 Mark Parisi.

Toss of a Coin

A person's a person, no matter how small.
Dr. Seuss, Horton Hears a Who

It was a hot August day when Mike and Jeff sat down in the shade of a maple tree to assign students to their respective classes for the coming year. This year, more than seventy twelve- and thirteen-year-olds were enrolled to receive the lessons and experiences of grade seven. But Mike and Jeff were no ordinary teachers. Rivaling their love of teaching was their love of sport. And thus, when the time came to assign students to their respective classes, Mike and Jeff did what any good captain of a team would do—they flipped a coin. Their plan was to assign the first pick to the winner of the coin toss, then alternate picks until all seventy students had been placed.

Mike held the coin firmly in his grasp and nodded to Jeff. When Jeff indicated he was ready, Mike caused the coin to flip end over end through the summer air. As the coin reached its peak, Jeff called "heads." With the smooth precision of someone skilled in hand-eye coordination, Mike grabbed the coin out of midair and placed it onto the back of his hand. Both waited with mock impatience as if something of extreme importance depended on the outcome. Little did they know how important this decision would be.

As Mike removed his hand from atop the coin, Jeff yelled out with exuberance, "Heads, I get first pick!" Despite Mike's plea for "two out of three," Jeff began reviewing the names of the students on the list. "Now who shall it be?" Jeff thought out loud. "Who will be the captain of my team?" After seemingly endless pondering, Jeff's eyes rested on the name of Joshua Kuntz.

Joshua was not your average student. Josh began seizing at five months of age following his immunization shot. The seizing increased in frequency and duration, despite the efforts of the neurologists at the local hospital. By the time Josh was four, he was seizing twelve to fifteen times each day, with seizures lasting up to twenty minutes. Seizures of this length deprive the brain of oxygen. The result is significant neurological damage. By the fall of his grade-seven year, the effects of the seizing had reduced Josh's capacity to the level of a two-year-old. Having Josh as a student would mean constant vigilance to keep him safe, as well as additional assistance to support his learning. And yet Jeff's eyes remained on Josh's name. Then Jeff raised his eyes to meet Mike's. In a soft, clear voice, Jeff declared, "I choose Josh."

Mike was a relatively new teacher to the school. He did not know each and every student, but Mike did know Josh. Josh's disabilities—both intellectual and medical—were well known at the school. "What?" exclaimed Mike in disbelief. "I don't understand. Of all the students you could have selected, why would you choose a child with severe disabilities for your first pick?"

Jeff smiled at Mike's question. It was not an unusual one. As a matter of fact, most people who meet Josh for the first time see only his "disabled" parts. Jeff knew it took time to see beyond the disabilities and notice the parts of

Josh that are wonderful and beautiful. Jeff responded, "Mike, I've been around the school for a few years, and I can't help but notice Josh. But even more important, I notice how the other children respond to Josh. I notice how they eagerly greet him as they pass him in the hallways. I notice children rushing to complete an assignment to earn the opportunity to read to Josh while the others finish. I notice boys and girls alike taking turns holding Josh's hand as he is wheeled in his chair. I notice children modifying a game so as to include Josh. I notice children rubbing Josh's back as he rests following a seizure. But most important, what I noticed is that the children are kinder and gentler when in Josh's presence. I believe having Josh in my class makes it a kinder and gentler place for all children to learn."

And so, on that hot August day, a wonderful thing happened under the shade of a maple tree. A young child whom many saw only as disabled came to be valued for his contribution. And what was Josh's contribution? Creating an opportunity, by way of his disabilities, for others to express their caring, compassion, respect, and dignity.

Anyone who happened to visit that particular grade-seven class noticed something different. They may not have known that the toss of a coin and the selection of a young student with disabilities were responsible, but the spirit of caring in the room was unmistakable.

Ted Kuntz

Ted Kuntz is the father of Joshua and author of *Peace Begins with Me*. This inspiring book captures the wisdom Ted acquired in making peace with his son's disabilities. To contact Ted or to order his book, visit www.peacebeginswithme.ca. To learn more about recognizing the contributions of individuals with a disability, visit PLAN Institute for Caring Citizenship at www.planinstitute.ca. Josh is now twenty-two years old. He lives in a home in Coquitlam, British Columbia, a suburb of Vancouver. While his seizure disorder has improved, the seizures have never been completely controlled. Josh enjoys going for walks with his dog, Miah.

Miniature Angels

The language of friendship is not words but meanings.

Henry David Thoreau

"I want a friend!" my five-year-old's clear blue eyes showed the pain of rejection. Noah is deaf, and the past couple of years have begun to show what the future holds for my little guy.

The first few years of his life, Noah had many friends in our neighborhood. Small children don't talk a heck of a lot and are content to simply play. As time passed and Noah got to the age where speech and hearing were a noticeable part of "hanging out," his friends started realizing he was different. Soon, no one came to play with my tiny son, and he too began to understand he was different.

My heart has ached, and I have spent endless hours in tears, begging God to send him a friend. "Just one," I have prayed. "If he just had one buddy, I know he would be happy." I have prayed this prayer for a very long time, but my little son has had to be content with only having friends at the school for the deaf, where he attends preschool. Noah has lots of friends at school, and they are all deaf like him, so this has been a blessing. But the children at school come from far and wide, and none live near enough to "hang out." It's just not the same when you're five.

Noah recently began the heartbreaking hobby of writing and leaving mail on the porch for his "friends." He tapes his own toys to the notes, thinking that he can somehow make friends this way. I often have to sneak outside to retrieve his notes so that he thinks someone is getting his messages of friendship. And I have to admit I have even "forged" notes left with stickers for him, so that his excited trips to the front porch the next morning would sometimes net him a feeling of having an unseen pen pal. It breaks my heart. This beautiful, hilarious, kind child deserves to have a friend.

But today was different. I got a miracle—in fact, three of them.

My phone rang, and I was distracted with a long-distance friend, catching up with each other's lives. I didn't notice Noah slipping out the front door.

It wasn't until my sixteen-year-old came home for lunch that Noah's absence was known. Panic-stricken, Nick and I scoured the house, yard, and garage . . . no Noah.

As I searched the house again, my heart pounding with a million frightened thoughts flitting through my brain, I began to tremble. A child off on his own is scary enough, but a deaf child poses hundreds of dangerous scenarios that gripped me in a panic.

"I found him!" Nick yelled from around the side of the house. "You have to see this, Mom." I could hear awe in my teenager's voice, and I hurried around to see. I couldn't believe my eyes at first. I thought I was hallucinating.

A few houses down the street from ours, four children

were playing gleefully. One of them was Noah. My neighbor runs a day care, and three of her charges were in the front yard, dancing and jumping and doing little-kid things—and Noah was right in the middle of it.

I watched with tear-filled eyes a scene that most mothers see every day, but that I had dreamed of and prayed hard for, for the past two years. Two little girls and two little boys who looked enough alike to be brothers chased each other around the trees, laughing, falling, and giggling, and generally having a silly time of it. Tears slid down my cheeks.

I watched from a distance, and sheer joy filled my heart. Three little kids, who had no idea what a gift they were giving a little boy who was deaf, looked like miniature angels to me. My heart just filled with gratitude. Watching them, you couldn't tell Noah was any different, and his laughter rang with the exact same impishness as the others. I absolutely wanted to kiss and hug those three children.

I let them play until lunchtime, at last walking down the street to retrieve my child like a million other mothers do a million times a day. I felt like I was floating, and my grin was greeted by four chubby, dirty, and happy faces.

"Hi! I'm Noah's mommy," I greeted them. I wanted to empty out my purse and give them all my money and credit cards.

"Is that his name?" the little girl in pink inquired of me. "I'm Jessica, and she's Carissa, and he's Nathan." The little hostess made introductions all around.

"Yup, Noah can't hear, though. His ears don't work very well." I tried to squelch the visions of rejection as I shared this news with Noah's new friends.

"We know, but he can CLIMB!" was the simple response. My son was proudly demonstrating this skill for her. Not missing a beat, the same little girl asked,

"Can he jump on the trampoline with us?" Children are amazingly uncomplicated. Overlooking what Noah couldn't do in favor of what he can do was a beautiful little lesson all in itself. I loved this little girl.

It was time for Noah to come home, so we made plans for another playdate. Noah waved good-bye, started off for home, and then turned back around. "Hug?" he signed to the mini-angels.

I explained the sign to them, and they each stepped forward to hug their friend. The tears threatened me again, and we made a hasty retreat before I embarrassed him.

"Bye, Noah! Come over later!" followed us home. Noah looked up at me, his blue eyes huge, and with a priceless grin signed "friends" to me. Holding his little hand in mine, I said a silent prayer of thanks for three miniature angels.

Susan Farr-Fahncke

Noah is now a happy nine-year-old and is active in Scouts, swimming, and art. He recently won his very first writing contest. He wrote about being thankful for his family and won a college scholarship! Dedicated to making a difference, **Susan Farr-Fahncke** is the creator of 2theheart.com, the founder of the amazing volunteer group, Angels2TheHeart, and is also a busy writer and mom of four. With stories featured in several Chicken Soup books, she is also the author of the beloved *Angel's Legacy*. She teaches online writing workshops, and you can sign up for a workshop and see more of what her readers fondly call "Noah stories" at 2theheart.com.

Milestones

Patience makes lighter what sorrow may not heal.

Horace

Life presents many milestone moments. Among the biggest is high-school graduation day—a sea of smiling faces, fond memories, hopes, dreams, and new challenges to face.

The graduation of the class of 2000, the first graduating class of the new millennium, was to be such a moment for Melissa. Instead, it would be one of the many milestone moments we would grieve after her death. But Graduation Day 2000 also served as a reminder that, while it may never be the same, life does go on.

Kelly was only seventeen when Melissa was born. She and her young husband, Tom, took their parental responsibility very seriously. Kelly left school thinking she could always finish later. Tom got a good job to support his new family. It seemed that everything would be fine, until they got the news that Melissa had cystic fibrosis, a terminal illness for which there was no cure. It was a devastating blow, but they found strength in each other, and Melissa was the joy of their life.

I met Kelly when Melissa was about three years old. Our husbands worked together, and we became close friends. Melissa dubbed me her "second mom," and we quickly developed a special bond that I will always treasure.

Six days after Melissa's fourth birthday, she got a baby sister. We prayed that Amanda would be healthy, but she, too, had cystic fibrosis.

Barely twenty-one, with two terminally ill children, Kelly's days were filled with hospital visits, medication, and treatments for the girls. Returning to school was the furthest thing from her mind. She was totally devoted to raising her beautiful daughters. I continually marveled at what a wonderful and selfless mother she was.

The years flew by, and there were many milestone moments to cherish. But there was also the sad realization that there would be many more milestones that would probably not come to pass.

In 1994, Melissa was twelve, and Amanda was eight. Amanda had been in and out of the hospital for most of the previous year. Her health was steadily declining, and the doctors had tried to prepare the family for the worst— as if it is possible to prepare for the loss of a child.

Then, in March, Amanda seemed to be improving and was home from the hospital when Melissa grew suddenly ill. She had been laughing, happily riding her bike on Friday. On Sunday, she was in the hospital, fighting for her life. By Wednesday, she was gone.

Shocked and grieving, Tom and Kelly tried to pull themselves together for their youngest daughter. They knew how frightened she must be, knowing that her sister had succumbed to the disease that had held her captive in a hospital bed for much of her life. They were frightened, too—for Amanda, for each other, and for the life that would never be the same again.

Amanda died less than three months later. I will never forget the words Kelly said to me, numb with grief, at Amanda's funeral. "I am a mother without children. What am I going to do now?"

Kelly had been a full-time mom her entire adult life. She had tried working out of the home a few times, but with the girls in and out of the hospital, a job was low on her priority list. Now she felt she needed to work. She knew that if she stayed home, she would find herself lost in sadness. But she wasn't sure what she could do. She didn't have much job experience, and she had never graduated from high school. Fear and self-doubt flooded her thoughts, but then she thought about her daughters and how they had faced so many challenges.

Drawing strength from their courage, and with the support of her husband, family, and friends, she quickly found a good job that she enjoyed. That job led to a better one, and she was soon in a management position. But, despite her advancing career, Kelly still felt a deep void in her life.

Work is a good distracter, but it doesn't heal the deep wounds of grief. It is said that time heals, and it does, but never completely. Holidays and other special occasions serve as constant reminders of the part of life that is missing. Milestone moments, like sweet sixteen, prom night, and graduation, are especially difficult.

Kelly had been dreading Graduation 2000. Several of Melissa's friends had stayed in touch, so she received invitations to attend the ceremony. Kelly knew that attending would be too difficult, but she felt a strong need to do something. Then the idea hit her. She would graduate for both of them!

Kelly was excited, but nervous. It had been so long since she had been in school. What if she failed? Doubts flooded her mind, but she was determined to do it, for herself and for Melissa. Soon, Kelly called me beaming with pride . . . she was going to be a graduate of the class of 2000!

It was a bittersweet moment, but Kelly found strength in something she dreaded and discovered a way to honor her daughters' memories through her own life. With newfound focus and a sense of self that had previously seemed out of reach, Kelly enrolled in college, something she never imagined she would do. Kelly received her bachelor's degree in May 2004 and is currently working toward her master's degree.

And life goes on, one milestone at a time.

Gina Morgan

Gina Morgan is a certified grief counselor and author of the children's book, *If Teddy Could Talk,* for families with terminally ill children. Gina was inspired to write this book by her goddaughters, Melissa and Amanda, who bravely faced life and death with cystic fibrosis. Gina is also a life coach and coauthor of the CORE Multidimensional Awareness Profile. E-mail Gina at gem@coremap.com.

Baby Steps Came in Her Own Time

No child is perfectly whole in mind, body, spirit, ability . . . nor can any child meet all of a parent's hopes and expectations. Yet there is a wholeness of each and every child, a wholeness that is unique and brings with it a unique set of possibilities and limitations, a unique set of opportunities for fulfillment.

Fred Rogers

Maybe I bought the book after Lucy was born, or maybe some well-intentioned someone gave it to me. I don't remember. But here it is, nearly three years later, still next to my bed. Back then, I read it, as well as lots of other books, looking for answers to questions. Lucy, my first grandchild, my oldest daughter's baby, was born with an extra chromosome.

"We're sorry," people said when they heard. And we were, too. Sorry and stunned and scared. *When Bad Things Happen to Good People* seemed an appropriate book to be reading at the time.

But I hold it in my hand now and think, *Bad things?* Lucy wasn't a bad thing. It was bad that she had three holes in her heart, but we didn't know that when she was born. All we knew was that she had Down syndrome. And yet we were sad anyway.

What was wrong with us? Why all the worry and fear? And why, even now, do we still, sometimes, more times than we should, continue to worry and fear when Lucy isn't doing something that some chart says she should be doing? Why can't we just relax and let Lucy lead the way?

She has dark blonde hair that curls at the ends, the prettiest almond-shaped blue eyes, and the tiniest nose, rosy cheeks, and a smile that we waited so long for. Even now, although she smiles all the time, it is still magic.

All babies are measured against charts. The average baby smiles at one month, rolls over at five months, walks at thirteen months.

Children with Down syndrome have charts, too. There, in black and white, are the anticipated dates when the child you love is supposed to be crossing some milestone.

And you look at the charts, and you worry every day when a child isn't on target. When the smile doesn't come when the chart says it should. When a first word isn't within first-word range. *What do these things mean? That she will never smile? That she will never talk?*

And then one day, she does. She smiles, and she talks, and you wonder: *why were we worried?*

I have been taking Lucy to church on Sunday mornings since she was ten days old. People whose names I don't know enveloped her from the beginning. "What a beautiful baby. What's her name? Lucy? Hi, Lucy." They prayed for her when she had heart surgery. And they prayed for her when she had to have more heart surgery.

"Look at how big she's getting. Look at her sitting up! And crawling! And standing!"

They have been cheerleaders to her progress. And they have witnessed her wonder: she loves the church lights and the music and the man who collects the money.

Last year, her cousin Adam, who is ten months younger, learned to walk. We watched him stand and take a step and grab on to a doll carriage and take more steps. Amazing! "Look at him learn," we said.

Lucy sat on the floor and watched him, too. Children with Down syndrome take a little longer to do things. The chart said she'd walk at twenty-five months. She was only twenty-three months. She had time.

But twenty-five months came, and she didn't walk. And then she was two and a half, and still not walking. And even two months shy of her third birthday, she wasn't really walking. She'd take a few steps, then sit down and scoot.

"Come on, Lucy," we said, clapping and cheering.

But standing upright and putting one foot in front of the other was clearly not on her agenda.

And then three weeks before her third birthday, as we arrived at church, I asked her, "Do you want to walk?" And she said, "Yes." So I unbuckled her seat belt, and she took my hand. And there she was, walking along the sidewalk, walking up the cement walk, walking up the big steps, walking into the church, walking into the foyer, and walking down the aisle, her pretty spring dress sashaying with every step.

And when she reached the pews, she sat down and clapped.

I held her hand again when it was time for Communion. But on the way back, she pulled away and continued on down the aisle, my little Lucy Rose, walking all by herself.

Beverly Beckham

Beverly Beckham writes a weekly Sunday column for the *Boston Globe*. She is also the author of *A Gift of Time*, a collection of personal essays, and *Back Then*, a memoir of childhood. She lives in Canton, Massachusetts, with her husband. They love watching Lucy Rose, who is now four years old, walking, running, and dancing! Beverly can be reached at bevbeckham@aol.com.

The Race

The morning dew clung to the grass,
As the sun began to rise,
A little girl stretched with a yawn
And rubbed her weary eyes.

A day just like all others,
Yet she managed still to smile,
She peered out through her window
And dreamed a little while.

This girl, like you, was special,
Unique in her own way,
Her legs just didn't have the strength
To run and jump and play.

She prayed each night that they would heal,
So she could share the fun,
To giggle and laugh with all her friends
Beneath the warming sun.

She longed to feel the soft, cool grass
And the sand between her toes,

To walk among the falling leaves
And the cold and crispy snow.

She'd watch the others in their favorite game,
In stance to start a race,
All crouched down in a single line,
Such excitement in their face.

She'd eagerly shout, ready, set, go,
And they'd take off with a flash,
Oh, she thought, how glad I'd be,
Even if I came in last.

And then one new and precious dawn,
Unlike the ones before,
She peered out through her window
And rubbed her eyes some more.

She thought she must be fast asleep,
For never had she seen
Anything quite as beautiful,
Not even in her dreams.

A chestnut horse with a golden mane,
With legs so large and strong,
"Surprise!" she heard her parents shout,
"He's now where he belongs.

"For this horse, he is not perfect,
"He's blind and cannot see,
"He'll trust in you to guide him,
"And together you'll run free."

They asked the girl to come and meet
The answer to her prayers,

For with her sight and his strong legs
They'd be a perfect pair.

Each day they lifted her atop
This horse with a golden mane,
And never again would another day
Feel quite the same again.

She practiced hard and learned to ride
This big and noble steed,
And knew that she could do all things,
If only she believed.

She brushed his coat until it shined
And whispered in his ear,
I never believed in miracles,
Before they brought you here.

And then one day, beneath the sun,
Her hands tightly on the reins,
Among the others, ready, set, go,
She joined them in their game.

She gave her friends a running start,
A fair and distant lead,
Then like a flash, she bounded forth
With her blind but trusting steed.

The wind, it rushed against her hair,
And she grinned from ear to ear,
Just then she looked ahead to see
The finish line drawing near.

She felt the spirit in this horse
Run hard with all his might,

For he now gave her legs to run,
And she gave him his sight.

This horse, he ran with so much grace,
Two longing hearts now soared,
A girl who prayed for two strong legs,
And a God who gave her four.

Together we can do all things,
If we only just believe,
Just as this girl who won the race
With her blind but noble steed.

Lisa J. Schlitt

Lisa J. Schlitt lives in Kitchener, Ontario, Canada, with her husband, Patrick, and four children. They are soon to expand their family with the addition of a seven-year-old boy. Lisa and Patrick work alongside the Bolivian Children's Mission in Cochabamba, Bolivia, and serve as the Canadian contact and representative. Lisa is hoping to publish "The Race" into a children's book where proceeds would be used to help sustain the Bolivian Children's Mission. For further details about the mission, please visit their website at www.vivabolivia.org/bcmission or feel free to contact Lisa by e-mail at p.schlitt@sympatico.ca.

In Life and in Death, Always Faithful

If you've had wonderful family relationships, you will be able to call yourself a true success in life, no matter what else you've achieved.

Vic Conant

Like most military children, Marc Tace knew how to wait.

He knew how to wait for his Marine Corps dad's next job, his next homecoming, and the next deployment. Marc knew how to wait even when his dad's absences only could be explained by the words "Semper Fi"—and for a child who's missing his dad, that's a hard concept.

But unlike most military children, Marc waited without moving. Diagnosed with muscular dystrophy at the age of four, Marc used a wheelchair by the time he and I were in elementary school.

I remember his wheelchair—decked out with 17th Street Surf Shop and USMC stickers—like I remember my grandparents' brown Volvo station wagon coming up the street. Marc's wheelchair was simply part of my elementary school experience, long before "inclusion" was a word tossed around in newspaper editorials.

And Marc's mom became somewhat like a beloved aunt. I looked forward to seeing Mrs. Tace in the school hallway as she helped Marc with the things he needed. She'd come down the hall, dressed in a jeweled sweatshirt with the American flag on it, singing something from the Barney show to me, and Marc would roll his eyes with feigned embarrassment.

But my favorite memory of Mrs. Tace and Marc was when they found me crying in the hallway of the junior-high school. "Now, we can't have our little Sarah crying," Mrs. Tace said, and then she let Marc and me play hooky from school and took us to get donuts.

Later, Marc and I went to the same high school and college. He was always there, and so was Mrs. Tace. While our dads were away on military assignments, our families spent Easters and Thanksgivings together. And over time, Marc's wheelchair got bigger and more complex.

Then I got married, moved away, and had children. In some ways, I had left my military childhood behind. I no longer knew exactly when my dad was out on detachment or home with Mom. In 1994, Colonel Tace died of a massive heart attack while serving overseas and never came home.

No one could have anticipated the strength and support of the greater military family that would keep them going. No one could have anticipated the way Marc would rise to the occasion and become the father figure for his family. And no one anticipated—although we should have—the way the Marines would take care of their own and embrace Marc and his family.

Last week, more than ten years after Colonel Tace's death, it was that same strength and support that cradled Mrs. Tace when she laid Marc to rest next to his dad.

With an American flag in one hand and the Marine Corps flag in the other, Mrs. Tace kissed her son's coffin and told him, "Don't be afraid. I'm here with you." Then, coincidentally, a military jet from nearby Naval Air Station Oceana screeched overhead, rustling the flaps of the tent where we stood. I imagined Col. Tace, from somewhere up above, smiling at the timing of those jets. I thought, *Leave it to a Marine to arrange a flyby for his son's funeral.*

On June 19, muscular dystrophy finally took Marc Tace's life, just a few months shy of his thirtieth birthday. Yet in some way, death also freed Marc because the morning Mrs. Tace found her son lying still in his bed wasn't any ordinary day. No, the day Marc slipped from this life to the next, to find what he'd been waiting for, was Father's Day.

And so it was, on the day set aside for fathers and their children, Marc went home to be with his dad, where this time the Marine stood waiting for his son. Semper Fi.

Sarah Smiley

Sarah Smiley is the author of *Shore Duty*, a syndicated newspaper column, and the book, *Going Overboard*. Sarah's book was optioned by Kelsey Grammer's company, Grammnet, and Paramount Television. It is now in development to be a half-hour sitcom for CBS. To learn more about Sarah, please visit www.sarahsmiley.com.

Perspectives

*I was one of the "puzzle children" myself—a dyslexic
. . . And I still have a hard time reading today. Accept
the fact that you have a problem. Refuse to feel sorry for
yourself. You have a challenge; never quit!*

Nelson Rockefeller

It was October 25, 1881, in Malaga, Spain. Two men sat comfortably chatting, waiting for the birth of a baby upstairs. When the midwife came in, she looked troubled, and when she started to speak, she cast her glance toward the floor. "I'm sorry, the baby was stillborn."

One of the men, the baby's uncle and a physician, put down his cigar and got up. He walked quickly up the stairs. He picked up his tiny nephew, unmoving and blue. Without hesitation, he brought the lifeless infant close to his face as if to kiss him and breathed into his mouth. The first breath that filled the baby's tiny lungs was still heavily scented with cigar smoke.

The baby's mother had already entered the dark recesses of her grief as she looked on in fear and wonder as her son took a struggling breath. Could she dare to hope that her baby might yet be saved? She had hoped for a healthy child, one who would live a full and normal life. She still wanted that. The story of the doctor who breathed life into a dead baby spread around the city. Some said it was unholy; others thought it might have been a miracle. Many thought it was foolish. Was it right to interfere with nature? Did the uncle's rash actions just delay the inevitable? Would this infant ever grow into a normal human being or contribute to society? Might it have been better to accept fate and simply let nature take its course? Yet, when the next day came, the baby was still breathing.

Soon, days became weeks, and weeks became years. Eventually, he learned to walk and talk, and to do many of the same things that other children do. He even learned to draw and paint. Of course, some people laughed when he would put the eyes in the wrong place or make silly mistakes on other details, but other people actually thought his drawings were quite good.

As it turned out, the uncle's action had only delayed the inevitable, and eventually the baby whose life was saved in the fall of 1881 died in 1973, but the art that Pablo Picasso created lives on.

Some people claim that his lifelong love for cigars started with that first breath. Picasso's story is about an uncle's hope. In a moment in which others might have only seen despair, Picasso's uncle had a moment of hope. His family was rewarded with a healthy child, and Picasso's genius transformed the world of art. It shows that great things can come from what seem like catastrophic beginnings, and a moment of hope can transform the world.

Dick Sobsey

Dick Sobsey is director of the JP Das Developmental Disabilities Centre and the John Dossetor Health Ethics Centre in Edmonton, Canada. Like Pablo Picasso, Dick was diagnosed later in life as having dyslexia. Unlike Picasso, he has no artistic talent and very little affection for cigars.

"I really hope Mrs. Picasso comes to Parents' Night."

4

BREAKING
BARRIERS

*There is no chance, no destiny, no fate that
can circumvent or hinder or control the
firm resolve of a determined soul.*

Ella Wheeler Wilcox

Music to My Ears

God is the answer. What is the question?

Jay Robb

During my pregnancy there had been no sign of anything wrong with the baby. I took my vitamins, ate lots of fruits and vegetables, and did my stretching exercises. I expected everything would go as smoothly as they had when my first son was born: an easy delivery and a "perfect" child.

In the delivery room, squeezing my husband's hand and hearing our baby's first cry, I was not prepared for what followed. The look on the nurse's face expressed her alarm as clearly as her words: "Mrs. Gardner, something's wrong here!" I looked in horror as she pulled back the blanket to show our son's face: one eye sealed shut; the other a milky mass; no bridge to his nose, and a face that looked crushed. Although I knew I should take him in my arms, I couldn't. I just couldn't. He was whisked away by the nurse as I was wheeled to the recovery room.

I lay on the hard hospital bed, the tightly pulled curtain shutting out the world. Still, I could hear other new mothers cooing to their babies. I heard one bemoan, "Not another boy!" and I was filled with jealous rage.

I thought of all the dreams I'd had for this child, of cuddling with him, of reading to him from brightly colored picture books, of his singing or painting or playing the piano like his older brother Jamaal—of his eyes, like Jamaal's, studying the keys.

Instead, my baby was blind and painful to look at.

Slowly, deliberately I walked to the phone and dialed my mom. My agony poured out between sobs: "It's a boy. His eyes won't open. His face is deformed. Mom, what am I going to do?"

"You will bring him home. You will bring him home and nurture him," she replied simply, firmly.

A nurse appeared at my side, led me to a rocker, and placed a small, blanketed bundle in my arms. Taking a deep breath, I looked down at my son. I had hoped he would look different—but he didn't. His forehead protruded. Under the sealed eyelid, an eyeball was missing, the other was spaced far from it. His bridgeless nose was bent to the side of his face. The doctors called it *hypertelorism*. I didn't know what to call it.

As we rocked, my mom's words echoed in my ears. I began to talk to him. "Hello, Jermaine," I said. "That's your name. I am your mommy, and I love you. I'm sorry I waited so long to come to you and to hold you. Please forgive me. You have a big brother and a wonderful father who also love you. I promise to work hard to make your life the best it can be. Your grandpa has a lovely voice, and can play the piano and sing. I can give you music." *Yes*, I thought, *that I can do. That I will do!*

Over the next few months, my husband and I poured our energies into filling up the darkness in Jermaine's life. One of us carried him in his Snugli or backpack at all times, constantly talking or singing to him. We inundated him with music—mostly classical, some Lionel Richie, some Stevie Wonder. His four-year-old brother was already taking piano lessons, and whenever he practiced, I sat next to him on the piano bench with his little brother on my lap. After a while, I began strapping Jermaine into his high chair next to Jamaal when Jamaal practiced.

However, I seldom took Jermaine out of the house because I couldn't stand anyone staring at my baby. Since blind infants cannot mimic a smile they cannot see, they often do not smile. It hurt that I got no smiles from Jermaine.

Every day my younger sister, Keetie, called, reminding me that God had a plan for each of us.

One day, Jamaal was practicing the piano, playing "Lightly Row" again and again, his little brother secure in his high chair next to him. Jamaal had just finished practicing and had come downstairs where my husband and I were sitting, when we heard a familiar *plink plunk-plunk, plink plunk-plunk* floating down the stairs. I looked at my husband, and he looked at me. It couldn't be Jamaal. He was jumping up and down on our bed. We stared at each other for a second, then tore upstairs!

At the piano, head thrown back, a first-ever smile splitting his face, Jermaine was playing "Lightly Row"! The right keys, the right rhythm, the right everything!

In response to my husband's immediate and astonished, amazing-news phone calls, the house filled with family and friends within an hour. I sat Jermaine at the piano in his high chair, as we all stood around expectantly.

Nothing.

I hummed "Lightly Row" and played a few notes. Jermaine sat silent, his hands motionless.

"It was just a fluke," my husband said.

"No," I replied unabashed. "It couldn't have been." I was certain our eight-and-a-half-month-old son had perfectly replicated a tune.

Two weeks later, he did it again, this time playing another piece his older brother had practiced. I ran to the piano and listened as the notes became firmer and the tune melded into its correct form.

From then on, there was no stopping Jermaine. He demanded to be at the piano from morning until bedtime. I often fed him at the piano, wiping strained applesauce off the keys. At first, he only played Jamaal's practice songs . . . and then he played Lionel Richie's "Hello" after hearing it on the tape recorder. At eighteen months, he played the left-hand part of Beethoven's "Moonlight Sonata" while my sister played the right-hand part. When he gave his first concert, I crawled under the piano to work the foot pedals his little legs could not possibly reach.

By the time he was out of diapers, I was desperate to find him a good piano teacher. I sought out a teacher at the Maryland School for the Blind and called, explaining that Jermaine was already playing the piano.

"How old is he?" the teacher asked.

"Two and a half," I replied.

"A child that age is too young to start piano lessons," he said disapprovingly, just as strains of "Moonlight Sonata" filtered in from the other room.

"By the way, Mrs. Gardner, who is that playing in the background?"

"That's the two-and-a-half-year-old."

"Bring him in!" the teacher replied promptly.

Soon, invitations for Jermaine to perform poured in. He appeared on national television. He played at the White House for two first ladies. Stevie Wonder invited him to play with him at his studio in California. A pair of Texas philanthropists who saw Jermaine on TV flew him to Dallas for a special surgery to rebuild his face.

As I reflect on his accomplishments, I think of my sister Keetie's words when I had despaired: "God has a plan for all of us," she'd said, and "God has a plan for your son." Indeed, I believe He did.

Jacqui Kess-Gardner

Jacqui Kess-Gardner is a nurse, author, motivational speaker, hair stylist, makeup artist, aerobics instructor, producer, and teacher. She has authored four books and has a passion for the elderly. Jacqui married her high-school sweetheart, James Gardner, thirty years ago, and the couple has two sons. Jacqui reports that after Jermaine played his audition piece "with the intensity of an adult but with the playfulness of a child," he was accepted to and attended Baltimore School for the Arts. He next attended Oberlin Conservatory of Music, from which he graduated in May 2006. Jermaine chose Oberlin because of the distance, and he wanted to be away from the doting eye of his mother, Jacqui. She was delighted with his choice and soon got used to the idea of him being independent. He has, since then, added four CDs to his credit and another is in progress. Jermaine states that he would like to start a music school for the blind. Jacqui can be reached by e-mail at jwriterG@aol.com.

Jermaine Gardner pictured with Stevie Wonder at Wonderland Studios.

Reprinted by permission of Jacqui Kess-Gardner.

I Am

I am not retarded.
I wonder how I got to be viewed that way.
I hear that dreaded word and shudder.
I see everything without quite looking.
I want trusting friends who don't utter that word.
I am not retarded. I am Dillon.

I pretend I don't hear it, but
I feel every nasty letter.
I touch the hearts and minds of all I meet, yet
I worry what they think.
I cry inside because
I am not retarded.

I understand everything, I understand it all.
I say what's on my mind, and people nod and smile.
I dream of true acceptance.
I try my very best.
I hope that people truly see
I am not retarded. I am simply me.

Dillon York

Dillon York wrote this poem as a school assignment when he was thirteen. He is now sixteen. He has autism and cannot speak. He uses adaptive communication technology to expose his thoughts. Without this technology, he could not write, and would remain silent. He is an advocate for greater understanding of autism, and for communication for all. He is currently working on a poetry anthology and a novel. Please visit Dillon's website at www.dillonsbuzz.com.

The Spirit of Travis

Today, we reconnected with college friends who were running in the Utica Boilermaker, a 15K run with more than 12,000 participants. Thousands more cheered the athletes along the hilly course.

Many spectators also wondered if they had the potential to run. Halfhearted boasts could be heard throughout the crowd about how "Next year, I'll be running instead of watching."

Everyone met at the finish line to celebrate the competition. Friends and families alike shared stories about the hardest part of the race, and how invigorating and inspired they felt upon finishing the course.

Thousands of people gathered together to listen to music and share in the joy of competition. Two hours after the last runner had crossed the finish line, the fanfare was interrupted by an announcement.

"We have just been informed that one runner is still out on the course," a race official said over the loudspeaker. "His name is Travis, and he's ten years old. He is in a traditional (non-racing) wheelchair and only using one arm to propel himself. And he really wants to finish the race.

The race sponsors have just informed us that they will give Travis a $3,000 racing wheelchair if he finishes the race. They are asking people to support him along the course and cheer him on during his last mile."

Within seconds, the crowd dispersed, forgetting their own moments of glory so they could reach out to Travis. Within fifteen minutes after the announcement, thousands of people—racers and fans alike—lined the street chanting, "Travis, Travis, Travis . . ."

Soon, Travis appeared over the hill, with a caravan of police cars and runners alongside him. Travis was filled with sheer exhaustion, yet radiant with the belief that he would reach what had once been a nearly insurmountable goal. The crowd cheered with as much determination as Travis was displaying.

While he could feel the outpouring of love, Travis could not "see" the crowd's support, since his focus was on the finish line ahead. With his mom by his side for four hours and fifteen minutes, he endured the journey.

Travis is blind to the limits . . . he could only see with his heart.

The cheering grew to a fever pitch, and tears flowed freely as Travis labored across the finish line.

Teresa D. Huggins

Teresa D. Huggins inspires people to live life fully, empowers others to transform obstacles into opportunities, and offers strategies that assist people to discover the possibilities within the problems. She facilitates weekend renewal programs and offers inspirational keynote speeches, one-day seminars, and teen leadership camps. She is the author of *Whispers of the Wind: Wisdom in a Moment* and *There's Another Way: Heart Centered Education,* and is the coauthor of *You Are Never Too Old to Dream, Dare, and Dance.* She can be reached at www.teresadhuggins.com or 315-853-5064.

Amanda's Triumphant March

The most striking fact about the disabled population is that it is the most inclusive. I will never be black, and I will never be a woman, but I could become disabled on the drive home tonight.

George Will

It was the end of summer vacation, 1965. In two days, I would join my friends and classmates at the new high school built in the center of town. I had just completed driver's education, and my new license was hot in my pocket. As I breezed through the school parking lot in my blue Mustang, I kept the windows rolled down and turned the radio volume full-blast for Top 40 hits like, "Stop! In the Name of Love," "Hang on Sloopy," and "My Girl."

The first days of school were filled with the pungent smells and polished sparkle of newness. An air of anticipation stirred in every new club and team tryout. The halls vibrated, and the bleachers rocked with chants: "We are the Titans, the mighty, mighty Titans!" I soon found my place performing in school plays and organizing pep rallies. I was, I admit, more interested in the social aspects of high school than academics. My life was not complicated. I had never encountered any obstacle worse than braces on my teeth or an untimely pimple on my face. In those days, I took perfect health for granted.

The young woman who would leave a lasting imprint on my life sat across the aisle in my second-period geometry class. Her name was Amanda. She was a slender girl with softly curled, shoulder-length hair. She had beautiful eyes and long lashes, although they were usually hidden behind oversized glasses. She always had her homework, and she never passed notes to friends or talked in class. That's all I knew about her, except that I did notice Amanda move through the hallways with an uneven gait. She kept her eyes fastened on her books, which she clutched to her chest.

One of Amanda's legs was shorter than the other, and she had a dropped foot that was malformed and tiny. Her smaller foot wore a serious-looking orthopedic shoe. Her other foot wore a beautiful shoe, color-coordinated with meticulously planned outfits. The "beautiful shoe" was always in the latest style, the most popular name brand.

If Amanda had been any other girl in class, I would have proclaimed, "I love your shoes! They're Pappagallos, aren't they?" But at the time, I couldn't imagine saying "I love your shoe" in reference to only one of them.

One afternoon, as the final bell brought the school day to a close, the air suddenly erupted with enthusiastic squeals. My friends and I stood around our lockers, laughing and talking. We decided our group should try out for our school's first-ever marching drill team. Wouldn't it be cool to march on the football field at halftime and hang out at the pizza parlor after the game? We pantomimed with imaginary pom-poms and laughed at our own goofiness. Still, we took tryouts very seriously.

My friends and I practiced every day. And we weren't

the only ones. Not one of us expected hundreds of girls to sign up with hopes of becoming one of fifty chosen for the team. Each girl took a number and performed her carefully studied routine, while the band director scribbled notes on a clipboard.

On day four of the tryouts, clusters of girls milled about the sidelines. Suddenly, the hum of chattering voices fell silent. The school lobby became perfectly still. Out of the silence, a number was called. A moment later, it was called a second time. "Who is she?" a friend asked.

Looking toward the starting line, I recognized Amanda from my geometry class. She was holding her head high and smiling, waiting for a nod from the band director. On cue, Amanda marched triumphantly across the school lobby with nearly 300 girls watching.

I vividly recall the rush of whispers, the bewildered expressions, and how my stomach tightened as some of the participants shielded cruel remarks behind cupped hands. I was hit by a tidal wave of remorse for their rudeness, followed by a second wave of admiration for Amanda.

That evening, I struggled to concentrate on my homework. I couldn't get Amanda off my mind. For the first time, I tried to imagine myself in her shoes—in *both* of her shoes. I tossed and turned that night as I thought about the drill team. I wondered if she was awake thinking about it, too.

By 8:00 the next morning, a crowd of anxious girls surrounded the list of names posted on the door of the band room.

By second period, I sat at my desk rushing to finish my geometry homework in the final two minutes before the bell. I glanced up from my work to see Amanda making her way to the seat across from mine. She paused in front of my desk. "Congratulations," she said. "I am really happy you made the team."

My friends and I had already waded through the early-morning frenzy to check the list of names posted on the band-room door. My name was one of the fifty that made the team. When I searched for Amanda's name, it wasn't there. I was not entirely surprised, but it took the joy out of seeing my own name on that list. My eyes welled up when I saw Amanda's sincere smile. "Thank you" was all that I could stammer.

I wish that I had told her how courageous I thought she was, but I never did. I was afraid it might embarrass her. I didn't want to say anything that might in any way call attention to her disability. How stupid is that? People with disabilities live with them every day. It was my own embarrassment, not hers, that was the problem.

The 1970s rolled in, and I joined the ranks of 54 million people with disabilities, which I learned was the largest minority group in the country. In my early twenties, I was diagnosed with rheumatoid arthritis. I spent five years in and out of hospitals and rehabs having my knees, hips, and shoulders replaced with artificial joints. Nearly a decade had passed since my high-school days, and I was just beginning to understand the empowerment Amanda demonstrated when she surmounted her disability and found the strength to try—just like anyone else.

One of the most important lessons I have learned is that sometimes life's greatest challenges serve as the stepping stones to a far bigger dream than one can ever imagine— if only we can summon the courage to take that first step. Thirty years from the time this story began, I cofounded Saint Francis of Assisi Service Dog Foundation. The non-profit organization empowers children and adults with disabilities by providing service dogs that love them unconditionally and help with daily tasks.

I could not have known the foundation would become a success, but thanks to Amanda's example, I was sure going to try! I've often recalled that long-ago march across the school lobby. A crowd of competitive young women witnessed Amanda's courage that day. How many remember? Were other lives influenced as dramatically as my own?

My only regret is that I never told her even once, "I really love your shoe." I think she would have been pleased to hear that.

Carol Willoughby

Carol Willoughby became an advocate for people with disabilities in the early 1970s. In 1996, she cofounded Saint Francis of Assisi Service Dog Foundation in Roanoke, Virginia. "Amanda's Triumphant March" is an excerpt from her keynote speech presented at the YWCA Women of Achievement awards in 2005. Write to Carol at carol@saintfrancisdogs.org or visit www.saintfrancisdogs.org.

The Need for Speed

The ideal attitude is to be physically loose and mentally tight.

Arthur Ashe

Every year, our youth group takes a three-day ski trip to White Face Mountain in Lake Placid, New York. But 2006 was special because Rebekah was old enough to attend the trip.

At age twelve, Rebekah has lived more in a lifetime than most. Born prematurely and with cerebral palsy, she has survived many surgeries, and also a battle with leukemia that was finally vanquished by a bone-marrow transplant. Embodied within this child are a strong will and a positive attitude. Somewhere along the way, she captured my spirit.

I invited Rebekah to attend the ski trip.

At first, her parents refused permission. I cannot even begin to imagine the internal struggle for them. This would be the first time that their daughter would be so far away from them. Rebekah's care would be in the hands of other people. I assured them that I would be there. I

researched and talked to the adaptive ski program administrators at White Face Mountain. I arranged for an accessible room. And, finally, seeing Rebekah's excitement and
insistence, they gave in.

I didn't anticipate the battles that would arise from
other sources. Other chaperones for the trip thought I was
crazy for inviting her. Her parents were criticized for letting her go. Her grandparents had long discussions with
me about all of her needs and how much work she can be.
Underneath it all, I sensed a deep, pervasive fear from
everyone around me. Her family feared letting her go. The
rest feared caring for a child with a disability who used a
wheelchair.

All I could see was a young girl, desperately wanting to
do something adventurous and on her own. I felt anger
and frustration. Why should Rebekah be limited by her
body? Why should she be limited by others afraid to take
care of her? Why couldn't anybody else see that she
needed this?

Rebekah came anyway, and I knew her parents were
walking on pins and needles back home, almost sick with
worry.

I will never forget the look on Rebekah's face when
Donald Dew, the adaptive ski instructor, first strapped
her into a specially made bi-ski. She glowed with excitement and adventure! Donald was remarkably prepared.
He had specially tailored lesson plans for skiers with cerebral palsy.

Rebekah took off! We all stood in amazement as Donald
taught her how to manipulate the bi-ski. Later, he told me
that she had accomplished in two hours what he had
hoped she would accomplish in three days. She was a natural at skiing.

In the middle of the first lesson, Donald asked me to
follow Rebekah by holding on to the back of the bi-ski.

Unbeknownst to me, she had been planning this moment all morning in her mind. She headed straight down the hill, accelerating to a breakneck speed, dragging me all the way. We were out of control! What if we hit a tree? What about all those promises I made to her grandparents to keep her safe? I started screaming, "Rebekah! Turn! Turn! TURN!"

With a giggle, she turned and halted our wild slide. "Mrs. Muzzey, I have a need for speed. They've been holding me back all morning. Now I finally got it!" By the time Donald got to us, we were both laughing, with tears rolling down our cheeks.

At the end of the lesson, Donald took her to his office and had her call her parents to inform them of her success. "Mom, Dad, I'm having the time of my life! And I think you need to get yourselves in gear and learn to ski, because I love this!" I later found out that this phone call made all the difference to her parents. They were finally able to relax and get rid of the pins and needles.

Every night of the trip, we had group devotions. On the first night, I couldn't keep quiet about how awesome it was to watch Rebekah ski, about how far she had progressed in one day, and about the crazy trip she had taken with me in tow. I was so proud of her.

The next day, different people wanted to ski with her. One of them was the speaker we had hired. He was trying to explain what happened during that day's lesson. Instead of someone holding the back of the bi-ski, she had a tether attached from Donald to her bi-ski. But he wasn't getting the words out in a way that made sense. Rebekah finally piped up to explain, "Look, people. It was like a dog leash. I was on a dog leash!" I know I was holding my gut with pain from laughing.

By the end of the ski trip, almost everyone from our group took some time to come and ski with Rebekah.

Everyone was talking about her. In those three short days, that precious soul captured many more spirits with her attitude and wit. No one was afraid of the girl in the wheelchair anymore.

Linda Muzzey

Linda Muzzey is a stay-at-home mom, a youth director at her church in Delaware, and cofounder of Treasured Girls, a Christian abstinence-education program for girls. Rebekah has been bitten by a "ski bug" and now skis as often as she can. No one stands in her way anymore! She is now in ninth grade and is hoping to obtain her own ski equipment someday. Please contact Linda by e-mail at dlmuzzey@comcast.net or write P.O. Box 190, Elk Mills, MD 21920.

The Most Famous Kid at School

Excellence is the result of caring more than others think is wise, risking more than others think is safe, dreaming more than others think is practical, and expecting more than others think is possible.

Howard Schultz

It was that simple birthday party invitation that brought home how far we had traveled. For five years, we had sought answers to why Adam was so inconsistent, so unpredictable. Our bright and beautiful child could charm a stranger as easily as he could haul off and punch another child for a crime only he could perceive. Life with Adam was never balanced; it was a tightrope walk from one good moment to the next. Two bulging file folders— each the size of our Philadelphia phone book—bore testament to the volume of misdiagnoses, unanswered questions, missed workdays, and sleepless nights. Each report represented another series of tests—and another disappointment when the latest expert gave us no more promise of resolution. PPD, SID, ADD, ODD, NVLD—the pages contained an alphabet soup that spelled out our family's uncertain future.

Finally, in our most trying year (a year filled with increasingly unnerving behaviors, a potential legal battle with our school district, and fallout from our other children), two letters broke the code: TS (Tourette syndrome). A relatively common disorder, so misportrayed in popular culture, we could never have added up all the clues to get this answer. Dr. Anthony Rostain, the genius from Children's Hospital of Philadelphia, finally made the diagnosis. He explained, "Parents of children with simple problems never make it to me. I get the families like you, who have been seeking answers for years, and whose children defy diagnosis."

His hourly fee drove home the truth in his words, but by this time, cost and additional debt had become secondary to uncovering what made our child tick (or should we say, tic). A birthday party invitation he received in second grade—the first that Adam had received from a school friend—was to us a sign that we had crossed some invisible divide. Our son was no longer the pariah who had parents calling the principal because they didn't want their child in the classroom with "that" boy, the one who barked like a dog and tried to yell out closed windows. The little girl who invited Adam to her party is still his close friend and will remain in our hearts forever. So will all the schoolchildren who, empowered by knowledge, compassionately befriended Adam in second grade.

Teaching the children about Adam is at the heart of our story, and perhaps where we should have begun. For us, understanding Adam's behavior instantly made him easier to accept. Once we learned about Adam's TS, we quickly discovered that many of his quirky behaviors were tics he could not control. One of the most troublesome, which received unwanted attention at school, was picking his nose and eating the contents. His frequent tantrums, inconsistency, and impulsivity were all manifestations of this syndrome. As politically incorrect as it may be to admit, even as parents, Adam became immeasurably more lovable once it was clear these behaviors were involuntary. In fact, there was immense guilt that we had allowed our son to be disciplined for actions he couldn't control, and even greater relief that these behaviors were not signs of terrible parenting. Too strict, too lenient, inconsistent—we'd second-guessed ourselves in all directions, as had teachers, caregivers, relatives, friends, and the other parents on the playground.

If knowledge and understanding impacted our feelings about our son so dramatically, they could also change his social stature at school, we reasoned. We just had to find a way to help the other children understand what made Adam tic.

Our angel this time was Laura Umbrell at the Pennsylvania chapter of the Tourette Syndrome Association. Nothing in our experience was new or surprising to Laura, whose job included visiting schools to teach children about TS. She offered to visit Adam's school to talk to the students and the teachers. We were game, Adam was game, and even his big brother was game. *Who wasn't?* The school, unfamiliar with TS, was inclined toward ignoring the elephant in the room. Although popular folklore encourages parents to avoid labeling their child by treating developmental disorders as private family matters, it was clear that we had two choices: trust in the other children's compassion or relegate Adam to a lifetime of being viewed as inexplicably weird. Once we brought the school on board, Laura worked closely with Adam to prepare him for the experience.

When the day finally arrived, he was excited and nervous, and so were we. We had gathered the troops, so Adam had the support of his siblings, grandparents, aunts, uncles, and cousins. We quickly realized he didn't need us; the assemblies were working just as we'd hoped. That day, Adam stood up in front of five different groups of children (one assembly per grade) and spoke about his TS—how it felt, what it made him do, and how he hoped the children would treat him from then on. All of the adults in the room laughed nervously each time he demonstrated his nose-picking tic. The children laughed, too, but this time they were laughing with Adam. Our vision of our son was forever changed. He spoke with such bravery, reflection, and self-awareness that we (and every other adult in the room) were moved to tears. Adam, on the other hand, was all smiles.

That was the day his world changed. We saw the first inkling of it when his entire class created cards for him, recognizing his courage and labeling him their friend. Our older son was no longer asked by his peers, "Why can't you control your brother?" Adam stopped hearing, "Eew, you're gross." Our phone started ringing with accolades from other parents, eager to tell us how their children came home from school excited to share tales of Adam's bravery. Playdates even became a two-way street, with calls coming in from Adam's new friends. Perhaps more life-altering was Adam's realization that he had the power to change his world and the world around him. Phrases like "I'm the most famous kid at school," and "I made the world a better place" replaced "Everyone hates me" and "I'm a maniac." He began making plans for delivering his message beyond the school walls with the belief that he really could make the world a better place by helping children understand one another's differences.

Today, it barely matters how many children invite Adam to their birthday parties, because he is filled with the confidence that only self-understanding, genuine acceptance, and loyal friendship can bring. Now, if asked, Adam will tell you that, although he doesn't like having TS, he does not wish to be "typical," because the insight gained since his diagnosis has made him a better person who gives others grace and cares deeply about his community. And, he adds, "Now I have all the friends I need."

Rachel Ezekiel-Fishbein and Joel I. Fishbein

Pennsylvania couple **Rachel Ezekiel-Fishbein** and **Joel I. Fishbein** often bicker when writing together, but easily agree when communicating about their son, Adam, who was diagnosed with Tourette syndrome and ADHD in 2005. Ezekiel-Fishbein is a freelance writer and publicist; Fishbein is an attorney, known as "defender of all that is right." Ezekiel-Fishbein has been a driving force for improving special education and family advocacy in her community. Contact them at makingheadlines1@comcast.net.

Trials and Tribulations

To win without risk is to triumph without glory.

Pierre Corneille

I was thirteen when my Binghamton, New York, Boy Scout troop planned a camping trip. I wasn't afraid of being out in the woods at night, but the thought of being with a group of people terrified me. I stammered severely, and kids sometimes made fun of me.

However, I summoned up the courage to go on this outing for I knew that there would be at least one person I could spend time with: my best friend. A friend who had never been put off by my disability, whose father owned a meat market a block away from where my father operated an Army/Navy store. A friend with a "fantastic" imagination. Sitting apart from the other campers, in the dark of the woods, alert to the spooky night sounds, my friend would tell stories of life on other planets, of beings he imagined would be found there, of time traveling to other worlds, of ghosts, of the meaning of dreams, of reincarnation, of the ability to read minds. I sat spellbound as he elaborated a string of "what if" stories. He wanted to be a writer, and I was certain he would be.

My friend's name was Rod Serling. He became the fantastic writer he dreamed of being and more. As creator of the television show *The Twilight Zone*, his influence on science fiction has been "astronomical."

I was so certain that Rod would attain his dream that I was almost too embarrassed to tell him mine. I wanted to be a defense attorney like Clarence Darrow and Sam Leibowitz. I'd read everything I could about them, including transcripts from their trials. I'd spent hundreds of hours alone at the library, imagining myself a golden-tongued attorney pleading sensational cases before juries.

But I knew I could never be like Clarence Darrow and Sam Leibowitz because of my speech impediment. "You'll make it," Rod would say, never once discouraging me. "Don't worry. The stammering will go away, and you'll be a great lawyer one day." When I felt discouraged, Rod would cheer me up with a tale about an attorney defending a three-eyed creature from another planet. I'd laugh and feel better, his confidence in me encouraging my own confidence in myself.

Eventually, I did attain my dream of becoming a lawyer. Still, it was preposterous to think a stammerer like myself could perform in a courtroom. I conceded as much and planned to return home, to help my father run his Army/Navy store, and then perhaps to branch into legal research where I could silently earn a living.

Thoroughly depressed, I sank into my chair at the 1951 University of Miami Law School commencement. When I looked up, I couldn't believe my eyes: There at the podium stood the keynote speaker, Sam Leibowitz! Leibowitz was the famous New York attorney who had saved the lives of nine Alabama black men falsely accused of raping two white women in the famous "Scottsboro Boys" case. That afternoon Leibowitz, his voice filled with conviction, told us that defense attorneys were the key to keeping America free, that the protective ideals of the U.S. Constitution and the Bill of Rights were constantly under attack, that "authorities" were chipping away our rights to a fair trial, to the presumption of innocence, against unreasonable search and seizure, and to proof beyond a reasonable doubt. He warned us that the old guardians were dying out and that without a new generation to take up the fight, America would succumb to a reemergence of robber barons and torture chamber confessions, and that the average man and woman would be stripped of dignity and liberty, and would then be legally and economically enslaved.

Leibowitz challenged us to take the torch he was passing, to become defense attorneys, and to protect America. I felt as if he were speaking directly to me.

Because of Leibowitz's speech, I remained in Miami to become a defense attorney, stammering or not. Soon I got my first case: A black man named Henry Larkin, who had shot and killed a man in the hallway of his apartment building, was charged with murder. Larkin said the man he shot had come after him with a knife.

Since there were no public defenders in those days, groups of young attorneys would mill around the courthouse volunteering for cases and hoping to be appointed. I was doing just that when someone told me about Henry Larkin. He nearly cried when I offered to represent him.

The day before the trial (my first!), I read in the *Miami Herald* that Leibowitz, then a New York judge, was back in town for another speech. I searched him out, and soon I stood at his hotel door, briefcase in hand. Stammering an apology for my intrusion, I asked for his help.

"I was in the audience at your ca-ca-commencement address here; I became a defense attorney because of you.

Now I'm facing m-m-my first case tomorrow."

Leibowitz smiled and invited me in. I told him about the case. He raised his eyebrows every time I tripped over a word, but never said a thing about my speech impediment and then proceeded to outline my entire defense.

The next day I stood before twelve people in a court of law, with the life of Henry Larkin in my hands, or more precisely, in my misfiring mouth. Then something strange came over me: not fear, but confidence.

My own troubles vanished, replaced by the far greater problems of Henry Larkin. He was a good man who had never broken the law in his life. It was up to me to convince a jury that he had acted in self-defense. I talked for four hours that day, remembering everything Sam Leibowitz told me as I pled for Henry Larkin's life. The jury took three minutes to decide he was "not guilty."

One thing missing from the next day's newspaper report is that I had not stammered once during my entire argument. I tried to call Sam Leibowitz, but he had left town. Needing to share my multifaceted victory with someone, I called Rod and told him about the miracle of my untangled tongue. He exuded elation, and then grew serious. "Ellis, it's a sign! You've found your place in time. You were destined to speak for the innocent and oppressed. Never forget that!" Rod was quick to see some unexplained, universal phenomenon in practically everything. In his eyes, what happened was the result of what can only happen in *The Twilight Zone.*

For whatever reason, Rod's words have stayed with me throughout my life. I've been in thousands of trials and have always tried to do my best to defend the "poor and defenseless." Some people, including my wife, feel I've overdone it. I have spent a great deal of time on "pro bono" cases.

I've also had my share of wealthy clients, including

celebrities, rich businessmen, doctors, and a billionaire Arab oil sheik. Payments come in many forms, such as a handshake, a hug, a baby's smile, a holiday card, a home-cooked meal, a friendly face in court, even a picketer carrying a sign outside of jail. Henry Larkin, my first client, came by every Friday for the rest of his life and handed me an envelope with a five-dollar bill in it. He never missed a week.

Ellis Rubin
As told to Dary Matera

Dary Matera is the author of fourteen books, including *Get Me Ellis Rubin!, John Dillinger, Most Wanted, Quitting the Mob, What's in It for Me?, Taming the Beast, Childlight, The Stolen Masterpiece Tracker,* and the *New York Times* bestseller *Are You Lonesome Tonight?* Mr. Ellis Rubin passed away in December 2006. He was eighty-one. Dary lives in Chandler, Arizona. E-mail him at dary@darymatera.com.

"My imaginary friend says 'get real.'"

Reprinted by permission of Jean Sorensen and Cartoon Resources. ©2005 Cartoon Resources.

You Didn't Give Me a Turn

A winner is someone who recognizes his God-given talents, works his tail off to develop them into skills, and uses these skills to accomplish his goals.

Larry Bird

"Welcome to the parents, family, and friends of our 1998 graduating class . . . As your name is called, please step forward to receive your diploma."

Looking at the somber faces glowing among the sea of blue and gray caps and gowns, I am overcome with nostalgia. It seems like only yesterday that they were my active and inquisitive first-graders. As the almost-adult girls totter forth one by one in newly purchased heels, and the boys shuffle by in their self-conscious gaits, the public-address system announces their names while I find myself immersed in memories.

Another name is called, and suddenly I am consumed by a vivid flashback of a little, freckle-faced strawberry-blond named Adam. He was a smiley, quiet kid, a conscientious student with beautiful penmanship and detailed, creative artwork.

His mother and I bantered often. She always joked and laughed a lot. She wasn't laughing the night she called to say that Adam might not be in school for several days.

"Why not?" I asked.

"Well, he'd probably have trouble zipping his pants. He cut his fingers off," she replied.

Appalled, my immediate response was, "That's not funny!"

"No, but it's true," she said.

Adam had been at his grandfather's farm. The family had butchered a cow and was making hamburger. Adam, trying to be helpful, stuck his hand into the meat grinder, severing his fingers and part of his thumb.

I could tell you about the challenges this presented—wearing sweatpants to avoid zippers, anchoring his paper as he learned to cut and once again become the neatest printer in the room, the curiosity and questions his peers asked. But, instead, I want you to meet the little boy who was not willing to accept help. It was the end-of-the-year picnic. I had set up an obstacle course with seven stations to test their athletic abilities and coordination (boys against the girls). All activities except the overhead horizontal ladder were done. The score was tied three to three. Ten girls tried, and eight made it across the "alligator-infested pond." Eight boys tried, and all eight made it. I declared the score tied, everyone a winner.

Adam said softly, "You didn't give me a turn." How could I explain to him that he couldn't do it? He had no fingers on his one hand to grasp the rungs. "It's my turn!" he repeated a little louder and climbed the ladder. I stood below to catch him when he fell, ready to hug him and tell him I was proud of him for trying.

I watched with barely contained tears as Adam hooked his left wrist over the first rung. His feet came off the steps, and for a second he was suspended in space. Then with a jerk, his good hand grabbed the next rung. He hooked his wrist over that one and began to advance, one rung at a time.

At first, the class stood frozen silent, almost like a picture. Then one boy chanted, "Go, Adam, go!" He was soon joined by the whole class, all competition forgotten, as their classmate and friend grasped and advanced, grasped and advanced. His little body swung from side to side. "Go, Adam, go!" Clapping, chanting, "Go, Adam, go!"

As beads of perspiration formed on his forehead, determination etched his face. He never gave up. He made it to the other side, dropped to the ground, raised his mismatched hands in a victory sign, and beamed!

Tonight, once again with tears streaming down my face, I applaud loudly as he steps forward to receive a scholarship to pursue a degree in engineering.

Yes, graduation and commencement are an ending— and a beginning.

Mary Henderson

Mary Henderson taught for the public schools of Calumet, Laurium, and Keweenaw (in Calumet, Michigan) from 1967 until 1999. She truly loved all of her "little people" and tried to always teach with patience, humor, and respect for the individual differences each child brought to the classroom. Although she had a soft spot in her heart for many of her children, Adam was special. She followed his accomplishments and successes, and cheered him on as a starter on the varsity basketball team. Mary has been published in *Guideposts, Reminisce Online, Reminisce Extra, I Love Cats, International Library of Poetry,* and self-published a book, *Out of the Mouths of Babes.*

I'm a Dancer

Be the change you wish to see in the world.
Mahatma Gandhi

It was my first dance-team performance, and I was so excited! My entire family came to my school to watch me dance. This first dance program was so important to everyone in my family—even the whole school!

I came early to the school, and I went into the girls' bathroom to change into my new dance-team outfit. The other girls on my team were already there changing. As I put on the outfit, I began to think how beautiful my outfit was and how it looked on me. It had silver, blue, and black pants, and a top. The collar on the top was made with silver sequins that itched and made a red place on my neck that hurt. The top was blue and black with silver sequins across the bottom with blue fringe. The pants were black and shiny with one blue stripe at the bottom. My shoes were black, but they were too little. They hurt my toes! It bothered me a little because I had to curl my toes to dance.

My mom helped me fix my hair with a brown hairpiece. She curled the front of my hair with a hot curling iron. Then she pulled my hair back in a bun and put in the hairpiece. It was really curly. I looked so beautiful!

It was finally time to dance. I felt fine and ready. We lined up in the hall. I looked in the gym. Many people were there, and the players were sitting with the coach to watch us dance. My heart started to beat really fast. We walked into the gym. I knew I must look at the other girls as we went into the gym. I looked at my mom, too. We walked in the gym and stopped in a line in the middle of the floor.

We waited for the song to start. My head was down when the music started. I could feel the beat in my feet, and I could feel when it stopped. I felt the song start, and I started to dance. Mom sat on the first bleacher and pointed "right" and "left," and signed "jump" and "turn" for me. I didn't watch the other girls; I always watched Mom! When the song stopped, I saw the people clap! I could see Mom smiling and clapping, too. Mom was proud of me. I knew because she was smiling.

We marched out of the gym. As we got off the floor, I felt very happy and proud of myself that I had finished the dance and done a good job.

People from the other school did not know about me, and why this dance was so special. My family and teachers did. When I looked at the crowd after the dance, they were crying. *Why?* I'm deaf. I hear no sounds. I did the dance by watching the other girls' positions, watching my mom sign the directions to me, and by "feeling" the beat. I was the first deaf girl ever on our school's dance team!

Briana Hobbs

Briana Hobbs is in seventh grade. She likes to swim and talk with her friends on the Internet. Briana loves animals and wants to be a veterinarian. Her large family is very proud of her accomplishments in and out of school.

One Special Olympian

Setting goals, following dreams, giving it all you've got, making it happen . . . these are the things that make all the difference in your life!
Dominick Castellano

It was the final attempt in the competition.

CJ had successfully completed eight out of eight lifts and, amazingly, all his efforts were performed with the power and control of a hydraulic lift. As always, he was well prepared. Still, his face was drawn and showed the fatigue of a long day of competition. His 350-pound squat lift and 220-pound bench press lift eclipsed the world records, the most anyone had lifted in his weight class and division in history. He still had one final attempt left in the dead lift. I told him he had truly earned the respect of everyone and had done all he needed to do. His performance was 150 pounds more than the winner of the last world event! If he really did want his final attempt, it would be his decision; I felt he was spent, and injury was a concern. All the noise and excitement of the final attempts of the other lifters in heavier weight classes made it hard to communicate. CJ was lifting the same amount of weight as competitors twice his body weight. The cheers of the crowd, and the voices and the clanging of plates, produced a surreal bubble of atmosphere, sound, foggy images, and haze. I impatiently awaited his decision. CJ carefully thought for a moment, much more composed than I was. He softly said, "One more attempt, please." I went to the control desk and told the official that CJ Piantieri would take his final attempt at 420 pounds. She abruptly looked up at me as if I could not be serious, but confirmed my request, repeating, "Piantieri, 148-pound weight class, 420-pound final attempt."

As I chalked his hands, my own focus cleared to what he faced. I explained that he would need a supreme effort to make this lift. The bar would likely stall halfway up, he was tired, and he had to stay with it and keep it moving. He would have to pull with more force than he had ever put forth in his life. The massive weight was loaded onto the bar. The crowd grew quiet, sensing the intensity of the moment as the announcer proclaimed this the final lift of the entire competition. CJ approached the bar. His 143-pound body was small but muscular. The bar seemed ominous and defiant . . . so many plates, so much to lift. With the focus of an Olympic champion, he placed his feet, adjusted his grip, took a huge breath, lifted his head, and with eyes on fire, he began to lift. The crowd erupted as the bar rose from the floor and slowly began to rise. Slowly, surely, the bar gave way to CJ's will. I screamed at the top of my lungs . . .

"Stay! Stay! Stay!"

CJ held on, but the bar's ascent slowed. The crowd's screaming was ear-wrenching. With inches to completion, the massive weight almost overcame him. The crowd was now in a frenzy! CJ strained with every fiber of his being for every quarter-inch of movement. I was helpless and could only watch in awe as he again showed the courage of determination. Each second was agony. CJ refused to give up, refused to submit, refused to fail. Gravity was saying no, but he was not listening. The final effort was intense and painful to watch. I could not accept this was happening. It was too much to ask of any athlete. I wanted it to end. Forget the lift; I didn't want him hurt. I thought out loud, "I am going to stop this . . . he can't take it anymore!"

But on this day, he would not be denied. With a resounding yell heard round the auditorium, CJ found something deep within himself and conquered the weight. The crowd erupted.

Dominick Castellano

Dominick Castellano is a world champion powerlifter and participated in eight varied sports. He is an Olympic trials rower, marathoner, ironman triathlete, swimmer, and kayaker, racing all over the world! But what defines him is thirty years of motivating and coaching people, especially his speaking and coaching for Special Olympics, schools, city programs, cooperation, colleges, police/fire departments, prisons, and the U.S. military. Contact Dominick at DomCas1@aol.com.

CJ deadlifting 415 pounds. He is now close to 450, weighing only 140 pounds! He is working hard to bring home the gold for the United States in China at the World Special Olympic Games!

[POSTSCRIPT: *At birth, CJ had a stroke that caused neurological damage, seizure disorder, learning disability, and physical disability. These are just a few of the things that CJ has lived with throughout his thirty-one years. His training is as intense as you would expect of any world-class athlete.*]

5

COMMUNITY

One should guard against preaching to young people success in the customary form as the main aim in life. The most important motive for work in school and in life is pleasure in work, pleasure in its result, and the knowledge of the value of the result to the community.

Albert Einstein

An Appalachian Miracle

The differences are great, and the differences are small. That's just part of the beauty of it all. . . .
                                        Red Grammar

Jimmy Beckley, born on a 1973 winter night in a small town, did not breathe for the first seven minutes of his life. It might have had something to do with Deborah Mae Beckley's drug use during the late stages of her pregnancy, the town's ladies gossiped in hushed tones. No matter the reason, those first seven oxygenless minutes carried a heavy price tag. Jimmy suffered extensive brain damage.

In the next two years, Deborah birthed two more children, and Jimmy's needs quickly overwhelmed the teenage mother. Social services placed Jimmy in the care of Walter and Margaret Beckley, Deborah's parents. Though they lavished the child with love, the senior Beckley's were limited in their abilities to tend to Jimmy's increasing physical needs. Both had arthritis, and as Jimmy grew larger and heavier, caring for him became a nearly impossible. By the time Jimmy was eight, they were providing care for three more of Deborah's children and had to make the heart-wrenching decision to sever legal custody of the child.

Tears did little to wash away the pain, but they were consoled with limited information provided by the authorities. Jimmy was adopted into a good home in a far-away state. The years passed quickly, but the Beckley's never forgot the smiling little boy in the wheelchair.

As is often the case in Appalachia, the church became a haven for Walter and Margaret. Rising to the position of deacon in the local Baptist church, Walter was a true believer in the power of prayer. Walter and Margaret began to think about Jimmy more and more during 1996, the year Jimmy would turn twenty-three. The doctors had predicted since Jimmy was an infant that he would not live beyond twenty-one. Walter and Margaret began to pray fervently, asking the Lord to intervene in their pain, which just would not go away. Soon the entire congregation took up the cause for the ailing deacon and his wife's prayers.

And what had become of the little boy in the wheelchair? Jimmy raised in a small town in Michigan, his doting parents had instilled in him the spirit of independence, teaching him to challenge his physical limitations. As he grew, he became an adept driver of his electric wheelchair; he moved into his own apartment, assisted by daily visits of skilled nursing professionals. Weather permitting, Jimmy went on short solo jaunts throughout the neighborhood. On one such trip, he rode into a local 7-Eleven and encountered a dozen bikers, a motorcycle club quite unlike the stereotype.

One of the scruffy Harley riders noticed that the young man in the wheelchair was riding on rubberless steel rims. Unable to ignore Jimmy's indomitable spirit, the bikers decided to help—first, by repairing his wheelchair wheels, and later by making him an honorary member of their club. Blazened with his own vest and colors, encased in a sidecar, Jimmy joined the club members for his first-ever motorcycle ride.

As Jimmy and the bikers came to know each other better, Jimmy told his newfound friends what little he remembered about his past. His mother's name, his grandpa's name, and the name of a little town in Tennessee. He told them that his doctors had predicted that he had perhaps two more years to live, and that he wished to find his birth family and show them how much he'd learned—how far he'd come from his days of total dependency and noncommunication.

Two of the bikers decided to help. And so it was that I heard one day from my Michigan nephew, Tim. He told me about Jimmy, about his adoption, prognosis, and dream. Tim asked me if the wonders of computer database technology could find Jimmy's birth family.

I tried a few tricks and got lucky. I found an address for the two people whom I believed were Jimmy's grandma and grandpa Beckley. But adoption locates can be tricky, the results not always happy, so I penned a short letter to the elder Beckleys.

"I have reason to believe that you are the grandparents of Jimmy Beckley. If this is true, and you'd like to know more about your grandson, please call me at . . . "

Soon thereafter the phone rang. "Mah name iss Walter Beckley," said a heavy Appalachian voice. He was difficult to understand, not only because of his unfamiliar accent, but because he was crying. "My wife and I put our faith in the Lord," he said, "and we've been praying every day and every night. We're both in failing health, and the one thing we want more than anything else before we go to glory is to talk or see our grandson Jimmy."

Following a flurry of long-distance telephone calls, culminating in the biker boys talking directly to the happy deacon, plans were made.

Next Sunday, the biker club will take Jimmy for another ride. They plan to share the good news at that time and make a videotape to send to Walter and Margaret. The next step will be to coordinate schedules and secure a motor-home that will accommodate Jimmy to Tennessee —and witness firsthand the miracle of a dream come true.

Cookie Bakke

*Some names have been changed to protect their privacy.

[POSTSCRIPT: *The bikers did indeed outfit a van to hold the wheelchair—and then drove Jimmy down to the small town where he'd spent his earliest years. They arrived on Christmas Eve. I heard that when they pulled into the driveway of the ramshackle mountain home, that two young women (the two sisters that Jimmy still had vague memories of) came running out of the house and toward the van. They were yelling, "Bubba, Bubba, Bubba . . .," tears streaming down their faces.*

I suppose that we all have to judge for ourselves how and why these events unfolded the way they did. All I know for sure is that most of those involved in this Appalachian Miracle will remember the experience and their own parts in it for as long as they live.]

Cookie Bakke is a writer and speaker who primarily covers insurance and financial fraud. She currently serves as the executive editor of the *John Cooke Fraud Report*, as the associate editor of *The Bulletin* (magazine of American Mensa, Ltd.), and as a director of Fight Fraud America, Inc. Please e-mail her at JCFR@aol.com.

❧ Out of the Mouths of Babes ❧

I took my six-year-old son Nicholas, who has autism, to the doctor's office for his flu shot. I didn't want to tell him what the doctor was going to do for fear that he would refuse to go, so I told him it was going to be just a checkup. While I distracted him to prevent him from seeing the needle, the nurse gave him the shot. He never saw the needle, but, of course, he felt it.

But surprisingly, instead of crying, Nicholas was furious! All the way from the doctor's room and through the crowded waiting room, he was shouting: "That woman right there *hurted* me! She took a sword and stab me! Right here in my arm! You are in *big* trouble, lady! Say you are sorry! Doctors are supposed to make children feel better, not *kill* them! You are in time-out until you say you are sorry!"

Nicholas ranted and raved all the way home. I think I'll try a different approach next time. I hope the nurse isn't still in time-out.

Rosita Ferro

Rosita Ferro is the mother of three. The youngest, Nicholas, was diagnosed with autism at age four. He is now a tenth-grader, attending the Habour School in Maryland, and looking forward to college.

A Classy Kind of Love

No one ever exceeds their wildest expectations unless they first begin with wild expectations.

Source Unknown

Bud was the kind of kid that every teacher wants in her classroom—a kind, funny, gentle giant of a boy who had a talent for making people laugh out loud. At ten years old and five feet, six inches tall, he towered over many of the other students and staff in our elementary school. His heart was even bigger than his body, and Bud was always willing to lend a hand to anyone in our school who needed help. It mattered not that reading eluded him and he was only able to do very basic math. His capacity to love and assist others more than made up for his struggles with academics. Bud often encouraged his classmates, and his enthusiasm made even the smallest gain seem like a trip to the moon.

Whether it was cheering on Elliot as he painstakingly navigated the hall in his walker, or praising Rachel for remaining in her seat during reading, Bud was the glue that sometimes held our uniquely diverse class together.

Bud had one habit that was sometimes annoying, but often endearing: when he became interested in a topic, he fixated on it. He would talk for days about the same issue, rehashing it over and over until something better to discuss came along. Over the course of his three years in my class, I worked on trying to fix this, but by and large, Bud had the final word. Literally. He just kept on chatting away.

One day, Bud came to school and announced that one of his dreams in life was to be able to ride in a limousine. All week long, I heard about how wonderful it would be to cruise around town in a limo. But unlike many other topics before it, this one didn't go away. Like a bad penny, the "riding in a limo conversation" kept coming back as Bud's voice reiterated all of the wonderful, cool comforts that came with riding in a flashy black car with a soda bar. After a while, I got to thinking, *Why couldn't Bud ride in a limo? In fact, why couldn't we all?* Our little class of six was certainly small enough to fit into one.

I began thinking about each of my students. So many of their families struggled just to make ends meet. If we didn't try to do it now, most of these kids would never get the chance to go again. This was an opportunity that we couldn't pass up. After getting approval from the principal and making a few phone calls to limousine services, I hit the jackpot. One new company was willing to give us a discounted rate to take the class somewhere in town.

Excited, I couldn't wait to share the news with Bud. "Wow, we really get to ride in a limo!" he shouted. "Where are we gonna go?" *Hmm . . . where are we gonna go?* A few more phone calls later, and we found a restaurant willing to foot the bill for drinks and dessert. A plan had been launched!

Excitement mounted as the date for the trip approached. We obtained copies of the dessert menu from the restaurant, and the kids pored over it to determine what they would order. We practiced table etiquette, and the children carefully planned what to wear to the special event. Since a few of the kids had never been in a restaurant either, this field trip was going to be doubly special. Overjoyed and exuberant, Bud exclaimed, "We should call the newspapers!"

Well, why not! Bud was thrilled as I placed a call to the local paper during recess, and he jumped for joy when the reporter agreed to cover our special event. By this time, the entire school knew of our trip. Children from the fourth and fifth grades were intrigued—and more than a little envious of their counterparts.

Almost overnight, my students, who so often struggled to maintain the most basic of social skills, were the stars of the school! Finally, the big day arrived. Bud was in the classroom early, chattering a mile a minute, and hopping up and down with excitement. Dressed in a suit and tie, complete with boutonniere, he was positively glowing. The other children soon followed, all dressed to the nines and anticipation showing on their faces. That electric energy that only children can produce was permeating the air!

We waited anxiously for 10:00, when we were to be called to the front of the building to leave. Minutes seemed like hours to the kids, who were having difficulty focusing on anything that didn't tell time. Finally, over the intercom came the voice of the secretary. "Room 5, your limo has arrived!" Cheers went up, and the kids quickly fell into line to go out the door.

Since Elliot was the line leader, I opened the door for him so that he could maneuver his walker as we exited the room. It was eerily quiet as we traveled down the hall. It seemed odd that no one in our wing was in his or her classrooms. We slowly made our way down the corridor and past the front office, with Elliot setting the pace as he determinedly led the line. Finally, we turned the corner and headed out the door. As my eyes adjusted to the bright March sunshine, it took me a minute to realize what I was seeing.

We had opened the door to a sea of faces—602 of them, to be exact! The entire student body and staff had lined up along the parking lot to see us off! The clapping started quietly and quickly grew thunderous as six little bodies and two adults were escorted into the stretch limousine. A camera flashed and a reporter asked Bud to spell his name. It was glorious watching these children have their moment in the limelight! Rachel blew kisses to the crowd, and shy little Anton tried to hide his exuberantly smiling face. Elliot squealed in glee, Jonathon hugged all of his classmates, and Katrina flashed a peace sign to her friends. Once safely inside the limousine, the driver honked our good-byes to the onlookers while Bud exclaimed, "Wow, this is really amazing! I think this is the best day of my life!"

For a brief moment, time stood still, offering a generous helping of grace to these six children. Six hundred and two people gave back to Bud what he had so often given to them during his time at school. Six hundred and two special souls made six other special souls feel like a million bucks.

That electric energy that permeated the air earlier? It was still there, but in such a short time it had grown and multiplied exponentially. And this time, we had a name for it. LOVE.

Patricia Gillule

Names of students have been changed to protect their privacy.

Patricia Gillule has been teaching students with disabilities for the past twenty-one years. She enjoys spending time with her husband and four children, writing, and adoption advocacy. Currently, she and her family are in the process of adopting a child with special needs. Bud is now twenty-two years old and has just finished high school. He has a job working in the Piscataway High School cafeteria. Everyone there loves him, and people go out of their way to check in with him. Bud puts the same enthusiasm into lifting boxes and stocking shelves that he does into speaking, so we're sure he's a valued employee! Patricia can be reached at stevepatg@aol.com.

Swimming with John

Success—*To laugh often and much; to win the respect of intelligent people and the affection of children; to earn the appreciation of honest critics and endure the betrayal of false friends; to appreciate beauty; to find the best in others; to leave the world a bit better, whether by a healthy child, a garden patch, or a redeemed social condition; to know even one life has breathed easier because you have lived. This is to have succeeded.*

Ralph Waldo Emerson

Last year, I read that one of our local autism organizations was partnering up with a local swim program. They agreed to pay half the cost for a six-week trial of one-to-one swimming lessons. I thought about this for months. I was so nervous to hand my son over to a stranger in the pool, even though I'd be right on the other side of the wall watching.

Jackson can be tough to work with if you don't understand him. He does not talk—he has never spoken a word—and so communication is definitely very limited.

For a three-year-old, he can actually be pretty intimidating. I was reluctant to sign him up.

I'm not sure why, but one day last fall, I changed my mind and decided to do it. I called the swim program and explained our situation. I shared my concerns about Jackson, and what I hoped his instructor would be like. They suggested John, and so we set up our first six-week session with him.

When we arrived at the pool, I couldn't believe my eyes. The instructor was a teenager! My heart started beating fast as I walked into the pool area. I blurted out, "He has autism, he doesn't talk, he doesn't really understand a lot," and so on.

John just smiled and said, "Okay, don't worry about it. I'll take it easy, and we'll be fine." And then I had to walk out of the room to the other side of the one-way glass. *I can't believe we're doing this*, I thought.

I sat with the other parents who were watching their children swimming, and I sobbed for the first ten minutes. But I need not have worried. My son was having fun. For the first time in his life, he was just like every other kid in the room. Most new things in his life are very stressful. This, however, was not. He was just a boy in the pool having fun.

We really couldn't afford one-to-one swim lessons, but Jackson kept swimming anyway. Month after month after month, we signed up—always with John. There were times when John would be out, and Jackson would have to swim with a covering instructor. It never worked out. Usually it was because the instructor was nervous or uncomfortable with Jackson. He didn't know what to do with him, or what he liked, or what he was capable of. I would end up walking back and forth into the pool room to talk to them. It got to the point where, if John was out, they would call us and see if we wanted to cancel. For Jackson, the lessons were wasted if they weren't with John.

In March 2005, after Jackson had been swimming with John for over six months, I wrote a letter to the owner, telling him what a wonderful experience swimming had been for us. It was all because of John and his natural way with Jackson. It amazed me how someone so young (John was only eighteen) could be so wise, so kind, just so good with my son. We were extremely lucky to have found such a good match. Jackson was very comfortable in the water. He was learning to kick, to dunk his head under, and to jump in the pool. His trunk strength increased from learning to climb out of the pool, and he was very interested in the other kids who were getting lessons around him. Swimming class was just so much more than we had hoped for.

And the benefits carried over into Jackson's daily life. He seemed more confident and independent. He became very comfortable in the water, and we really started to enjoy swimming together. It was a nice way to end the week—innocent, easy, typical fun, which was hard to come by for our son.

On Memorial Day weekend 2005, everything changed. I was away at an autism conference. My husband took Jackson to swimming class at 7:30 PM on Friday. He decided to take a picture of Jackson and John and send it to me on the camera phone. Later, when we spoke about that night, he told me Jackson was John's last student for the night, and that John's friends were waiting for him to get off work. Jackson swam with John that night and had a great time.

That was the last time.

The next morning, John was driving with a friend and had a terrible accident. His friend died. John was taken to the hospital where he was put on life support. We found out about it on Tuesday morning. John was taken off life support Tuesday night.

I have cried a thousand tears.

I am devastated by the loss of this young man, not only for the obvious reason—a young life lost, a sweet, kind young man taken away. But also for the not-so-obvious reason. This young man changed my life and gave me a gift that no one else has been able to give.

Jackson's three and a half years have been difficult, complete with both medical and developmental problems. He has had surgery three times. He has undergone countless medical procedures and evaluations. While I was pregnant with him, doctors told me that he might not survive the pregnancy. Jackson's life was difficult even before he was born. Almost every aspect of Jackson's life has been fraught with worry—except for thirty minutes, once a week, when I got to be just a mom watching her son swimming around and having fun. I got to see what life is like on the other side, thanks to John. And that won't happen anymore.

After John passed away, I went back to the swim program to bring some pictures for a scrapbook that they were going to put together for his family. I knew when I walked in that door that Jackson could never go back. I could barely stand there and hand over the pictures. I hardly made it out the door, crying through the parking lot, sobbing into my car.

Life just isn't fair.

A few weeks earlier, I had talked to John about stopping swimming lessons in August. At this point in Jackson's development, we knew that he was not ready to really learn to swim independently. He had gotten a lot out of his swimming lessons already—confidence, strength, socialization, and fun. He had achieved more than I'd ever expected. But we just didn't want to stop yet. Even though it was expensive for us, Jackson was just having too much fun.

When we went to the wake, we introduced ourselves to John's family. How could I explain to them what an impact he had had on our lives? What a special person we thought he was? How could we express how our lives would never be the same? My sorrow was so great that I could not even begin to imagine theirs.

I learned from his parents that John had always been a compassionate person. He had worked with children and animals for years. When he passed away, they donated his organs, and he helped save four people.

You saved me, too, John. You gave me a glimpse into a window that I hadn't seen before.

We keep a picture of John and Jackson in his room, from the last day they swam together. I will make sure that Jackson understands what John did for us. He gave us an amazing gift, and we will never forget him.

Michele Iallonardi

Michele Iallonardi lives on Long Island with her husband, Ralph, and their three boys. She is an advocate for her children and the community. Michele is a writer whose family was featured in the documentary *Autism Every Day* by Autism Speaks. Michele runs a group for families with three children on the spectrum. E-mail her at lumardi@optonline.net

Miracle Field

I'm not old enough to play baseball or football. I'm not eight yet. My mom told me, "When you start baseball, you aren't going to be able to run that fast because of your handicap." I told Mom I wouldn't need to run that fast. When I play baseball, I'll just hit them out of the park. Then I'll be able to walk.

Edward J. McGrath, Jr.

I've always heard that miracles happen when you least expect them. And yesterday I experienced it for myself. It all started with a phone call from a guy named Steve. "Hey, Scott," he said. "Do you remember me?"

I recalled meeting him earlier in the year at his brother-in-law's place of business. Steve had heard about my son, Evan, and about his terminal heart disease and Noonan syndrome. Even though Steve doesn't have a child with a disability, he is a warrior for the cause. His brother-in-law had told him about the stories I write, and Steve wanted to be added to the list of readers. I only met him face-to-face one time, but since then, we've stayed in contact through e-mail.

After I acknowledged that I remembered him, Steve asked me—knowing I was a builder/carpenter—if I would meet him at a construction site to help finish a project that was at a standstill. "Yeah, I'll take a look," I said. We agreed to meet the next day.

I arrived at the job site a few minutes early on a sunny March morning, very welcome after another harsh and gray Michigan winter. I was early, so I climbed out of my truck and wandered around the complex. I must admit, I was a bit in awe. The view that surrounded me was of a beautiful outdoor baseball stadium—one of the nicest I'd ever seen. The grass on the field was green—even in March!—and the surrounding areas were neatly kept. There were magnificent light poles standing around the field like soldiers guarding an encampment. I could only imagine how magical a night game played on this field would be.

Just then, Steve walked up, and we shook hands. As we stood in the middle of the impressive field, he began to explain how he'd started the project a year ago, and now he needed help to wrap it up. He told me how he'd become a part of the "Miracle League." I started to think he was talking about the movie with Kevin Costner, *Field of Dreams.* You know the famous quote: "If you build it, they will come." Yep. And here I am, a builder. So I said, "But the field looks great! It looks finished. I'm curious as to why you think you need me."

"No, no, no. That's not what this is about," he said. He continued telling me about the Miracle League—that every player bats once each inning, that all base runners are safe, and that each team and each player wins every game. I pictured in my mind what a game played by those rules would look like, and as I continued to listen in the early spring sunshine, I started to daydream about the field.

In my mind's eye, the empty bleachers began to fill with spectators, cheering like they were in a pennant race. The sounds of the players chanting and calling to one another filled the air. I swear, I think I even picked up the scent of hot dogs wafting from the concession stand. The excitement in the air was exhilarating. And then, from behind home plate, I heard: "You're safe!" The umpire rumbled his call, and the crowd stood and cheered.

I found a spot right behind the backstop—the best seat in the house. I leaned into the chain-link fencing and yelled at the umpire, "What? He can't be safe; everybody who's gotten up to bat this inning has been safe. How can that be?"

The heavyset umpire, dressed all in black, turned around and gave me a quizzical look. He snapped back at me: "Can't you see these kids have medical issues? Buddy, this is the Miracle League, where everybody is safe. Everyone gets at least a base hit, and there's no such thing as a recorded error."

Hmm, I guess I really hadn't noticed that the last kid to cross home plate was in a wheelchair. I started to look around, and, to my surprise, I noticed a lot of wheelchairs and walkers in the dugouts.

As I continued to dream, a boy with an oversized head approached the plate. This player, a bit small for his age, wasn't in a wheelchair, but he needed help getting to the plate. The man who walked alongside the wobbly kid must have been his dad. It wasn't a mystery who his mom was. She was the pretty blonde gal in the stands, smiling and crying all at the same time. The closer the boy and his dad got to the batter's box, the more she jumped up and down.

I looked back at the boy. He had a plastic tube in his neck that must have been there to help him breathe. He also had a noticeable wet spot on the front of his uniform where it appeared that another tube protruded from his belly, like one of those tubes that a sick child is fed through. His dad, still in his worn-out work boots and dirty jeans, got down on one knee to hand the bat to his son. He communicated to his boy in sign language. It was obvious to me that he was signing: "You can do it, son, you can do it."

The boy never swung, not even once, as more than ten balls pitched past him. To tell you the truth, I wondered if he even could. Suddenly, the umpire straightened up and yelled, "Run, run, go to first base." The player and his dad held hands and struggled for first base. It seemed to take forever, but they made it. The umpire ran out to first base and yelled as he waved his arms in familiar fashion, "You're safe!"

Wow, that was close, I thought.

But before I could wake from my dream, the first base coach yelled, "Keep going!" as he pointed to second base and started to swing his arm like a windmill.

In the stands, I saw the mother again. She stood up, and her voice rose above the rest. She yelled, "C'mon, son, you can do it!"

So off the boy went. His dad continued to help him. It was almost too painful to watch as the simple act of running the bases seemed like such a struggle for the boy. The pair eventually rounded third base and headed for home plate. I was now screaming like the rest of the fans in the stands, acting like a fool as I cheered for the little guy.

His breath was coming hard now. The air sounded raspy as it passed through his tube. He was worn-out, but he had the hugest smile on his face. He was definitely having the time of his life.

The umpire was still out in the middle of the field, almost on purpose, as father and son crossed home plate. He nodded at me, letting me know that it was up to me to call the play.

So I did. I yelled as loud as I could, "You're *safe!*"

The boy, so tired by now, turned and looked at me. I recognized the blond curls peeking out from his helmet. I saw that familiar face. I looked into the eyes of the boy I love and know so well. He was my son. The boy everyone was cheering for was my little guy. The father who was crying and hugging him now was my own reflection.

Once again, I started to wake from my dream, but before I could, the umpire, bless his soul, held up his chubby arms and called the game because of rain. Of course, you all know the flood of drops was not coming from the sky, but from me and all the spectators in attendance that day.

I awoke from my dream, still standing midfield with my friend and kindred spirit, Steve. As we shared the vision of all that was in store for this baseball field, he said to me: "Yes, Evan will play here someday, and he'll run the bases. He'll hit a home run, and he will know he is safe."

And that, my friend, is a miracle.

Scott Newport

Scott Newport is the father of Evan, who was diagnosed with Noonan syndrome and hypertrophic cardiomyopathy as an infant. Evan spent the first 252 days of his life in the hospital, only to leave with a death notice. Now five years old, Evan uses a ventilator to breathe and has various developmental delays. The Newport family endures happily in Royal Oak, Michigan. Read Scott's blog at www.eparent.com/resources—blogs/index.asp.

The Dance

The last day of camp has arrived and with it, the big dance—and the first time the girls will be trading their shorts and T-shirts for cool party clothes. Just old enough to have first crushes, they're all excited, commiserating discussing what to wear, what's the best color to paint their nails, and who they'd like to dance with.

They ask Megan for her advice on nail color because her nails are the prettiest and always look perfect. Someone guesses blue—since it's the "in" color this year. She glances to the right—that means no. Someone guesses red. Again she glances to the right—no again. Someone guesses pink, and Megan, who has cerebral palsy and communicates by looking in one direction or the other, smiles and glances to the left. All the girls decide to go with pink; it's a good idea to take Megan's lead on nail fashion.

The boys' main concern is the tunes. They have some strong opinions on what is cool and what is lame. They try to persuade their counselor to go with their music choices; after all, they know what a happenin' tune is much better than some ancient twenty-year-old.

Now it's almost time for the dance to begin. The girls are

in the locker room for some final primping: applying makeup, curling hair, approving one another's outfits—and trying to guess which counselor each has a crush on. When Megan glances to the left with a big smile, they all agree he is the cutest.

While the girls are taking great care perfecting their look, the boys are all trying to see who can have the most outrageous luau costume. It's actually a theme dance, but no one is quite sure what a luau is. Their laughter and rough-housing has taken on a slightly nervous edge: girls at a dance is a lot different than playing co-ed kickball or trying to impress them with a bull's-eye in archery.

For some campers, this is the first time they've even been to a dance. Many have never gone to camp or been included in much of anything—and certainly have never been in a place where they could feel that they were just like everyone else.

The counselors win out and get to choose the music, and it turns out to not be so lame after all, and they even turn it up really loud. A disco light sparkles but not nearly as brightly as the eyes of these kids as they share the dance floor and everyone forgets who is a little different.

The counselors now form a circle and take turns cutting loose in the center. The girls all giggle and the boys express their approval with exclamations of "awesome!" and "sweet!" The counselors invite the children to join them; but there is no way the boys are going to dance in front of the girls or the girls are going to dance in front of those cool counselors. So everyone just stares and the circle remains empty.

That is until Cara jumps in. With her signature sweet smile, she claims the spotlight and begins to move to the music with the most unique dance moves ever. Everyone starts to clap, and the boys nod in agreement that *that* is the way to dance. Chants of "Cara, Cara, Cara," begin to fill the hall. In this moment, Cara is not a girl who is different because of her Down syndrome. Cara is different because she is the girl who broke the ice and is leading the group with her extraordinary dance.

One by one the others follow her until the circle is filled with kids who no longer care who is watching—they're just having the time of their lives.

The resident heartthrob grabs Megan's wheelchair and twirls her around the floor and the other girls express their approval with discreet thumbs-up.

The happiness that permeates the air is almost palpable as the parents who know their children's daily struggles so intimately are overcome with emotion. With tears in their eyes and hearts filled with gratitude, they watch from the sidelines thinking *this is the way the world should be.*

And as this magical night comes to a close, and everyone is saying their tearful good-byes with promises of "I'll call you," and "Let's stay friends," one lone camper remains on the floor, her parents waiting patiently as she continues to do her version of ballet until the last song is done.

I look over at her and think how long it's been since I've had the courage to dance like nobody's watching me. I guess I just needed someone to show me the way. Another bit of magic on this unforgettable night.

Kristy Barnes

Kristy Barnes is the director of marketing and services of the Bubel/Aiken Foundation. In this role she directs the administrative and business management functions, programs, technology, and communications. Before coming to TBAF, she worked with YMCAs across North Carolina to build youth and family programs and facilities. She graduated from the University of North Carolina at Wilmington where she earned her bachelor's degree in psychology. For more information about the Bubel/Aiken Foundation and Kristy's contact information, please visit www.bubelaiken.org.

Silent Grace

Silent initiation changes the hearts of all.

Sri Ramana Maharshi

Quietly entering the kindergarten classroom for the first time, Grace did not appear much different from the other children. Obviously timid and quite silent, she found the bright green paper frog bearing her name and duti- fully sat in front of it. I reassured Grace's mother, con- cerned about the well-being of her child, that all would be fine. I work very hard to establish a warm, safe, friendly classroom environment for my students, and I had no doubt that Grace would be happily adjusted in a matter of weeks. As the weeks wore on, however, it became apparent that Grace was more than a shy child. Constantly isolating herself from the other children, she often cried silently. She refused to make eye contact, feared the bathroom, and found herself too anxious to eat. Grace refused to do her work when she was seated near other children, and did not participate in the usual move- ment songs and games that most kindergartners adore.

It was exactly one month into the new school year, and

Grace had yet to speak her first word within the confines of our campus. The majority of the eighteen other children in our otherwise close-knit classroom began to ask questions. One child remarked, "She's weird."

The severity of Grace's disability became apparent to us one cool, rainy September morning when the fire alarm sounded. The whole class obediently lined up and briskly walked outside, all except one. After a hasty head count that came up one short, my classroom assistant, Mylinda, rushed back inside to find a terrified, yet silent five-year-old sitting in the same place we had left her. It was then that I knew something more had to be done for this unusually shy child who was already touching our hearts.

As Mylinda walked silently hand in hand with Grace around the campus, I held a classroom meeting. These meetings, intended to establish boundaries and promote discussion and ownership on the part of the students, were common in our classroom. This one, however, was different. For the first time we were excluding one of our own, and the children immediately noticed. "Why did Grace have to leave the room?" Though a difficult question, the answer was one that my kindergarten students would hold fast in their hearts for the remainder of the year.

"Grace is afraid when she is in our classroom with us," I explained. "Remember how you felt when you first came into this classroom? You were not sure what to expect. You did not know if school would be hard or if your teachers would be nice. You were afraid."

"I was afraid I would not have any friends!" Jessica, one of my more thoughtful students, noted.

"We all were," I replied. "But we have all become great friends now. We take care of each other, and we love each other. That is why we all need to work together to make sure Grace knows that we love her, too."

Five-year-old Brandon was immediately intrigued. "What do we do?" he asked.

I proceeded to explain to my captive audience how they could best help their classmate.

"Grace wants to be our friend, but she is afraid. She is afraid we will not like her or that we will laugh at her. You can be a great friend to her by letting her know that you love her. Invite her to play in centers with you, and tell her hello when you see her. Be very careful not to frighten her, though. When you talk to her, make sure you do not scare her. When you say hello, do not stand and try to make her talk to you. When she is comfortable talking, she will, but we cannot force her."

What followed was a thirty-minute conversation in which the children in Room 113 discussed ways they would try to help Grace feel more comfortable. At the end of the conversation, Laura raised her hand and quietly spoke, "We will be like her family."

I did not realize the truth of Laura's words at that moment. As the year progressed, however, I watched a classroom of nineteen children become a true family.

As Grace entered the classroom each morning, still unwilling to talk or interact, the kind voices of my kindergartners quietly resonated through the room: "Good morning, Grace!" "You look pretty today, Grace." "Maybe you can play with me today, Grace." The response was always the same—silence.

During free time, many of the children wrote letters or drew pictures for Grace. Though seldom received with expression, these sentiments were always carefully stored away in her backpack. Each one would be examined and read once Grace was in the safety of her home.

These kind gestures and words continued tirelessly throughout the year. Despite the lack of response, the children never gave up hope that they would be able to afford Grace the same emotional comfort they enjoyed daily in the safety of our classroom and school. Never forcing her to interact, they learned the perfect median to express their care for Grace, without seeming overbearing. They protected her fiercely, never again leaving the classroom without first ensuring that Grace was in our line. I was pleased to overhear a conversation between an employee in the cafeteria and one of my more outspoken students. The lady was gently berating Grace for not speaking when Brandon spoke up in her defense: "Grace is still afraid to be at school," he explained. "It is our job to help her and make her feel happy." With that, Brandon turned to Grace and asked if she would like pizza, to which she nodded her head "yes."

For the duration of that kindergarten year, the silence continued, though changed. Compliments and invitations to play were no longer met with blank stares, but with shy smiles and, sometimes, even hugs. The family that began on that rainy September day had endured and will continue to endure for a lifetime in the hearts of those nineteen children and their two teachers.

It is sometimes said that the goal of a teacher should be to learn at least one thing from each of her students before a school year is completed. That year, we all learned a heartfelt lesson about love, friendship, family, and the ties that truly bind them together. A family is not always defined by the blood in their veins, but by the care, trust, and commonality in their hearts. It is a truly remarkable child who can touch so many hearts and change so many lives without ever uttering a word. . . .

Ashley Carroll

Ashley Carroll received her bachelor of arts degree from the University of North Carolina-Chapel Hill in 2003. She teaches in North Carolina. Ashley enjoys reading, traveling, and working with children. Please e-mail her at Ashley_Carroll@alumni.unc.edu.

The Goal

To be a good friend, remember that we are human magnets: that like attracts like and that as we give we get.

Wilfred Peterson

Ryan had another soccer game tonight. Once again, like every other game in the last seven weeks, Ryan opted to sit in the hallway while his teammates played on the indoor soccer field. Ryan's ears were sensitive to the sound of the buzzer. To Ryan, the tone of the buzzer was like hearing the noise of thunderous rocket engines in a closed room.

Unfortunately, the buzzer was connected to the scoreboard and clock at the Centennial High School in Circle Pines, Minnesota, and was not capable of being disconnected. We had tried earplugs, earphones, and simply warning Ryan of the timing of the buzzer so he could be prepared, but it was all in vain.

As parents of Ryan, we would have done anything to see our son on the playing field with his teammates, who also have developmental disabilities. But our plan for the adaptive soccer season was simply to have Ryan practice with the team after school and then sit in the hallway during the games. Our hope was that hearing the buzzer's sound from a distance would desensitize Ryan's ears so he would gradually get used to it.

So week after week for two months, our family rushed through dinner only to sit in the hallway with Ryan during each home game—all with the goal of Ryan playing just five minutes toward the end of the season. The season progressed, and Ryan continued to support his team from the hallway. With just two home games left, Ryan's big five-minute goal was coming up. The coach approached me and suggested that the time had come for Ryan to have a chance to play in his first game. I was so nervous!

Ryan's needs were much more severe than the other athletes on his team. Ryan was thirteen years old and weighed a mere sixty pounds. He has Down syndrome, aspects of autism, and is nonverbal. He has had so many medical problems that he has endured forty-nine surgeries in his short life span. I questioned my motives for putting Ryan on the team, and at the same time primed Ryan for his big moment. Ryan's coach had come up with a plan. Ryan would come out on the field immediately after the five-minute buzzer was activated, and then she would stop the clock with a few seconds left in the game. The buzzer would never go off when Ryan was on the field.

It worked! Ryan got on the field and kicked the ball! After the game, a team player's dad approached me and said that Ryan must have kicked the ball three or four times. I proudly responded, "Six, but who's counting?" Ryan had met his five-minute goal, and at the same time made his teammates and parents very proud!

With one home game left in the season, I had high hopes for what Ryan could accomplish at his last game. *Could Ryan actually sit on the bleachers with his other teammates? Could*

Ryan play for six minutes? Well, it turned out that Ryan was too scared to sit on the bleachers with his teammates, but he did sit on the top row of the bleachers with his hands cupped over his ears! This was a huge step, and we were very proud! The opposing team was from South Minneapolis. They were big, athletic kids and had a reputation for being very good players. With only one loss for the season, the South Minneapolis team came on strong from the start. After three minutes of play, the score was already 3 to 0. The game was going to be a blowout. As the evening progressed, the score became 12 to 0, and it was evident our team was going to be defeated. But it was also time for Ryan's second chance at playing. He entered the field with ten minutes left and looked dumbfounded at the crowd. They were standing up and cheering for Ryan like he was in the Olympics going for the gold. Anybody observing from the outside would think there was a championship game in progress. Ryan dubiously stood on the field and didn't know where he should run or what he should do. The coach saw Ryan's confusion and, in an unprecedented action, joined Ryan on the playing field and guided him in play.

Ryan ended up standing directly in front of the opponent's net. The South Minneapolis goalie was probably two and a half times the size of Ryan. He was a sharp-eyed, competitive player who took the game very seriously. I think he was the best player on the team. The ball was kicked to the goalie, who quickly grabbed it in search of an open teammate. Then, something came over this goalie—something that changed my life. After a short hesitation, the goalie set the ball on the ground and gently rolled it toward Ryan, who was standing about four feet away. Then the goalie walked over to the side and left the net wide open. Ryan kicked the ball and made a goal! Anybody in the stands who was not cheering was crying.

Ryan celebrated one of the greatest moments of his life by impersonating Rocky, with his fist pumping high in the air and his feet in a celebratory trot. Ryan had just scored against the Minneapolis team!

Suddenly, I was overwhelmed with the compassion of the South Minneapolis goalie. *Who had taught him this level of benevolence? Was there any forethought put into his action, or did he suddenly have a burst of tenderness?* Wiping the tears from my eyes, I thanked the goalie for his actions. He simply shrugged his shoulders and said, "Yeah," like it was nothing. But it was something—an act of selflessness for the benefit of his competitor. The goalie may not understand the impact of his actions until much later in life, but I will never forget the true meaning of the word "victory."

Susan McMullan

Susan McMullan received her bachelor's degree in journalism and studied international journalism at the City University in London, England. She has worked in the field of radio advertising and recently taught a creative-writing class. Ryan continues to play soccer for Centennial High School's adaptive soccer program. He graduated from the hallway to the bleachers and loves being a part of the team. Susan, along with her husband and two other children, are still cheering him on. Susan can be reached at SusanMMcMullan@aol.com.

What I Learned in Middle School

A community that excludes even one member is no community at all.

                                                        Dan Wilkins

As one of only a handful of white teachers in a low-income, minority middle school, I had learned over the years that black or white, rich or poor, dig down a bit and kids are still pretty much kids. Most want love and approval from the adults in their lives, no matter what they would have you believe. Another thing I learned was not to expect miracles for the junior-high child with a disability. By this age, familial, academic, and behavioral patterns were often entrenched and slow to change. As a special-education teacher, I had learned to measure progress in small increments.

Such seemed the case when I read the file on Carlos, a fifteen-year-old Hispanic boy with a dysfunctional family and a long history of school failure. As a fifteen-year-old eighth-grade student, he was two years older than his classmates. Although Carlos functioned at a third-grade level in reading and a fourth-grade level in math, he had only recently been identified with a learning disability in language processing. In addition to this delay in identifying his academic difficulties, several days into the present school year, Carlos had yet to attend my special-education classes, and he wasn't getting any younger. I marched down to the social worker's office to get some answers.

"Where's Carlos?" echoed Lena, the school social worker. "In bed!" I admired Lena's ability to continue to maintain her optimism despite an overwhelming caseload of children and families.

"We can't get him out," she continued. "He's only been with his permanent foster family for a few weeks. With his pattern of school phobia and depression, a new school and a new placement has just pushed him over the edge." With sadness, she elaborated on some of the details of Carlos's life. Carlos had lived with his mother and two younger brothers in a depressed neighborhood in a nearby city. He had been removed from his home and placed in a temporary foster home when his mother was convicted for selling crack cocaine. Carlos became a guardian of the state halfway through his seventh-grade year. He had been denied special-education services throughout his life due to his mother's refusal to grant permission for the psychological and academic testing needed to identify him.

However, once he became a guardian of the state, the school wasted no time in evaluating Carlos and developing an Individual Education Plan to address his learning disability. Finally, after a lifetime of failure, Carlos would get the help he so desperately needed. But there was one small problem: Carlos wasn't having any. Damage done.

Later that same day, Lena came to tell me that an emergency meeting had been scheduled to develop a plan to get Carlos to school. His new foster parents, Fernando and Jose, would be attending the meeting.

"Yes, you heard right," Lena said, in response to my raised eyebrows and look of surprise. "They're a same-sex couple."

"I didn't know they allowed same-sex couples to foster,"

I replied. "Don't you think that would be confusing for Carlos at this point in his life?"

"See for yourself," Lena said with an enigmatic smile.

It was quickly apparent at the meeting exactly what she meant. Well spoken, caring, and concerned, Fernando and Jose clearly had Carlos's best interests at heart. Together, we developed a plan for his first few days of school.

"I thought I'd let you see for yourself," Lena said after the meeting. "They've fostered other difficult kids for us successfully, and they have a lot of experience."

"They're going to need it and more," was my response. I had seen too many like Carlos to share Lena's eternal optimism.

The next day I was teaching as usual, facing the front of the class with my back to the door, when a sudden hush filled the room. Eyes, easily distracted by the smallest event, shifted eagerly toward the door. Then came the thumping sound of jaws dropping to the floor. *What could have possibly affected my students this way?* I thought irritably as I turned to see the source of all the excitement. Tall, well dressed, and movie-star handsome, Carlos had arrived. Though he shook my hand politely, his eyes remained firmly fixed to the floor to the complete disappointment of all the teenage girls in the room.

Over the next days and weeks, the girls were doomed to further disappointment. All their titters, giggles, and flutters were for naught: Carlos wanted to learn. And what a joy he was to teach! Once he learned strategies to help him to process and retain information, there was no stopping him. Voraciously, he gobbled up whatever I taught him in big gulps. Almost as much fun to watch was the shock of the other students in the class. Carlos's go-get-'em attitude was unprecedented in the typically tormented lives of the middle-school special-education child. If Carlos were a truck, the school year was a wild ride down a steep highway. The day he received his first report card was the first day he met my eyes. It was then that I saw the first shy smile dawn reluctantly on his face.

I was almost as impressed by Fernando and Jose, whom I largely credited with Carlos's transformation. There was never a day that Carlos was not well dressed or prepared for class. I had received several phone calls at night with homework questions from both foster parents. It was clear from my conversations that there were established rules and routines in the household for Carlos and his other foster sibling.

Then came the day that Carlos actually strode into my room, bursting with excitement: Fernando and Jose were taking him to see one of his biological brothers! It was the first of many such happy visits.

Graduation day was unusually bittersweet that year. Fernando, Jose, and all of Carlos's brothers, both foster and biological, watched with obvious pride as Carlos accepted his diploma. After graduation, as I shook Carlos's hand in congratulation, he whispered in my ear: "Miss, I have really good news!"

"Well, I heard you now have a girlfriend, is that it?" I answered with a twinkle.

"Oh, Miss, even better than that," Carlos said with a light blush. "Fernando and Jose are going to adopt me!"

Like the spring crocus determined to push past the rocks and snow to reach grateful arms to the sun, Carlos had come home at last.

In the end, I learned something else that year—it's never too late for love to make miracles happen.

Donna Larkin

Names have been changed to protect privacy.

Donna Larkin received her master's degree in special education from Southern Connecticut State University. She currently teaches seventh grade in Trumbull, Connecticut. She is happiest encouraging living things to grow.

Motherhood

Mother is the word for God in the eyes of children everywhere.

Eric Draven

I worked in a group home in Sherwood Park, Alberta, caring for eight adults with severe disabilities. At 3:00 every day the phone would ring.

"How are my children today?"

"They're fine, Mrs. Dreichel, just fine."

"Did Katie eat her lunch today?"

"Oh, yes, Mrs. Driechel, she ate a good lunch."

"She doesn't like tuna, you know."

"I know, Mrs. Driechel. She had soup today."

"How's Clifford?"

"Clifford is fine, as well."

"Did Clifford walk today?"

"Oh, yes, Peggy and Mona walked with him for twenty minutes."

Then came that all-too-familiar pause that I failed to prepare myself for again and again. With a tremble in her sweet, little Ukrainian-accented voice, she'd say, "I miss my children so much, Donna. I wish I could take them home with me. If Mister was alive, we could manage. I know we could. I love my children so much." There was a sense of loneliness and desperation in her voice that I felt great compassion, but could not truly embrace.

Mrs. Dreichel was eighty-one years old. Her husband had passed away six years prior. Her children were fifty-three and fifty-two. Both were incontinent, nonverbal, suffered from seizure disorders, and had limited mobility. There were no limitations on Mrs. Dreichel's love for her children. Once a month, she would take Katie and Clifford home for four days. When approaching Mrs. Dreichel's neighborhood, Katie would clap her hands and scream with delight. Clifford, on the other hand, always seemed to be just amazed with the traffic. Upon their arrival, Mrs. Dreichel would be standing on her doorstep, delicate and fragile in stature, yet larger than life and beaming with anticipation. As soon as they were taken off the bus, she would smother them with hugs and kisses. "I missed you so much," she'd say.

As we stepped inside, the aroma of freshly baked bread welcomed us. The sweet sound of Jim Reeves playing in the background filled her home with a peacefulness that needs no explanation. There were times when I wish I could have stayed.

Katie would be placed in her rocking chair. If there were two things in life that Katie loved, it was rocking and old country music. By this time, Clifford would be crawling to his bedroom. He would sit on his bed and play with his yellow truck. This was something that always made Clifford smile.

Mrs. Dreichel's daughter Rose was a great help as well. She would come daily to assist with their personal care and daily medications.

Although Katie and Clifford were not with us for the next four days, I still felt a sense of responsibility for their well-being, and I would call Mrs. Dreichel the following day to see if everything was okay.

The conversation was much shorter now. She reminded me of a woman who had just returned from the hospital with her newborn. Within minutes, she'd say, "I have to go now." The transformation was heartwarming and magical. Her voice exhibited no loneliness. The next four days belonged to her.

Although the return trip became very routine for us, it was heart-wrenching. When I arrived at the house, you could tell that Mrs. Dreichel had been crying. She would have her children bathed, fed, and ready for departure. Clifford would sometimes hold on to her and push us away. This, you could tell, left her very emotional. Katie would often scream. Katie's screams were no longer foreign to me and were always anticipated. This was her way of communicating.

Although we had a deadline to meet, we always allowed extra time for Mrs. Dreichel to say good-bye. Again, she would smother her children with hugs and kisses, and tell them she loved them more than anything. "I may never see them again," she'd whisper. Standing on her doorstep, wiping away her tears, she would wave to Katie and Clifford until the distance between them became unknown. Her posture changed. She no longer stood tall and proud. The loneliness and desperation once again intruded upon her.

Mrs. Dreichel passed away in 2004 while sitting in her living room. There was no burden too heavy, no challenge too great for Mrs. Dreichel. She was, in my eyes, what motherhood stands for.

Donna Judge Malarsky

Donna Judge Malarsky is employed at a Christian school in Sherwood Park, Alberta, Canada. She grew up in an extremely small town, Small Point, Newfoundland. She moved to Edmonton in 1991, and married the love of her life in 2003. She has two grown children and three grandchildren, whom she loves dearly.

An Angel Among Us

Instill the love of you into the world, for a good character is what is remembered.

The Teaching for Merikare

All teachers remember that one student who reaches into the depths of their hearts and touches their souls. Jackie was mine. She had lived most of her nine years in and out of hospitals and homebound classrooms by the time she arrived at mine. I joined the platoon of all who taught and cared for Jackie, astounded by her amazing spirit, as we witnessed her bravely fighting the dreaded disease that was maliciously robbing her body of its ability to survive. Having spent so much of her short life being poked with needles and fighting to breathe, Jackie did not totally trust anybody, always keeping her distance. Only her mother was allowed close enough to hug Jackie and give her the love and affection we all wanted to share.

Most of my students that year were little rough-and-tumble boys who avowed often that they had absolutely no use for girls. However, they had not reckoned with

Jackie. With her curious combination of an adorable sense of humor and understandable caution, she drew each of us into her web and made us her protectors. I would often hear "You know, she's just like one of the guys," and "Jackie's here!!!" coming from my little guys' mouths.

Two days before Jackie's last hospitalization, her mother brought her to my classroom late one afternoon after the dismissal of all the school's students. Collecting her belongings on that final day, Jackie finally succumbed to the world around her—and my prayers—and let someone besides her mother get close enough to her to kneel down and give her a long hug, a show of long overdue affection. I shall forever be grateful to the God I worship that I was that person. As her mother snapped a picture of the two of us, I could feel the fragile bones of Jackie's body and was sadly aware of just how pitifully and painfully ill Jackie truly was.

As the three of us walked down the school corridor together, I knew I would never see Jackie again, that this would be her last hospital stay. I could feel the tears rolling down my cheeks, and an intense sadness cover me with a shimmering and shivering fog. Jackie turned at the end of the hall, clutching her Barney, and waved a final and somewhat shy good-bye. Jackie's mother gave a wavering smile that I knew was overflowing with her immense bravery and sadness.

Three weeks later, I heard a quiet knock at my classroom door. One of my closest teacher friends stood before me with tear-filled eyes, holding a slender newspaper clipping in her shaking hands. "What is it?" I asked, so afraid of the answer. She quietly handed me Jackie's obituary and gently hugged me as I cried profuse tears of loss. I was finally able to return to my classroom to give the hardest and saddest news I had ever had to share with a class. We gathered together as I told the children of Jackie's death and the disease that had taken her from us. We cried and hugged and spent a special moment in time, remembering a little girl who had meant so much to us all.

One of the quietest little boys said what we all felt, "She always was an angel, and now she is one." At the students' suggestion, we dedicated a bulletin board to Jackie. I watched through my own sadness and tears as the class produced pictures and stories in honor and memory of their special friend. I now knew, as those little boys showed, an angel had indeed been in our midst. But still I grieved with intense pain and the empty feeling of a terrible loss.

Several weeks after Jackie's funeral, I heard a soft knock at my door and was overjoyed to see Jackie's mother standing before me. "I'm so sorry" were the first words out of my mouth. As we hugged and cried together, she told me quietly, "Thank you so much for loving my child." Very timidly, she handed me an envelope. Inside was the picture of Jackie and me in that one last hug. "Oh, thank you," I said, knowing I would treasure that picture always, as a memory of someone too special to ever truly be lost or forgotten. "Thank you for lending Jackie to us."

I invited her into the classroom. At first she declined, but I told her I had something special to show her. I introduced her to the class, and a hush settled. One of my shyest students walked up to Jackie's mother, silently took her hand, and led her to Jackie's bulletin board. She read each letter and stared at every picture, including Jackie's obituary, touching each lovingly. As she turned to look at us with tears of sadness streaming down her face, a tiny quaking voice said, "We want you to have our pictures of Jackie."

While taking them down, I watched Jackie's mother walk from child to child and give each a shy kiss. She said her good-byes to the students, and we walked down the school hallway together, both knowing it would be the last time we would meet and talk. We stopped to hug, and then I watched her walk out of my life just as I had watched her little angel do. As she turned to wave good-bye in the same way as her child, I noticed her clutching the pictures and letters to her breast, as if hoping to keep Jackie close. Tears rolled down my cheeks as I realized I was holding Jackie's picture in the same way.

Margaret Prator

Margaret Prator, a "born" teacher of twenty-five years' duration, with concentration on children with disabilities, has also been a freelance writer for as long. Several of her nostalgia pieces have been published in regional publications. Her column, STATION K-I-D-Z, narrated by Church Mouse, appears in her church's newsletter. Please e-mail her at mprator@satx.rr.com.

6

SIBLING REVELRY

Brothers and sisters are as close as hands and feet.

Vietnamese Proverb

Something About Benny

A brother is a friend given by nature.

Jean Baptiste Legouve

There is something about Benny that is strange. My little brother Benny doesn't look strange, but sometimes he acts like he is from a different planet. He thinks he is a dinosaur, and roars in restaurants and growls in the grocery store. My mom tells him not to growl so loudly, but he doesn't always listen.

There is something about Benny that is different from other little boys. Most little boys want to grow up to be firemen or astronauts. Not Benny. He wants to grow up and be a building. He likes to hold up the walls at the school and stare at the bricks very closely. I think he can see right through them, but he never tells me what he sees.

There is something about Benny that is magical. He can make a whole room of people disappear just by closing his eyes really tight and saying, "Go away!" *Poof!* They're gone. When he wants them to come back again, he just opens his eyes. Sometimes I wish I could do that magic trick, too.

There is something about Benny that is smart. He never forgets where he puts his toys, shoes, books, coat, or chocolate-chip cookie. He has memorized all of his favorite movies, from beginning to end. He can say them line for line and not miss a word. He knows all of his colors and the alphabet and the bones of the tyrannosaurus rex, but he won't always tell you.

There is something about Benny that is unique. He doesn't care what the other kids are wearing to school or what the weather is like outside. Last summer, when the sun was melting ice-cream cones faster than we could lick them, he wore a blue snowsuit and a green knitted cap every day. In the winter, when the ice cracked beneath our feet on the driveway, he wore his swimsuit and his favorite short-sleeved T-shirt. My mom told him he couldn't wear it outside, so he laid down flat and closed his eyes and made her go away.

There are lots of things about Benny that are funny. He makes silly faces and rolls his eyes and giggles to himself. He hides in the bushes and thinks he really is a tyrannosaurus rex. He wants to eat leaves, because that is, of course, what dinosaurs do. But my mom won't let him. She makes him eat chicken.

There is something about Benny that is athletic. He climbs trees and walls and doorways, and makes it look so easy. He can hike farther than any of my friends, and he can ride his bike for miles and miles without even breathing hard. He can also swim for hours and never get tired.

There is something about Benny that is tender. He loves babies, and wants to touch their eyes and nose and mouth. He wants to hold them and feed them a bottle. He loves animals, too, and pets their soft fur and feathers.

There is something about Benny that makes me sad. Kids say, "What's wrong with you, kid?" and "Why do you talk so funny?" Benny just ignores them, but it makes me sad inside.

There is something about Benny that makes me mad. Sometimes I get mad because I have a brother who screams and yells and acts so strange. Sometimes I get embarrassed and wish that he had a different brain, a typical brain like mine.

But then he wouldn't be Benny.

There is something about Benny that is out of this world. When he babbles and banters and barks to himself, I don't call it nonsense. I pretend he is speaking with angels.

There is something about Benny that many people don't see. They see a five-year-old boy saying silly sentences and parroting protests. They see a child whose body never seems to stop moving. Sometimes they get mad and sometimes they just stare, but sometimes they say mean things to him or my mommy. But they don't see what I see.

There is something about Benny that is just like you and me. He wants to feel loved and needed and special. He wants to be included in the playground games. He wants to have a best friend. He wants to help others.

There is something about Benny that makes me want to reach out to those who are different from me. Sometimes I see people's differences on the outside. Sometimes I see people who don't look any different on the outside, but I know they are different on the inside. I can see it in their eyes and feel it in my heart.

I know that Benny is here to teach me to be patient and kind and forgiving and compassionate.

There's something about Benny that makes me thankful that I have a brother who speaks to angels.

Kimberly Jensen

Kimberly Jensen graduated with a B.A. in communication from the University of Utah in 1991. She is the mother of three children and writes children's books focusing on loving children with disabilities since her youngest was diagnosed with autism in 2001. Please e-mail her at kcjensen419@msn.com.

"Sharon doesn't say much,
but she communicates well with animals."

Believe

*Nothing in the world can take the place of per-
sistence. Talent will not; nothing is more common than unsuccessful men with talent. Genius
will not; unrewarded genius is almost a proverb.
Education will not; the world is full of educated
derelicts. Persistence and determination alone
are omnipotent.*

Calvin Coolidge

Little did I know that Emily's unconditional belief in her
little brother's can-do ability would someday help her
recover from a devastating car accident.

When life as we know it shatters and dreams evaporate
too soon, we lose our ability to believe that goodness can
come from tragedy, that overwhelming grief can lead to
future healing.

I was so young, and I knew so little in 1985 when our
second baby, Mark, was born. I had survived a tempestu-
ous childhood of enormous sadness and loss, and my only
dream was to be a kind and loving mother to the happy,
healthy babies God would surely bless us with.

But babies didn't come quickly, and we spent years visiting fertility specialists. When Emily was born with bright light in her eyes and a joie de vivre that filled our home with wondrous energy, I believed she was a miraculous answer to years of prayer.

I selfishly wanted more for us and for Emily; I wanted another baby to share our blessings. Years passed, with more tests and several miscarriages. And then, on one of the prettiest spring days I've ever seen, my husband Russ and I celebrated the birth of our son Mark. God had blessed us once again, we merrily told friends and family, near and far, with a rich man's family—a girl and a boy!

Mark was a sweet baby, quiet and undemanding, sleepy and content. Pretty, too, with his older sister's dark brown hair and hazel eyes. But the morning after his birth, the pediatricians told us that Mark had one microscopic flaw that changed our lives forever—an extra chromosome, or Down syndrome.

Mark's diagnosis shattered me deeply and gravely, but I had to keep living, to go through the motions for our four-year-old daughter. Somehow, I gathered enough composure and grace to show Emily her baby brother without sobbing through the visit. She loved him immediately, glowing as she held "her baby." She was never jealous of him, never complained about all the medical appointments and therapists and emergencies that consumed the next year of our lives.

She adored Mark. She even angrily told me one day when I had let him cry too long that he didn't want me anyway. "He wants me to be his mommy, not you! He's my baby!"

The years passed, and Mark flourished. Milestones were significantly delayed, but he eventually reached them. The light in his eyes grew brighter as a magical little boy emerged from the shadows of doctors' first gloomy predictions of "He can't . . ." and "He'll never . . ." I began to see that Mark was a happy, loving child who worked incredibly hard to do all the things his therapists and teachers asked of him, slowly but surely learning and doing so much more than I ever believed he would.

Emily was his favorite teacher. She didn't know that other baby brothers and sisters didn't have speech, physical, and occupational therapists coming into their homes several times a week. She didn't know that all babies don't begin school when they are three weeks old to learn how to track with their eyes, to hold up their heads, or to roll over. On days when I just couldn't do all the infant-stimulation exercises with Mark at home, Emily would excitedly "play" with him, holding bright, musical toys for him to see, hear, and reach for. She always cheered his every move! He crawled to her before he ever crawled to anyone else, racing—at his own speed—for a hug from his big sister. I'm quite sure his very first smile was for Emily.

Before she was five, she had given Mark everything I struggled to give him—unconditional love and unconditional belief in his abilities. She taught me how to be Mark's mom.

Little did I know that Emily's unconditional belief in Mark's can-do ability would someday save her.

On a Sunday afternoon in December 1998, when Mark was thirteen and Emily was seventeen, I was waiting for Emily to come home after an overnight with Melanie, her best friend. Mark, his little sister Carolyn, ten, and little brother David, eight, and I were home baking Christmas cookies and singing carols with friends and their kids. I was conscious of how happy I felt, how blessed I was to be surrounded with so much love.

The phone rang. Melanie was sobbing. A car had broadsided them, and Emily, in the passenger seat, wouldn't wake up. They were less than a mile from our front door. Life was shattered again.

As I choked out what had happened, Mark dropped to

his knees and prayed, "Please, God, Emily can't die; she's my sister. Please help her."

Emily had suffered a traumatic brain injury, broken pelvis, broken back, broken ribs, and massive internal injuries. She remained in a coma for three weeks. The doctors gave her less than a 40 percent chance of survival. If she did survive, they warned us, "She'll never be the same and may have to spend the rest of her life in a nursing home."

Therapists had given Mark so much so many years ago. Physical therapists, speech pathologists, and occupational therapists had taught Mark things his pediatrician thought were impossible. Emily's unconditional love and belief in Mark's ability had once been his greatest motivation. Now Mark's lessons would help Emily relearn everything—words and their meanings, names of her friends and relatives, how to drink from a cup, hold a fork and a pen, how to stand and then walk, understand what she read, and believe in herself again.

"You can do it, sis," Mark would encourage Emily as she tried to walk five feet down the hall using a walker. And she'd take a few more steps just for him.

She'd snarl at me when I'd make her use the right word instead of "thing" or "it." But for Mark, she'd show off her latest mastery of the names of various fruits.

Head-injury patients are often angry and lash out at everyone around them. We all bore her wrath many times—all of us except Mark. She never screamed at him, or pushed him away, or slammed the door in his face. She always smiled for him, held his hand, and tried just a little harder to do a little more whenever he was with her.

Her recovery was miraculous. After just twelve weeks of intense rehabilitation, she returned to high school to finish her senior year. Many days were overwhelmingly hard; as she recovered, she became more aware of what she had lost. Some friends treated her differently, and a few teachers just sent her to a desk in the back of the room to work "independently." Facts accumulated over years of education had to be relearned, math skills and formulas rememorized, and metaphors and similes reunderstood.

"I just have one thing to say, Em. Believe in yourself," Mark counseled.

Now, I wonder as I look back: *Could we have encouraged Emily with the resolute belief that she could, indeed, relearn everything without all we'd learned from Mark's intense early-intervention programs? Would Emily have graduated from college in just four years, run a half-marathon, and mentored thousands of high-school students as buddies to special-education students if Mark had not been her little brother?*

Every day of his life, when we've been astute enough to pay attention, Mark has taught us that life's little victories add up to triumphs. As an infant struggling to make his own muscles lift the weight of his head, he taught Emily to persevere even when the task seems impossible. He showed her that sometimes the greatest rewards are a pat on the back for a job well done and belief in your own inner resolve. His very being taught his big sister that a person's worth cannot be measured by IQ, class rank, or worldly riches—it's measured by an unconditional love that many of us never experience, and very few of us are wise enough to truly understand. He taught us to believe.

Jennifer M. Graham

Jennifer M. Graham, mother of four unique kids, has written about the inspiring abilities of individuals with intellectual disabilities for twenty years. Her articles have appeared in national and regional magazines, and the anthology, *You Will Dream New Dreams*. She is a family educator on transition. Contact her at jennifer-mgraham@comcast.net. Emily graduated from James Madison University in 2004 and currently works for an international nonprofit serving children with disabilities. Mark graduated from high school in 2006 and has two part-time jobs in the community. He bakes the best chocolate-chip cookies and believes in the best in everyone.

Silent No More

I am a young man in a verbal world. I am silent. My mouth doesn't work in the usual way. I have autism. For ten long years, I remained silent in a lonely prison. Locked away in darkness as vast as the universe is big. I expressed myself through negative behavior that no one could understand. My mom tried everything possible to help me break out of my lonely wasteland. I used picture communication systems, which were useless. I tried sign language, which was hopeless. My family resorted to the only real thing that works—praying a lot. My dad is a minister, so our whole church prayed for me.

One day, an amazing angel in the form of a purple-haired lady arrived at my school. She brought a Lightwriter, which is a special voice output device for silent people. The angel lady explained the device to me, and then took my hand in hers, and my silence changed to golden words of freedom. I am now able to type all my thoughts with the help of my trained support staff. My parents bought me my own device, and I have been a paroled prisoner ever since.

Our story doesn't end there. Our family has been blessed twice with two silent young men. My brother,

Jonathan, has Down syndrome, and he too has been locked up in his own silent, tortured world. Once I started typing my thoughts, the purple angel thought it would free my brother, too, so very recently my brother was released from his silent world. One day, my brother came into my classroom, and we had the opportunity to talk to each other for the first time in our lives. It was so amazing to actually converse with my older brother in real words. The conversation was videotaped as a gift to my parents. My mom and dad watched it a hundred times. It was Christmas time, so we made a Christmas card video of our conversation for our church and friends who had prayed long and hard for us. My life is now filled with endless possibilities.

Jordan

Jordan is a fifth-grader at Hope Technology School in Palo Alto, California (www.hopetechschool.org/index.htm). The school practices inclusion, where typically developing and special-needs students learn together. Jordan enjoys parks, movies, and attending an inclusive E-soccer program (www.e-soccer.info/index.html). He also attends a spiritual resources class for families with special needs.

Jordan and Jonathan talking for the very first time using their Lightwriters presented by Janna Woods, whom the family calls a very special purple-haired angel. The Lightwriter is a designated communication device sold by Assistive Technologies. The device can be viewed at www.assistivetech.com.

Photo reprinted by permission of Gail Ewell. ©2006 Gail Ewell.

Teaching by Example

Tell me and I forget.
Teach me and I learn.
Involve me and I remember.
Benjamin Franklin

"Joyce is two years younger than me," I told the director, "and four years younger than my other sister. When she was born, the doctors recommended that my parents institutionalize her. They chose to keep her home unless it became too difficult."

I had thought my interview for admission was finished, but the program director wanted more insight into my character. "Whose influence was most important in making you who you are today?" he asked.

"My sister Joyce," I answered.

He leaned back in his chair. "Tell me about her."

I hesitated. It was, well, complicated.

Joyce and I went for walks and liked the same music. We ate cookies and ice cream together. We both had brown hair and blue eyes. But Joyce and I were different. Very different. I was looking for admission into a competitive college major. Joyce was finishing her years as a student in the special-education system. I was developing my independence as a young adult. She remained nonverbal and dependent on others for assistance with daily tasks.

Out in public, I had seen pity, horror, disgust, mockery, and curiosity on the faces of strangers as they watched Joyce and our family. Sometimes people reacted to her in ways that made me mad. I yelled at a woman once because she pulled her children out of a pool as we entered. "My sister hasn't got any disease your kid is gonna get," I hollered.

As I got older, I recognized ignorance as the source of people's stares. It saddened me that people saw only the shell of disability instead of my sister's humanity. Now I had to explain Joyce to this Ph.D. who held my admission in his hand. I wondered if he would understand how this person with limited abilities could teach me so much. I took a deep breath and continued. "Joyce learned to walk when she was five and feed herself when she was eight. She was toilet-trained by twelve, and then tried to learn other practical things, like setting the table." I laughed at the memory. "We had to get unbreakable plates and cups. She was so excited to help that she dropped things or put piles of dishes and silverware in the middle of the table.

"That excitement never changed. No matter how many times she was asked to set the table, get ready for a bath, or watch at the window for my dad, she would rush right into the task. She loved being part of the family activities. She tried everything with gusto.

"By Joyce's example, I learned to enjoy routine tasks. Everyday jobs give my day rhythm and keep me part of a bigger whole. Joyce taught me that things don't have to be exciting to be fun. It's all the way you look at it."

The director pressed his fingertips together while I continued. "Learning to do anything took Joyce a long time. Even a simple thing like learning to brush her hair took months." I giggled at another memory. "She was taught tooth-brushing and brushing her hair during the same time period. More than once, she got confused and wound up with toothpaste in her hair. But she would try again. Joyce taught me patience and perseverance in spite of multiple failures." The director's nod urged me on.

"She showed loyalty and love of family," I continued. "She would watch at the window for my dad's car to pull down the street. As soon as it came into view, she'd race to the door, open it, and bring my father inside by the hand. Sometimes she'd even let him get his coat off before she led him to the dinner table." I smiled at the memory before I continued. "Joyce has an innocent charm. When she sneaks cookies from the cookie jar, the rattling of the ceramic lid gives it away. Doesn't bother her at all. During hide-and-seek, she hides behind the shower curtain with her shoes sticking out below. She may look like a young adult, but she functions like a young child, trusting, simple, and pure."

"And that has influenced you?" the director asked. I hesitated as I tried to put these complex thoughts into words. "Joyce enjoys who she is and where she is. Her dignity and worth come from that, not from worldly accomplishments. I find that admirable."

I was admitted into that program and graduated a few years later as a physical therapist. The lessons Joyce taught influenced not just my choice of career, but virtually every aspect of my life. She taught simplicity, acceptance, patience, and love by example, touching my life and allowing me to touch hundreds of others. I am forever in her debt.

Jeanne Moran

Jeanne Moran has worked with children with disabilities for most of her twenty-nine-year career as a physical therapist (PT). She teaches pediatrics to PT students in the classroom and in the clinic. In her spare time, she enjoys her family, church, tap dancing, and writing. Unfortunately, her sister Joyce had major surgery at age nineteen and lost most of the skills that had been so hard to gain, including walking and some self-care. She has been living in a long-term care facility in Goshen, New York, since 1980. She enjoys sunshine, car rides, and cookies, and visiting with her family. E-mail Jeanne at jmoran@epix.net.

Just Tori

He who knows that enough is enough will always have enough.

Lao-tzu

They tell me she's different, but to me she's just Tori. She stood there in line in her uniform—blue shorts, white blouse, white ruffled socks, and black shoes. She wore her long brown hair down, and a smile that I can never say "no" to widely spread across her face. She tugged her Care Bear backpack behind her, the one with the wheels. She said to me, "Don't get me," and ran off, as she often does, so I chased her for a few minutes, strategically dodging the other students.

A bell rang, and she had to get back in line. Her aide was waiting for her. She marched with the other kindergartners up the steps and into the school. She was so proud to be on her own. I was scared for her, but she was oblivious. *Would she make friends? Would the other kids make fun of her? Would she be accepted?* They tell me she's different, but to me she's just Tori.

The wheels on her backpack remind me of the day she

was born. I had never held such a young child. The feeling was unexplainable. After nine months of anticipation, my dream of becoming an aunt had finally come true. For an eleven-year-old, this was the most important thing that had ever happened to me, yet there was a feeling that something was wrong. The ride home in my mother's minivan was a long one. Nobody spoke. I just watched the wheels out the window as car after car rolled by. My mom tried to explain something to me. She told me that Tori would have a flatter nose bridge, less-defined muscle tone, and that she may never do things other kids would. I cried that night. She was my niece. I was supposed to take her shopping and teach her about boys, but I would never be able to do that. They said she would not walk properly, learn to read, have friends, work for a living, or make much of a life for herself at all. They tell me she's different, but to me she's just Tori.

The wheels of her backpack remind me of the tricycles Grandma and Grandpa got her and her younger sister, Gilli, for her fourth birthday. This was the tricycle they told me she would never be able to ride because she was different. She rode it all right. Up and down the block for hours and hours, I watched the wheels of that tricycle turn in a blur of red and white. This past year for their birthdays, the girls got big-girl bikes. I watch the wheels on those bikes turn, too, rolling Tori past places they said she would never even get to.

I spend time almost every week with Tori, and every week she does something new they told us she would never do. Most recently it was writing her first name, counting to ten, and reciting the alphabet. I sit on the phone for hours listening to my sister's struggle to have Tori in the best educational setting possible. She tells me of the people putting restrictions on what Tori can do because of her disability, and all I want to do is tell her to keep fighting. If we would have listened to them six years ago, who knows what kind of a person Tori would be right now. She would not be the Tori I know and love. They tell me she's different, but to me she's just Tori.

Tori gives everybody in the family something to believe in when she runs in the door and shouts out their names with her arms wide open. She has no idea of the ways that I am different from other people, and I am oblivious to the ways she is. They tell me she's different, they always have, and I've never listened. To me, she's just Tori.

Katherine Schroeder

Katherine Schroeder studies communication arts and journalism as an undergraduate at the University of Wisconsin-Madison. She treasures her boyfriend, family—especially her two nieces, Victoria and Gillian—and the White Sox. Kathi can be reached at kaschroeder@wisc.edu. Tori loves playing at the park and taking ballet and tap classes where she is the only student who can do the splits. She has grown the last few years, and she continues to surpass expectations placed upon her both at home and at school. And her hugs still give everyone who knows her more to believe in than ever.

Switching Roles

I have a beautiful older sister, Sarina, who just so happens to have Down syndrome. From my earliest years, I was made to believe that I was to take care of her, as she would never be able to care for herself. I remember promising my mother that I would.

When I went off to college at seventeen, Sarina stayed home with my parents. I lived in Nevada, and she lived in Massachusetts. When I turned twenty-one, Sarina wanted to move to Nevada with me, as my parents were not giving her as much independence as she wished, and she was steadily regressing. I thought about this, wondering if I could take care of my sister and finish off college. *Wouldn't she be a lot of work? Could I actually get her all the things she would need and still maintain a life of my own?* We decided to try. In all honesty, I was not prepared for all the challenges that faced us. I worked nights, went to school during the day, and slept when I could. In between, I was teaching Sarina the ins and outs of taking care of herself. I took her along to everything—parties, clubs, casinos, vacations—all over the West Coast.

On Halloween 1992, we were going to a nightclub in our

costumes. She was Catwoman, and I was a gypsy. A car ran a red light, hitting us head-on. Sarina went through the windshield, and I was a mess—broken knees and hands, and a fractured skull. Sarina sustained no injuries but a scratch on the nose and neck.

When we were discharged from the hospital, I could barely walk and was in constant pain. Sarina had to cook, assist me in the shower, help me get dressed, and do my hair—basically everything I had done for her previously. She was amazing! She had retained all that I had taught her and was able to apply it to real-life situations, not only for herself, but also for another. We had switched roles—I was now being taken care of by my sister.

After five years, I decided to move back to the New England area. Sarina and I climbed Calico Basin in Las Vegas on Christmas day, and when we got to the top I told her that I wanted to go back. She very clearly said to me with a smile, "You go, my sister. I stay here."

I asked her who would take care of her, and she said, "I take care of myself." I had little doubt she could, but I just couldn't leave her alone in Las Vegas, so she gave in and moved back to New England with me. After we got settled, she got her own apartment with twenty hours of assistance and took college classes.

I will never forget how I wondered if I could take care of Sarina. Now I wonder if I could have accomplished all I did if I didn't have her in my life. She has shaped my career, my personality, my parenting skills, and my life. I love you, my sister.

Gina Favazza-Rowland

Gina Favazza-Rowland is a holistic counselor in Portsmouth, New Hampshire, and a case manager for folks with "different abilities," not disabilities. She is currently writing a book about Sarina and their lives together. Sarina and Gina each have their own MySpace account—feel free to look them up at www.myspace.com/gypseahealer and www.mspace.com/angelface38!

Big Brother Time-Off

"He's ruining my life," Clayton yelled as he ran upstairs to his bedroom and slammed the door. Clayton was talking about his younger brother, Bennett, who resides in the same bedroom. The two boys share not only their room, but also their clothes, toys, friends, and, on occasion, underwear.

As I followed Clayton upstairs, I glanced at the Lego tower he had just finished building. It was now in pieces, and in the middle of the destruction was, of course, Bennett, quietly gathering up all the red Lego pieces.

"How is Bennett ruining your life?" I asked Clayton.

"He follows me everywhere. He ruins our games. He growls too loudly in my ear. He won't let me sleep at night. He breaks my stuff. He's just ruining my life!"

Bennett entered our family when Clayton was three years old. Clayton didn't have to share much with his little brother for the first year. But after Bennett's first birthday, he moved into Clayton's room. Bennett was still in his crib, and Clayton slept in a bed. Three feet of space separated the two sleeping boys. At night, I could hear Clayton sing songs to his little brother and attempt to tell him stories with his limited speech. In the morning, I would find Clayton's favorite stuffed animals scattered in the crib with Bennett. Very often, Clayton would be in there, too.

We soon moved to a bigger house with an extra bedroom, but we decided it was best to keep the two boys together. That was also the same month that Bennett turned three and was diagnosed with autism.

The boys continued to play somewhat independently. Bennett was content to play dinosaurs by himself, leaving Clayton to his own friends, and games of Legos and Pokémon. Then, one day, Bennett became Clayton's unshakable shadow, stuck fast to his back, front, side, and even his head.

That's when Clayton first declared, "Bennett's ruining my life!"

My husband and I just smiled, thinking we knew how he felt since both of us had had to share a room with a younger sibling who ruined our lives as well. My own childhood memories didn't stop me from forcing our two boys to spend every waking moment side by side. My voice could often be heard encouraging their twosome. "Include Bennett. Let Bennett play. Let him take a bike ride with you. Let him go outside with you. Share your pop. Give him a cookie. Let him hold your Pokémon cards. Let him have all the red Legos. Give him the frog."

Clayton obliged most of the time, albeit begrudgingly, and I knew there was little he could do on his own as long as Bennett was around.

I thought I knew how he felt since I had a little sister who was my shadow for eighteen years. One night, I found out how little I knew about how he felt.

I had just put the boys down for bed and was settling into my book and a bowl of popcorn when I heard what sounded like crying from the upstairs bedroom.

I sighed and hesitantly climbed the stairs. "What are

you crying about?" I demanded angrily. Clayton had used the crying stall tactic many times at bedtime.

"I ... I ... I ... wahhhh!"

"What? Slow down, I can't hear what you're saying," I said, softening my voice and sitting down on his bed.

"I just wish Bennett had a different brain ... wahhh!"

That's when my heart sank in my chest. I had never realized until that moment what a burden my oldest son was carrying as he tried to be a big brother to Bennett.

"Why do you wish Bennett had a different brain?" I asked, sincerely wanting to know how he felt.

"I just get so mad at him, and then I feel so bad because I know he can't help it. It's just not fair that I can't have a normal brother who understands things like I do."

My throat tightened, and tears filled my eyes. I knew exactly what Clayton was talking about. I knew how Bennett's disability had impacted me, but I had never really thought about how it had impacted his siblings.

I rubbed Clayton's back softly as he continued to sob. "Do you know why Bennett was given to our family?"

"Yes, I know. So that I could protect him, and that he could teach us and others to love people who are different than us. I know. I know. But I still wish he had a different brain and that he didn't have autism."

"Do you think he knows that we love him even when we get mad at him?"

"Yes," Clayton said, sitting up and looking over at Bennett, who was playing on his bed unaware that a conversation about him was happening just three feet away. Bennett continued to crash his plastic dinosaurs together, making gnashing and gnarling sounds as they wrestled on top of the bedspread.

"Benny, do you want to sleep in my bed tonight?" Clayton asked with tears still staining his cheeks.

Bennett grabbed his pillow, his blanket, and twenty toy

dinosaurs, and crawled onto the foot of Clayton's bed, curling himself around his big brother's feet.

"I love you, Benny," Clayton said.

"I wove you, Benny," Bennett replied.

After tucking the boys in for the "this is the last time, and I mean it" time, I pondered Clayton's words and realized he needed some time away from Bennett. He didn't know how to say it and probably didn't even realize he needed time off from being "Big Brother."

I found babysitters for Bennett so Clayton could spend some uninterrupted time with Mom and Dad. I also arranged more playdates for Clayton away from home. Clayton still gets angry and frustrated with his little brother, but he knows when he needs time alone that he can ask. When Clayton comes to me and says, "I need to be alone," I find a special spot for him to be alone with his thoughts and his Legos. After a little while, he returns, looking for Bennett, who greets him with a toothless smile.

The boys still share their clothes, their bedroom, and their toys. But as this mother found out, they don't always need to share their time. They needed time off from being full-time brothers.

And at the end of the day, when the lights are out, I still hear two brothers at the end of the hall, trying hard to whisper as they fly their toys off the end of the bed and battle plastic dinosaurs until they fall asleep, sharing a bed and possibly each other's underwear.

Kimberly Jensen

Kimberly Jensen is the mother of three children, and writes children's books focusing on loving children. Today, Clayton and Bennett have separate bedrooms after a move to a new house and a heartwarming essay by Clayton entitled, "A Room of My Own." That essay solidified Kimberly's decision to separate her growing boys after reading the line where Clayton expressed the need for "a room to be me." Please e-mail Kimberly at kcjensen419@msn.com.

✑ Out of the Mouths of Babes ✑

My husband and I are the good-humored parents of four children with autism. Not many people come to visit, but when they do, they are sometimes surprised at what they may experience. One day, a repairman came to our house. Upon seeing our 110-pound dog, he fearfully asked if the dog bites.

My eleven-year-old son with Asperger syndrome said to him, "No, our dog is very well behaved and does not bite. However, you may want to make sure that you do not get too close to my three-year-old brother. He has sensory problems, and biting is his way of checking you out. So if he gets too close, run." At that moment, our three-year-old was in the process of biting the dog, who just looked at me as if to say, "Please, help me. The toddler is biting me again."

The repairman, looking a bit surprised, commented that our dog was very well behaved indeed.

Deana Newberry

Deana Newberry received her master's degree in Spanish education from the University of Buffalo in 1994. She is a teacher in western New York. She is currently completing a Spanish lesson book for her special-education students. You can e-mail her at deanie6069@hotmail.com.

$\overline{7}$

EARLY LEARNING

Isn't it splendid to think of all the things there are to find out about? It just makes me feel glad to be alive—it's such an interesting world.

Lucy Maud Montgomery, Anne of Green Gables

The Slide

*There are two ways of exerting one's strength:
one is pushing down, the other is pulling up.*
                                        Booker T. Washington

I have worked with people with disabilities since I was
in college. Honestly, though, I have always said, "This
really isn't where I belong." I did not study special education in college. I was a psychology major. When I pursued
my master's degree, I chose early-childhood education
hoping to open a parenting center in my community to
teach expectant parents the wonders of newborns and
very young children.

Yet, time after time, I kept finding jobs and opportunities in the field of developmental delays and disabilities.
My husband and I were blessed with two little girls when
I was working as the director of an early-intervention program for children from birth to age three with developmental delays and disabilities. My young daughters were
raised around a kitchen table where stories were shared
about the triumphs, challenges, joys, and struggles of parenting children with disabilities. They heard many of my

"soapboxes" about stereotyping people with disabilities. They cried or laughed at wonderful stories from those infants and toddlers and their families who opened their lives to me.

Each year, our program had an end-of-the-year graduation for those children who would be moving on to the next stage of their lives. For some, that would be community programs; for others, they would begin the special-education process. It was a big to-do at a local park with many families in attendance. All of the staff's families attended, too. There were balloons, fried chicken, graduation certificates, lots of pictures, and certainly many hugs and a few tears. The graduation picnic was just getting started when my youngest daughter, Gracie, age four, asked if she could go down the slide. This was one of those "cool slides" with about ten steps and a steep incline. The slide was all metal and slippery.

Since my husband had a work commitment that night and was unable to join us at the picnic, I greeted families as they joined us and kept one eye on the slide as I watched my two little ones head off. The picnic paraded on with the charm of a small town. Parents laughed and reminisced. Children ate ice cream and chased lightning bugs. Gracie could hardly take time to come down from that slide to eat.

Pretty soon, a little girl who had been in my program several years earlier made her way to the slide. She, too, wanted a turn on the "cool slide." Lena, who was seven, had Down syndrome. Due to complications from heart surgery, she had incomplete paralysis from the chest down. She wore a body brace and "bear-walked" on her hands and feet. Lena had been the very first baby I had seen as an early interventionist. Lena's mother was now a member of the staff at the early-intervention program. Quickly, I went to find Lena's mother to see how she wanted to "handle" this. It took me a few minutes to locate Lena's mother in the crowd. When I explained the situation, both of us went running back toward the slide.

As we made our approach, we both stopped, frozen in our tracks. Lena was pulling herself up the first few steps of the slide ladder. Gracie was behind her, lifting one of Lena's feet onto a step. She then moved to the other side, lifted the other foot, and gently pushed her bottom. Lena then used her arms, which were very strong, to pull herself to the next rung. Gracie then began the process again, lifting one foot and then the other, with a little bottom nudge. When Lena made it to the top, she smiled triumphantly, laid down on her belly, didn't even blink, and *whoosh!* Down she came! In a flash, Gracie was on her belly right behind her, squealing and laughing all the way down! At the bottom, the girls giggled and carried on, and slowly made their way back to the ladder. It was time to do it all again! Lena and Gracie played on the slide until the last flicker of evening light gave way to the early glow of the August moon.

As we drove home that evening, I thought I would try to talk to Gracie about how proud I was of her. I also thought that perhaps all those talks around the table had made some impact, and maybe, just maybe, I had played a role in this remarkable child's ability to relate to a child with a disability. And so I said, "I guess you see that Lena is really much more like you than different from you."

Gracie was very quiet in her car seat. Finally, she said, "Oh, you mean, how her eyes are squinky." For the life of me, I could not understand how we could be talking about Lena's eyes when Gracie had just spent the last two hours lifting Lena's legs and helping Lena get up a slide because she could not move the same way as Gracie.

Ever the early interventionist, however, and never one to pass up a "teachable moment," I decided that Gracie must be talking about Lena's facial features related to having Down syndrome. I began a monologue about facial features that people with Down syndrome may have. When I finished and asked Gracie if she understood, she simply sighed and said, "Lena's eyes are squinky because she smiles so big when she laughs!"

At that moment, humbled by the wisdom of this little child, I knew that God was teaching me many lessons through Gracie and Lena. When we truly look at the person, we see beyond all disabilities. Lena's smile captured Gracie's heart, and a friendship blossomed. And for that moment, on that August evening, all that mattered was how many times you could ride on that cool slide!

Corinne Hill

Corinne "Cori" Foley Hill received her B.A. from the University of Virginia and her M.Ed. from James Madison University. She provides personnel training in early intervention in Virginia where she lives with her husband and two daughters. Cori dreams of living in the Caribbean and writing children's books. Gracyn "Gracie" Hill is now in middle school in Augusta County, Virginia. She plays travel soccer and AAU basketball. Gracyn loves to dance, especially lyrical, hip-hop, and Irish step. When she grows up, Gracyn would like to find a job working with babies or young children. Lena Campbell is an AB honor roll student in middle school in Rockingham County, Virginia. She recently became the first cheerleader/pom-pom girl with Down syndrome in Rockingham County. Lena won a blue ribbon for her artwork entitled "Pom-Pom Girl."

Three Houses Down on the Left

Make education a continuing, never-ending process.

Nido Qubein

In 1964, Millside Heights was a new town with new houses built to lure the baby boomers away from the city. This acreage—once a dairy farm with roaming cows—was now filled with colonial, split-level houses, but no stores, post office, schools, or churches. How great life was when you had a master bedroom and a master bath, hardwood floors, a fireplace, and four choices of wallpaper! My parents bought the split-level design, perfectly placed on a wooded lot facing a freshly paved black-top road named after a top-notch Ivy League university. We were a family of three: my mom, my dad, and me.

In the surrounding area, there were three Catholic schools, which most of the neighborhood kids attended. I thought it was fascinating: students got to wear a uniform, buy their schoolbooks, carry a lunch box, and ride on a big yellow school bus. I went to a small Quaker school, so small that no buses transported the students. I wore whatever clothes I wanted, got a hot-cooked meal at lunchtime, and was driven back and forth by my mom. While my mother made every attempt to reinforce how privileged I was, the other children made it clear that I was "different," decidedly not one of them.

The only kids more different than I lived three houses down on our left. Nobody was allowed to play with these kids. I was too young to understand what really went on in their home, but there was gossip. Sometimes the police would come in the middle of the night and handcuff the dad while the mom screamed obscenities. Sometimes I would see the parents in the daylight as they staggered down the driveway, unable to keep their balance. Their four children, all skinny and pale, wore hand-me-down clothes. And, it was rumored, the kids had lice. They did not have new bikes, and the few toys they did own were broken and left out on their front lawn. As I remember it, the mom died tragically, and the dad was left to take care of the four children. Prior to the mom's death, none of the children were registered in school, but a lot of things changed after she died. Three of the children were sent away—we never knew where. One boy remained at home, sometimes supervised, sometimes not.

One day, we noticed a green and white VW bus pulling up in front of the house three doors down on the left. The remaining boy got into the van every morning and was returned in the afternoon. Rumor had it that he went to a school for "bad boys" and that he was "retarded." Around the neighborhood, the green and white VW bus became known as the "retarded kids' bus." It was around that time that my school connected with the local school district, agreeing to provide transportation. Believing that on the first day of school I would get to ride in a big yellow school bus like the other kids, I was thrilled. I would no longer be different, at least not when it came to that.

But as I stood at the front door waiting for my ride on the opening day of school, to my horror the small green and white VW bus pulled into our driveway! The neighborhood children on their way to catch their buses stopped to stare as I climbed aboard.

"See, I told you she was retarded," one of the boys yelled from the back. My face burned, and tears streamed down my face, as I waved good-bye to my mom. The bus driver told me that "everything would be all right." But for the next five years, I heard the same horrible, hurtful words—even when they were not said out loud.

I wonder now if this is how the boy who lived three houses down on the left felt every morning when he went to school.

Words like "inclusion" and "accessibility" were not part of society's daily vocabulary in the sixties, and the thought of accepting individuals who were different into our lives was unthinkable.

Forty years later, I am a social worker for adults who have developmental disabilities. I am also the parent of a child who has a developmental disability. I work daily to break down physical and attitudinal barriers. Every day I am blessed ten times over by my daughter's smile and good-morning hugs. I treasure her accomplishments and am so proud of the effort she makes when attempting to master a task. Through four years of early intervention and thirteen years of schooling, my daughter has learned to stand, walk, and assist with dressing and feeding herself. She makes choices, has learned her colors and shapes, and has worked on learning her alphabet.

After reading Mitch Albom's *The Five People You Meet in Heaven*, I was left wondering who in my life has made such a profound difference in who I have become. I believe that the skinny little boy who lived three houses down on the left will be the first person I meet. I hope I get the chance to tell him about my daughter and to thank him for teaching me what I needed to know. Until then, I hope he is in a place where he is cherished and accepted. I hope he is somewhere he is never ignored or isolated. Even more than that, I hope he will forgive me.

Deborah McIntire

Deborah McIntire resides in Jenkintown, Pennsylvania. She is the director of Special Gifts, which is dedicated to adults who have developmental disabilities and helps others to be aware of the gifts that these adults have to share. Write to Deborah at Special Gifts, 412 West Avenue, Jenkintown, PA 19046, or deborahmcintire@hotmail.com.

Illumination

When people are made to feel secure and important and appreciated, it will no longer be necessary for them to whittle down others in order to seem bigger by comparison.

Virginia Arcastle

The lighting in the girls' restroom ceased. There were no footsteps, no click of a switch, no flicker as if the power had failed. No window to let in the light. Just darkness.

Abby sat perched on the toilet seat, gripping the rails. The terror on her face etched into the darkness. Sitting on the toilet was a challenge for Abby—her balance, or lack of it, a direct result of cerebral palsy. For her, to perch on a toilet seat meant the synchronization of many muscles determined not to coordinate. With no light to give her visual cues, the task was doubly difficult. Abby could only hope that the lights would be restored. She attempted to call out to her attendant, but speech did not come easily when fear had contracted every muscle in her body.

Kristen kept a steady pace, a straight face, held her head

high, and smiled as she strolled past the opening to the girls' restroom. She headed back to the fourth-grade classroom where she and Abby both belonged. She had smoothly extended her hand and, with one coordinated movement, flipped off the switch. She was proud of her stealth. There had been no whoosh of fabric, no squeal of a rubber sole. Ten seconds later, she slid into her seat in the classroom with an attentive look on her face and a smile that told the teacher that Kristen was back and ready to learn.

Diane, Abby's personal attendant, returned to the restroom to find a cavern of darkness and a panic-stricken Abby. Instantly, she knew what had happened. It was not the first time that this had occurred. The last time, Kristen's excuse had been, "Oh, I didn't know anyone was in there," and before that it was, "Oops, I slipped." Diane knew that today it would be complete denial and, in truth, no one had any proof that Kristen was responsible for the incident.

Angry voices rose from the office as the paperwork was completed. Kristen was called into the office, interrogated, and assigned to in-school suspension, one of many for her. Diane was instructed to watch Abby more closely and prevent the two girls from coming together. Abby was a magnet for bullies and no match for Kristen.

The principal penned the dreaded note home to Abby's mother. An "incident" has occurred—yet another "incident"—and the school staff would discipline the culprit. There was zero tolerance for bullying in this school. Abby's mother, Sandra, read the report and visualized the outcome. Abby's drive for independence would once again suffer a setback as adults rallied to hover around her with a protective wall. It sometimes seemed as though, in the end, Abby suffered consequences far greater than that of the bully.

Sandra sensed a long road. This was only the fourth grade. The "incidents" were likely to become more frequent and more creative. She strategized her own tactics. Sandra called and requested that the school lift the ban on interaction between the two girls. Like a coach, she sent Abby back to school the next day with the game plan.

"Hi, Kristen. I really like your shirt. That is such a cool color of blue. I wish I had a shirt like that," chirped Abby as Kristen passed Abby's desk. And at the lunch table, "Hey, does anyone want my bag of M&Ms? I don't have time to eat them . . . Yeah, Kristen, you can have them."

And later, "Bye, Kristen. Thanks for being my friend today." Abby ended the day with a perfect execution of the coach's play.

Returning to school the next day, Abby found Kristen taking off her coat in the hallway.

"Hi, Kristen. My mom is taking me to the store tonight to buy my secret-pal gift for tomorrow's party, and I get to invite one friend. I was wondering if you would want to come along, and we could pick out some things." The voice was small and hesitant. Abby was not at all certain that she wanted Kristen along that night, but her mom had assured her that it would be fun. "She gives us each five dollars, and we get to go in and pick out whatever we want. Then we go back to my house and wrap our gifts."

Opportunities for Kristen came far and few between, and so the message Kristen heard from Abby brought a lightness to her heart. Could it be she would finally have the opportunity to be just like the other kids at tomorrow's Christmas exchange? She envisioned herself placing her exchange gift under the tree that held all their ornaments. She would smile, knowing what was inside the package. It would have a red bow, and the wrapping paper would be creased perfectly. This year, she would have her own gift and not have to rely on the kindness of a teacher to provide a generic gift.

The match was made. Kristen took on the responsibility of pushing Abby's wheelchair through the crowded aisles. She helped Abby pick up and examine items. Together, they made their final selections. Both girls left with a gift for the next day, wrapping paper, and ribbon. Back at Abby's home, Kristen and Abby paired up to complete their project. Together, they laughed and giggled. Together, they made note cards and tied ribbons.

In school the next day, Kristen helped Abby tuck Abby's gift in just the right spot under the tree. Proudly, Kristen placed her exchange gift under the tree. It had a bright red ribbon, neatly creased paper, and a card. Her contribution looked like all the rest of the packages.

Nothing was ever said about the past incidents, and the lights in the restroom always stayed lit for Abby. Sandra employed the tactic in several different forms throughout Abby's elementary and high-school years. When incidents made her want to strike out in anger, to shield and protect Abby, she moved forward with kindness. It turned out to be protection of another kind.

Jeanne Schmidlin

Jeanne Appelhans Schmidlin lives in Kent, Ohio, with her husband and two daughters, and is coauthor of *Thunder in the Heartland: A Chronicle of Outstanding Weather Events in Ohio*. She serves as a parent mentor in her school district, helping parents of children with disabilities negotiate the special-education maze. Jeanne enjoys travel, gardening, books, and volunteer opportunities.

One Egg at a Time

A true friend is one who thinks you are a good egg even if you are half-cracked.

Author Unknown

Raising a child with autism is never easy, but as most parents can attest, it's also never dull. Sometimes you just gotta laugh.

Max loves eggs, absolutely loves everything about them—the smooth, perfect whiteness of their shells, their shape, the way they feel in his hands (broken and unbroken). He loves rolling them, watching them spin on the table, or even better, cracking them and squeezing out all the goo until it coats his hands, clothes, and his mom's carpet. Max loves just about everything about eggs—except eating them. Won't touch the stuff.

Max loves to play with eggs. I can't keep him away from them. He's broken every fridge lock known to man, found every last egg hidden in there, gleefully, as if every day was a giant Easter egg hunt.

The first time I realized he had this unusual interest was right around the time of his autism diagnosis. That was back when I thought my child was extraordinarily creative because he played not with toys, but with everyday household items—a piece of string, a vacuum-cleaner hose.

Max sprung the egg fixation on me with what I like to call the "shock and awe campaign." I walked into the kitchen one day and found him sitting on the floor, surrounded by crushed eggshells and the slime of egg yolks. He looked at me with a huge, joyous smile as he held up his yellow, slimy hands for me to see. It took me a moment to understand what I was seeing, and then figure out how exactly to clean it all up. I hoped to God my son didn't come down with violent salmonella poisoning resulting from his new hobby.

That was the beginning. Then came the struggle—me against the eggs. Trying to outsmart my son was exhausting because, deep down, I know that my four-year-old is much smarter than I am. For instance, once in the summer while mowing the lawn, my husband found four or five eggs strategically hidden in the backyard. I guess Max had gotten his hands on a bunch of them and decided to put some away for later.

I tried buying him toy eggs, but he tossed them aside dismissively. I went a long time without buying eggs at all, tired of scrubbing goo out of my carpet and off my kid, and still frightened of whatever kind of nasty illness he could come down with.

After a few eggless weeks, I decided tentatively to bring another dozen into the house. In desperation, I came up with a compromise. I boiled an egg one day. I took a marker and drew eyes and a mouth on it.

"Max," I said as I handed it to him, "here you go." He looked up at me, disbelieving. Here was Mummy giving him an egg. Freely. It was almost too good to be true. He looked down at the egg. "Mike," he decided. He reverently took Mike downstairs. This was working. Suddenly, after months of this unsolvable problem, I was the smartest mother in the universe.

I came downstairs a few minutes later, and Max was sitting on the couch quietly watching TV. Mike was sitting next to him. "Now remember, Max," I said, "be gentle with Mike. No squishing Mike! Be gentle."

"Gentle Mike," he echoed. I figured Mike probably wouldn't have a very long life, but at least a smashed hardboiled egg was safer than a raw one (and easier to clean up).

But Mike made it all the way to bedtime intact. "Good night, Mike," Max said, kissing the top of his pointy head and putting him "to bed" in the fridge. I truly was Mother of the Year.

The next day, I had a doctor's appointment. It was with a great amount of anxiety that I arranged for someone to babysit Max and his twin sister, Olivia. Finding a babysitter for Max is not always easy. Actually, it's never easy. My sister Jenn agreed to do it, assuring me that everything would be fine.

I was in the waiting room for twenty minutes when I called home the first time.

"How is he?" I asked nervously.

She ran down a rap sheet of only minor misdemeanors— nothing out of the ordinary, no bleeding, abrasions, broken bones, or major catastrophes to speak of.

"Oh, and by the way, the funniest thing happened. He got into the fridge and was running around the house with an egg. I chased him all over the place, but I finally got it away from him. Boy, you wouldn't believe how he held on to that egg," she said.

"Where's the egg now?"

"I threw it in the garbage," she said.

"You threw Mike in the garbage?" I shouted into my cell phone. I got some strange stares from the others in the waiting room.

Jenn felt really bad about it afterward. She did make a good point, though. "If you are going to let your children play with food, you really have to tell the babysitter," she said, ruffling Max's hair. As I boiled another egg, I realized how different my family is from other families. In my house, eggs and string are toys. If you take your eyes off your child for a second, he might jump into a tubful of water fully clothed, dunk his head in the toilet, or try to escape out the front door. (It's happened!)

I started thinking about all the stuff I couldn't do with Max that other "typical" families could do. Going down that line of thinking started to make me feel sad.

But then I looked at the egg cooling on a plate and saw a minor victory. As I drew another face on the new Mike and watched Max's smiling eyes when I handed it to him, it occurred to me that no challenge is insurmountable if you just learn to take it one egg at a time.

Dawn Morrison

Dawn Morrison is a communications manager at Dalhousie University in Halifax, Nova Scotia, and mother to beautiful twins, Maxwell and Olivia. She received her bachelor of arts in community studies from Cape Breton University and a bachelor of journalism from the University of King's College. She writes humorous and upbeat nonfiction about life with twins and caring for a child with autism. Maxwell, at five, remains as intelligent and curious as ever. Thanks to early intervention, Max's vocabulary has grown greatly. To the delight of parents Dawn and Jason, he is interacting more than ever with his family and friends. "This egg makes me perfect," he offered one day recently. Although Dawn's not sure what that meant exactly, it reminds us of Max's gift of finding joy and beauty in ordinary things. Please e-mail Dawn at delightful2828@yahoo.ca.

🐚 Out of the Mouths of Babes 🐚

One evening, I came home from work to find my son, Jonny, stark naked, sopping wet, and glistening from head to toe with clear deodorant. I said, "Jonathan, what on Earth are you doing?"

Jonny replied, "I just wanted to see if it worked, Mom."

"If what worked?"

He picked up the deodorant, pointed to the label, and said, "Well, this says right here 'provides protection against wetness,' so I got in the tub to see if it worked! Well, as you can see it *didn't* work!"

Karen Simmons

Karen L. Simmons is a mother of six, two with special needs, and the founder of Autism Today, an award-winning information and resource center shining a new light on autism worldwide. Karen's first book, *Little Rainman,* was inspired by Jonathan, who has autism and is now sixteen years old and, as always, the life of the party!

"If it's night that 'falls' why is it day that 'breaks'?"

The Case of the Silent Kindergartner

*Sometimes the best way to convince someone he
is wrong is to let him have his way.*

Author Unknown

I always imagined it like this: my mom would be sitting
in a dim corner of a dusty room, arms folded across her
chest, cigarette dangling from her mouth (though she's
never smoked in her life). "That kid can talk," she'd say in
a way not unlike a cocky detective. My mom would reach
into the inside pocket of her trench coat and pull out an
unmarked audiocassette tape with the proof. The school
guidance counselor, my kindergarten teacher, Mrs.
Gonzales, and other elementary-school authorities would
huddle over the tape recorder. "Not so fast!" they'd
exclaim. "You ain't proved nothin' yet."

But Mom would. The contents of the tape would reveal
me, at age five, faithfully reproducing the songs I'd learned
in class, as well as some of my favorites. Later in the tape,
I discussed the nuances of each class play station and cite
which three kids were my best friends that day. Ha! My
mom would show them.

Such banter would normally come as no surprise to anyone who works in an elementary school. The only thing
odd about the situation is that my mom secretly did exactly
that: she recorded a car trip home from kindergarten. Even
that could be rationalized as a bored housewife's attempt at
posterity, or re-creating a *Columbo* episode.

The guidance counselor and my teacher were shocked
and embarrassed at the revelation. The two women had
jumped to conclusions about my intelligence and abilities
too soon. Since September, I hadn't spoken one sentence
in school. In a silent shell, I followed every instruction,
colored every picture, and always maintained order in the
lunch line. Often, I smiled and laughed. I was just very
shy and missed my little sister, my big-kid friends, and
mostly, my mom. At school, everyone was convinced I
couldn't speak.

My teacher, Mrs. Gonzales, had been nice at first, but
her few squats down at my desk while I colored weren't
enough to build a close, trusting relationship. I still didn't
feel comfortable enough to speak to her, and she began to
put bright red bear cards in my pocket on the behavior
chart. The chart was at the front of the class, and the red
bear was the worst card you could get. It was reserved for
kids who started fights and said bad words, or in my case,
said nothing at all.

Eventually, Mrs. Gonzales started to slip the red bear
card in my pocket early in the day and send me to the
guidance counselor. A battery of tests ensued. I liked
the hearing test, where I had to indicate my detection of
the world's faintest beeps. I felt clever when I learned my
hearing was perfect. My second-favorite test involved picture puzzles. But the worst one was when the counselor
would sit in front of me for what seemed like hours at a
time, point at her nose, and ask, "Amanda, do you know
what this is?"

Of course I did, but the guidance counselor, with her too-soft voice and liver spots, was particularly frightening to me. I began to wish Mrs. Gonzales still liked me. Then I could return to the play stations, the songs, and my classmates. But now she never smiled or even tried to have a conversation. Mrs. Gonzales had given up.

My mom apologized to my teacher each day when she picked me up, asserting that I really could be quite talkative at home. She said that she suspected I was bright. Perhaps I just liked observing the class. Mrs. Gonzales and the guidance counselor weren't so sure. They announced they'd made up their minds that another year in kindergarten was the best thing for me. "Amanda is just not cognitively or emotionally ready for first grade," they said.

The secret tape surfaced in *National Enquirer* fashion. Could the child's voice be inauthentic? How could we have found out about this so late? The elementary school agreed to promote me to first grade, provided I was enrolled in the small English as a Second Language (ESL) class with Mrs. Edwards. My life was changed forever.

Mrs. Edwards never punished me for my shyness. Instead, she made me feel safe by providing personal attention, compassion, and warmth. She could hear what I wasn't saying. Soon, I wanted to talk to Mrs. Edwards and anyone else who'd listen. She was the first person other than my parents who said, "I know you can do this," when I attempted to read, write, add, jump rope, and more.

When I graduated from high school years later, I thanked Mrs. Edwards in my valedictory address. It was fortunate I hadn't been held back a year. If I had, I might have been labeled a student to pass up, a student who wouldn't amount to much anyway. Every child has needs—not all come with a label.

I strive to emulate Mrs. Edwards now that I'm a teacher

by working under the idea that every student is unique and can be successful. Without a teacher like her, or cunning undercover detective work by my mom, where would I be? Probably booked long ago for a crime no one is ever guilty of—the inability to learn.

Amanda Green

Amanda Green teaches reading at a public middle school in Harlem, focusing on at-risk and special-education students. She moved to New York City to pursue a teaching and writing career after graduating from the University of Texas at Austin with a bachelor of arts degree in English and a UTeach Liberal Arts teacher certification. Amanda enjoys reading, writing, photography, and exploring the East Coast. She welcomes all e-mail at amanda.louise.green@gmail.com.

🐚 Out of the Mouths of Babes 🐚

My husband, my daughter, and I are all deaf. Our first house was accessible in the sense that we had flashing signal lights for our text-phones and doorbell. When our daughter was a toddler, she came to accept that every time the lights flashed, I would go to the phone to answer the calls. One day, we were driving to California in a thunderstorm. When bolts of lightning lit up the sky, my daughter quickly turned to me and said, "Mom, phone!"

Ava Crowell

Ava Crowell is currently an American Sign Language specialist. She received her master's at Northern Arizona University in educational leadership in 1989 and bachelor of arts in social work at Gallaudet in 1982. She's married to Tom, has two children, one of whom is deaf. She enjoys hiking and working in the deaf community.

Ace of Hearts

To the world you may be just one person, but to one person you may be the world.

Brandi Snyder

We had been going through an especially difficult time. My eight-year-old son, Eric, who has high-functioning autism, had been at a new school for over a year, but he was still having a hard time making friends, and being accepted at school and in the neighborhood.

I had been lobbying hard with administrators and the school board to get supports in place, and to get staff and peers educated about "differences." But things just didn't seem like they were coming together. As a parent, I felt very limited in my power to effect change in the system. Days and weeks and months had gone by with a lot of planning, strategizing, and attending difficult meetings. Uncounted hours had been spent identifying resources and laying them at the feet of educators. I had researched workshops and professional development opportunities and forwarded them to school staff, hoping they would agree to attend, but I would attend these events myself and not see a single familiar face.

Each day, I would watch my charming, affectionate, intelligent son run up to classmates and, albeit standing a little too close, greet them cheerfully. They would stiffen and turn away. "Mom, I just can't seem to get to know those kids," Eric would say, perplexed.

With these difficulties in the backdrop of our lives, Eric, and his younger sister, Sabrina, had recently become interested in card games. It was especially good for Eric, who has always had difficulty with freewheeling conversation, but thrives on structured interaction. Here we had hit upon something that provided the needed structure, showcased Eric's math skills, and was fun for the whole family. We bought a book of card-game rules and proceeded to learn variations of rummy and whist.

One morning during this time when I was feeling most discouraged about my son's social life, I was trying to get the kids up and out for school. This had been a particularly bad morning. No one got up before the third or fourth call. We couldn't find the lunch boxes. The kids fought over breakfast cereal. The homework was not done. I was sleep-deprived and behind in my own freelance work projects. The house was a mess, and so was I. I was pretty much feeling like a failure in every quadrant of my life.

The kids were both talking to me at once, and they kept getting distracted from the morning routine. It was getting later and later, and nothing I said seemed to bring them to focus on their tasks. Finally, I blew a gasket. I had a full-blown "mommy tantrum." I ranted and raved about how I just wanted us to feel successful about *something!* Getting to school on time was part of being successful. I raved about my frustrations with the school and the neighborhood, and how nothing seemed to be working. I went on about everything that was bugging me, whether or not it was related to getting out the door on time for school. Of course, I felt terrible afterward. What a way to set them up for a full day of learning!

Finally, we got out the door and were walking to school. After about a block of silence, I apologized and explained that I was just crabby and overwhelmed, and that my anger was about me, not them. After a few moments, Eric took my hand and said, in a voice that was crystal clear, earnest, and far more mature than his eight years: "I want to tell you something, Mommy. You are my highest trump card."

You are my highest trump card!

Those of us with children who have autism have heard all the stereotypes: difficulty understanding metaphoric language, little or no ability to empathize with others, inability to grasp social nuance, poor if any comprehension of the big picture, and so on. "You are my highest trump card." I have never heard sweeter words.

Three years have gone by and we have moved across the country. Continuing to educate people about differences has its highs and lows, and there are strengths and weaknesses in every school system. But no matter how unresponsive systems sometimes seem to be, I have come to understand the power of persistence and of focusing on a positive outcome. Most of all, I know that I have one *superpower*—love. And it will give me an unlimited supply of advocacy fuel for as long as needed. I have the *Ace of Hearts* up my sleeve.

Lynn Skotnitsky

Lynn Skotnitsky, M.A., F.M.B. is a client-centered coach and consultant with twenty years' experience facilitating planning and development for individuals, organizations, and communities. She has volunteered on various nonprofit boards and is an advocate for diversity and inclusive education. Eric, whom experts said would likely never talk, is now in Grade 5 French Immersion, and makes public presentations, most recently at York University. An inclusive child-care center where Eric had early opportunities to develop social skills with peers made the most significant difference for his outcomes. Contact them at lynn.skotnitsky@rogers.com or 778-327-9641.

Labels

I know of nobody who is purely autistic, or purely neurotypical. Even God has some autistic moments, which is why the planets spin.

Jerry Newport

I used to be very caught up in labels: Calvin Klein, Gloria Vanderbilt, Izod. Sure, I was only twelve and brand-new to middle school, where I quickly learned I was pretty uncool without them. I eventually grew out of the need to dress to impress, but I found myself once again caught up in labels.

This time the labels were different and much more important: ASD, PDD-NOS, SID—autism spectrum disorder, pervasive developmental disorder not otherwise specified, sensory integration dysfunction. All these acronyms and words buzzed around the aura of my son. While we thought Jack had officially been diagnosed with autism, we got a surprise when his paperwork was transferred to his new elementary school for kindergarten. It turned out his evaluation actually said, "Jack demonstrates many characteristics consistent with autism." He was never officially diagnosed with autism. The school wanted him reevaluated. They wanted to know his "label."

When he was first evaluated, the team of experts placed him at "moderate to severe" on that spectrum. It was hard for us to fathom. My husband and I thought he was just a late talker; autism never entered our minds. But we pursued a number of alternative treatments, and we were lucky enough to have a team of ten therapists and teachers working with Jack through early intervention. He flourished and did much better than anyone had predicted. One of his teachers called it astonishing. *But what should his diagnosis be?*

I shouldn't have worried so much about these labels. Surely, they didn't change how I felt about Jack. Diagnose him with Sassy Mouth Syndrome, whatever. No matter what the doctors came up with, he'd still be the same little boy who loved playing trains and tormenting his sister, but also stood up to people he thought were hurting her. But some of that was just brave talk. While it didn't bother me that a label could follow him his whole life, these labels did affect what I felt I could expect from Jack.

While the rest of the world might not understand it, I think most parents with children with "special needs" realize that a label doesn't define their child. It explains their child—the gifts they have and the help they need. It helps them understand why they struggle with certain challenges. So we were ready for whatever the experts were going to "label" our son. But it turned out to be a big surprise when the developmental pediatrician met with Jack. "I wouldn't place him on the autistic spectrum," she said after an hour interviewing our smiling little guy. We were shocked. She believes he has learning disabilities that have resulted in developmental delays. She did give him a diagnosis of mild Asperger's syndrome, but she said he just barely met the criteria and could test out of it at the next evaluation. This diagnosis ensures he will receive the needed services at school. Asperger's syndrome is traditionally listed as a disorder that falls on the autistic spectrum, but she is among the doctors who believe that Asperger's should not be on the spectrum. She thinks it's more of a learning disorder that Jack can outgrow or learn to overcome. She also said he has semantic pragmatic language disorder, which he can also outgrow or overcome.

This just shows that a label is a label, just like a rose is a rose. Another specialist could come up with a different diagnosis, or insist that Asperger's is on the autistic spectrum. I really don't care what the label says. He is and always will be my Jack. I think of it like a label on a shirt, offering directions to best take care of the child. And he will always have my own personal label attached to him: cherished son. Contents: 100 percent pure joy. Directions: love deeply on the gentle cycle.

Lisa Scott Macdonough

Lisa Scott is a TV news anchor in Buffalo, New York, and a freelance writer. Jack is flourishing in first grade in mainstream school without an aide and doesn't even meet the criteria for special education. He does receive some supports, such as occupational therapy, physical therapy, and speech therapy. His parents expect him to live a full, happy life. Contact Lisa or read more of her work at ReadLisaScott.com. Lisa is working on a novel with a young character who has undiagnosed sensory processing disorder.

8

FOSTERING INDEPENDENCE

*There are some aspects of a person's life
that we have no right to compromise. We
cannot negotiate the size of an institution.
No one should live in one. We cannot debate
who should get an inclusive education.
Everyone should. We cannot determine
who does and who does not get the right
to make their own choices and forge their
own futures. All must.*

Lou Brown

Joey's Gold Medal

Real power comes by empowering others.

Denis Waitley

In 1989, I had just graduated from high school, and it was my first summer working with the Special Olympics. I had volunteered that spring and was assigned as a trainer for a young man named Joey. Joey was eighteen years old, had Down syndrome, and was a delight to be with. Joey wore a perpetual smile and was quick to laugh and give a big thumbs-up to everyone he saw, peering at the world through his thick, Coke-bottle glasses, which he polished habitually. Standing just less than five feet tall, Joey was everyone's friend. His race was the long quarter-mile run, the full lap around the track. I would stand at the finish line and call out as he rounded the final corner, "What are we going to do, Joey?"

"We're gonna win!" he would shout back. We hit the track every Saturday for the six weeks preceding the race, and Joey's time slowly improved until he was making the finish line in just less than three minutes. We would follow up our practice with a trip to the local burger joint, where

Joey would tell the waitress, every week, that he couldn't have French fries because he was in training. He was going to win a gold medal, and he wanted a salad.

As summer neared, the girls at the restaurant would all come over to ask him what his best time was and how practice went. They patted him on the back and wished him luck. Joey basked in their adoration. The day of the race finally came, and I picked up Joey in my van. His mother kissed him good-bye, telling him she would be there for the race. We loaded up his gym bag and drove to a local high school where the Olympics would be held. Joey was so wound up he could hardly sit in his seat, his hands drumming constantly on his knees, stopping only to polish and repolish his glasses. We arrived, parked, and signed in, getting our race assignment and number.

It was then, on our way to the sidelines, that I realized that something was wrong. "Joey," I asked, "where are your glasses?"

Joey stared back at me, blinking owlishly. "I dunno . . . ." I got Joey started on his stretching and went back to search the van. Top to bottom, end to end, no glasses. All I could think was that he must have set them on the dashboard, and they were blown out the open window. I walked back through the parking lot, but there was no sign of the missing glasses.

When I returned to the field, Joey had finished stretching and was jogging in place, keeping his legs warm. Knowing that Joey was nearly blind without his glasses, my heart was breaking as I sat him down on the bench. "Joey, I don't know if you're going to be able to race today," I started. Joey was quiet as his chin began to tremble. "I just don't think it's safe," I continued. "Without your glasses, you could get hurt." His eyes began to fill.

"But we're gonna win," he said, his voice cracking. "I'm going to win a medal."

I sat there for a moment, struggling with my own disappointment and Joey's. Then a thought struck me. "Come with me, Joey." We walked over to the track, and I stood him in his lane. I pointed to the white line on his right. "Can you see that line?"

Joey peered at his feet. "Yes."

I pointed to the line on his left. "How about that one?"

"Yes."

"Okay," I said. "Now this is important, Joey. If you run today, you have to keep your eyes on those two lines. You have to watch very carefully, and not cross out of them. Can you do that?"

"Yes."

Still unsure, but out of options, I led Joey back to the starting area. He walked haltingly, squinting his eyes, one hand slightly out in front of him. "Is Mom here?" he asked. I scanned the bleachers until I found her and waved. She waved back. "Yeah," I said. "She's up in the stands watching." Joey waved in the wrong direction.

The other coaches and I got our runners into their lanes, and then headed toward the finish line to cheer them on. The starting gun fired, and they were off! Joey was doing well, holding steady in second place until they rounded the first corner. Another boy swerved from his lane into Joey's, and Joey lost sight of his white line. I winced as I watched one sneakered foot catch the back of the opposite leg and send him sprawling onto the tarmac. Joey had fallen before, and he seemed okay this time. He scrambled to his feet and, pausing to squint at the track, he found his lines and started off again, limping slightly on his left foot. The rest of the boys had passed him, and he was about a quarter track behind. He ran doggedly, arms pumping at his sides, around the far corner and into the straightaway. Just as he was starting to gain on the last boy, his foot slipped again and he dropped to the track, rolling onto his side and groping blindly around him for balance. I groaned and started forward, but Joey rose to his knees again. He was crying now and almost started back the wrong way, but he turned at the direction of the pointing crowd. Now he was limping heavily, worn out, his arms hanging limply. Twenty feet from the finish line, he fell again. It was too much, and I was going to stop it, but as I stepped out onto the track to lead Joey to the sidelines, I felt a hand on my arm.

I turned to look and found Joey's mother, tears in her eyes, standing beside me. "He'll be okay," she said. "Let him finish." Then she stepped past me and walked over to stand next to the finish line. "Joey," she called over the crowd. "It's Mom. Can you hear me?" Joey's sweaty, tear-stained face came up, searching blindly through a sea of blurred faces. "Joey," she called, "come this way, honey." I watched Joey rise to his feet for the third time. His palms and elbow were scraped, and blood trickled from his knees, but he began hobbling toward the finish line once more. "This way, Joey," his mother called again, and Joey's face broke like the sun through the clouds, a bright wide smile on his face, as he crossed the finish line and fell into his mother's arms. As I ran toward them, through the roaring applause of the crowd, I could hear Joey telling his mother again and again, "I won, Mom! Did you see me win? I won!" Joey took home two gold medals that day, one for his race and one for best spirit. He earned them both.

Perry P. Perkins

Christian novelist **Perry P. Perkins** was born and raised in Oregon. Perry dedicates this story to the memory of Joey, who passed in 2001. Perry's writing includes *Just Past Oysterville*, *Shoalwater Voices*, and *The Light at the End of the Tunnel*. Perry is a student of the Jerry B. Jenkins Christian Writer's Guild and a frequent contributor to the Chicken Soup for the Soul anthologies. Perry's work can be found online at www.perryperkinsbooks.com.

A Simple Question

Any path is only a path, and there is no affront,
to oneself or to others, in dropping it if that is what
your heart tells you to do.

Carlos Castaneda, *The Teachings of Don Juan*

Our family had lived on the same friendly street for over seven years—our daughter Anna's whole life. From the beginning, the neighborhood kids were sincere and open in their desire for information. Their questions about Anna were tough to hear at first, but I learned how to answer them. Books about disabilities provided the words for me; I used simple terms to explain complex realities like "cerebral palsy," "vision impairment," and the other challenges in Anna's life. I considered myself a capable veteran in responding to questions like "Isn't Anna too young to wear glasses?" "Why can't she talk?" and "When she grows up, will she still need a wheelchair?"

But Alexa, an energetic eight-year-old neighbor girl, had asked a question that was of an entirely different sort. I sensed immediately that it would affect me for years to come, but I wasn't sure exactly how. All I knew was that I wouldn't find the answer to this one on my shelf of books on disabilities. Standing by Anna's side, Alexa looked straight at me and said, "Bonnie, what does Anna get for her allowance?"

I tried to think of an acceptable response, but my silence gave me away. The truth was it had never occurred to me to give Anna an allowance! Alexa looked disapprovingly at me.

"Seven-year-old kids around here usually get a dollar a week," she said evenly.

Anna squealed. Now both girls were watching me intently.

I had always answered children's questions honestly, and I knew this was no time to do otherwise. "Alexa," I began, "I probably didn't think of it because Anna doesn't really have chores, like other kids do."

I felt sad, kneeled down, and stroked Anna's small hands. Wide-eyed and smiling, she touched my face. As always, her patience and tenderness comforted me.

My love for my daughter was so strong that I would do anything for her. Instead of resuming my career after she was born, I spent my days at home with her, applying early-intervention strategies given to us by specialists and therapists assigned to our family. My husband and I desperately wanted to give her a good start at living with multiple disabilities. Time was of the essence.

Alexa's question about allowance money stunned me because it had nothing to do with Anna's special needs. Why would I use Anna's valuable therapy time to think about something as ordinary as an allowance? Clearly, Alexa saw Anna's life differently than I did. She exclaimed, "Anna does TOO do chores. She's learning to carry her own dish to the table. She is trying to use her communication board to ask for things. She does exercises every single day!"

Anna was beaming as she listened to the unfolding drama. *How could I disagree?* Alexa was so very right. Her insistence that Anna receive an allowance for doing her chores, just like the other kids, was opening my eyes as well as my heart. "Okay!" I said with a nod. "We'll start today."

Kelly, another young neighbor, peered in through the screen door to see what was going on. In no time, the door flew open, and the two girls ran off to look for something to hold Anna's money, because, of course, a weekly allowance needs to be saved in a proper bank.

As Alexa and Kelly dashed out of the house and across the damp front lawn, a lovely breeze of spring air sailed into the living room. Anna's gaze followed the girls, and I closed my eyes in gratitude for this moment of discovery we were sharing. I began to wonder, *If I was feeling overwhelmed by all the special work Anna had to do, how was she feeling? And, on top of everything, without even an allowance to show for it!*

Anna reached toward the doorway, so I wheeled her outside to wait for her friends. Alexa and Kelly soon reappeared with a can and lid, and a small notebook and pen. Alexa made a wide cut in the plastic lid so Anna could easily drop her coins into the slot. The notebook was to keep track of whether I remembered to pay Anna every single week.

Each Friday, the girls helped Anna perform the ritual in which she proudly put her very own allowance in her very own bank. Other exquisitely ordinary activities ensued, much to Anna's enduring delight. The three girls counted allowance money together and entered sums carefully in the notebook. They examined magazines and catalogs for toys, and later, clothes, that Anna might want to buy. They cut out Anna's chosen pictures and made lists of items to track down at the store.

Every year, the girls, now firmly established as Anna's financial advisors, directed me to raise her allowance, and

I happily complied. We would accompany Anna to the mall where the allowance money was exchanged for her choice of wondrous treasures, including a bright orange wallet with matching orange sunglasses, a jewelry box with a delicate ballerina on top, a glow-in-the-dark jump rope, and glittery pink ballet shoes.

As we all returned home from one shopping trip, I noticed the van was unusually silent. My check of the rearview mirror revealed troubled faces. "Hey, what's wrong, everybody?" I asked. "Did we forget something?"

Kelly finally spoke up. "Bonnie, Anna does not have to buy educational games with her allowance."

"You mean the Memory card game I put in the cart? I thought everybody liked it. Nobody said anything when we were in the store."

"Yes," Kelly said with a sigh, "Anna wants the game. But parents are supposed to buy those things, not kids."

"Right again!" I answered, thrilled at the group's objection. I reimbursed Anna on the spot.

The simple question that Alexa asked so many years ago about her neighbor friend opened wide the door to ordinary life for our daughter. I see in retrospect that it was a door in danger of sticking shut while my husband and I focused so heavily on Anna's needs. Time truly was of the essence . . . time for the fleeting years of childhood.

Bonnie Mintun

Bonnie Mintun's international reputation continues to grow. She has been welcomed as a keynote speaker and panelist to conferences and seminars on disability, education, and assistive technology. Her blend of personal experience, as the mother of a child with disabilities, and compelling research gained as a teacher, writer, and advocate combine to inspire, inform, and challenge her audiences. Bonnie's daughter, Anna, is now a young adult, and lives in her own apartment with roommates who provide the full-time support she requires to live in her community. As part of her busy week, Anna volunteers at a local preschool, reciting poems and stories to children using her communication device. Bonnie lives in Davis, California, and may be contacted at bonniecm@sbcglobal.net.

Step by Step

Empower your child by giving him/her a choice and a chance. Let them learn to make their own decision, when appropriate, and learn to trust their feelings.

Doc Childre

"Mom, today is my day," says my daughter. With her black T-shirt and tight jeans, Talia looks like any twelve-year-old—except for her preschooler-type shoes. She insists on wearing sneakers that flash a light each time she steps.

Today, for the first time, she'll walk to school and home alone. For Talia, diagnosed with autism, it's a milestone I thought she'd never reach. But Talia has worked hard to earn this freedom. Over the years, along with learning to speak, read, and use facial expressions, she's memorized rules to keep her safe. "Three-step rule," she reminds me in the grocery store. In a crowded place, she keeps within three steps of the adult she's with.

But the three-step rule doesn't help her navigate the complex customs of the social world. Out in public she often says hi to everyone she passes. Then she looks back at me to see whether she's done the right thing. "Oops! Sorry, Mom," she says. "Was that a stranger?"

Once, while we waited in line to pay the cashier at a store, Talia patted the arm of the woman standing in front of her. "You're doing a great job waiting your turn," my daughter told her. The woman turned to me and smiled. I blushed. Others are not as charmed by my daughter's social eccentricities. They meet her comments with frowns and raised eyebrows. How do I protect her from that? So although she's ready to journey to school alone, I'm not ready to let her go.

For years, I've walked with her, acting as translator and bully protector. While Talia knows her safety rules, how can she protect herself from hurtful comments or being ignored?

I decide on a compromise. "I'll walk you just to the corner so I can watch you cross our road. Then you can cross the other road with the crossing guard," I tell her.

Her heavy backpack bulges with lunch, extra clothes, binders, and a pencil case. I start to sling it over my own shoulder.

"I can carry it," she says. We walk together, and then from atop the hill I watch her race down the sidewalk and stop abruptly when she reaches the curb. Standing still, she slowly swivels her head left and then right several times before venturing across the street. All during the day I think about her: How did she do? Realizing we left the house too early, I wonder how she spent the ten minutes in the schoolyard before the bell rang. Did she have anyone to wait with? Did she wander?

At 3:00 PM, I hear the school bell from my house. After eight years of being in the schoolyard before and after classes, it feels strange not being there now. Again, I wait on the sidewalk at the corner near our house. As I wait, I marvel at how much she's changed over the years. I remember her as a bewildered and unhappy four-year-old who communicated mostly by echoing phrases and crying. I remember endless car rides with Talia screaming "green, green" in the backseat every time we had to stop for a red light. I prayed the light would change quickly back to green. Anything, just so she'd stop wailing. And over the years, she has.

Soon, I see her striding up the hill alone. We meet and walk the final few minutes together.

"How was your day, Tal?" I ask her. No reply. At the table as she eats her afternoon snack (apple slices peeled to avoid the yucky skin), Talia is silent. Finally, she looks me in the eyes and says, "Mom, tomorrow, you need to stay in the house. Don't walk me to the corner. I can do this myself."

The next morning, she leaves alone.

"See you later, Mom," she says.

I run upstairs to peer through the blinds in her bedroom window to watch her. Her backpack bouncing, she skips down the hill.

Of course, Talia still has autism. But somehow she's emerged. She's active and present in the world, rather than constantly battling it. She happily checks her wall calendar for adventures she's looking forward to. "Only four more days til Emily's slumber party," she says.

It's hard to measure in a standardized test how far she's progressed. How would you score or categorize a child who brings me a tissue when my eyes well up? "It's okay to be sad, Mom," she says.

Like so many loving kids with autism, she defies the stereotype of being aloof and distant. I'm not sure why she's changed. When she was younger, we read frantically about therapies, specialized diets, medications, and ABA (applied behavioral analysis), but few resources existed in our community. So we pieced together bits of activities and therapies we thought might help—speech therapy, occupational therapy, one-to-one playtime and teaching, nursery school, and day care.

Mostly we took her everywhere in the community so she could experience different social situations and learn how to navigate them. We hoped these outings would help her develop new interests, skills, and language. We visited summer and fall fairs, stores, movies, restaurants, the library, parties, temple, concerts, hiking trails, and the YMCA. When she'd start to scream or tantrum, we'd scoop her up and escape back home.

While I enjoy her now, I often think about the future. Where will she live? What will she do? Who will be there for her when we can't be? My daughter, on the other hand, wisely lives in the present. Today Talia stands in the hallway and kisses me goodbye. "I'll see you after school, Mom."

I close the door. Though I really want to walk with her—at least to the corner—today I don't. Neither do I race upstairs to peer through the window blinds to watch her. Instead, I sit down and pour myself a coffee. And my own day begins.

Amy Baskin

Amy Baskin, M.Ed., is the coauthor of *More Than a Mom—Living a Full and Balanced Life When You Child Has Special Needs* (Woodbine House). A mother of two teens, her youngest has autism. She writes and speaks about parenting for magazines, conferences, and organizations. See www.morethanamom.net or e-mail abaskin@ sentex.net for details. Talia is thrilled to be traveling to Quebec City this spring with her classmates. An avid animal lover, Talia enjoys young Naturalist and Humane Society (SPCA) clubs on the weekends. She hopes to work with aninals or to be a chef one day.

Independence Day

Strength does not come from physical capacity.
It comes from an indomitable will.

Mahatma Gandhi

As a teacher, I have no favorites. But if I did, Jim would be one.

I met Jim when he was a sophomore in high school. As the inclusion facilitator for students with significant support needs, one of my first responsibilities was to teach Jim how to use his new electric wheelchair. Given the spasticity from cerebral palsy, the task would have been daunting enough, but Jim had another suspected agenda in learning to "drive"—his mother feared that he intended to do himself harm once he mastered it.

As with many families faced with living with a person with lifelong disabilities, Jim's parents, overcome with the stresses that go with them, had separated two years earlier. Jim did not handle it well, perhaps sensing that some of the tension in the family was due to the attention necessarily paid to caring for his daily needs. As a result, he attempted at his previous school to rock his wheelchair close enough to the top of an embankment to throw himself down it. Fortunately, a teacher's aide caught him, but he vowed to his rescuers that he would eventually accomplish his task. Regardless, we knew that if Jim was ever going to achieve any control in his life—any independence at all—which is the goal for all students, he would need to have the opportunity to move himself from one place to the next. So it was under this cloud of caution that we began his mobility training with an electric wheelchair.

Jim was motivated. From day one, his concentration in willing his contorted arms to even reach the joystick on his chair was at once both inspiring and excruciating. And while his speech was mostly unintelligible, when he was successful in getting the chair to move even slightly, it would be interrupted by his joyful expression—a loud, inhaling type of laughter that was infectious if not disruptive to everyone around him. This would cause him to have to start over, as his whole body convulsed with the laughter, but he would proudly do so, eventually containing himself long enough to make his chair inch forward.

Before long, Jim was navigating the halls. Eventually, he could access the elevator and his classes on the second floor. At first, we were obvious in monitoring his comings and goings, following him to classes and making sure that student assistants were aware that monitoring Jim was part of their responsibility. With the improvement of his ability to negotiate the halls came an improved demeanor as well; Jim seemed truly happy at last. The more proficient he became, the less we worried. Soon he was going from our resource room to his general-education classes unassisted, meeting his student assistant on arrival.

One day, Jim left our classroom and headed for the computer lab, where he was taking a modified keyboarding class. Shortly after the bell had rung, his teaching assistant came into the classroom with an innocent enough question.

"Is Jim out today?"

"No," I replied, with more than a little apprehension. "Didn't he meet you at the lab?"

"He never showed up for class."

Immediately, we headed out in opposite directions, trying not to panic. I checked the main entrance stairs near the elevator, while the teaching assistant took the west stairs, and we met on the second floor near the lab. Where could he have gone? I realized that the office should probably be alerted, but I was anxious to find him, hoping against hope that we hadn't misjudged his demeanor. I was just about to hit the call button in the nearest classroom when I heard a faint, unmistakable sound. It was the sound of Jim's inhaling laughter from quite a distance.

"Listen!" I motioned for the teaching assistant to go down one hall, while I went down the other. Because of the acoustics, it was impossible to tell from which direction the laughter had come; Jim was nowhere in sight. As I headed off down the hallway, it became obvious that I was getting closer. Near the end I found him, facing the door of an empty classroom. He had pulled into the doorway so that his chair had disappeared from sight. He had an unmistakably delighted look about him.

"Jim! What on Earth are you doing down here?"

My displeasure must have been evident, as Jim's laughter immediately stopped. His face did not reflect fear, however; moreover, it was a look of complete indignation. Wild-eyed, his head moved back and forth as he strained his neck forward in an attempt to get the words in his heart to come out through his taut, nonresponsive diaphragm. After a prolonged struggle, he was able to squeeze out a three-syllable response.

Even when Jim was calm, he was nearly impossible to understand. In the months that we had gotten acquainted, I had become pretty adept at interpreting him, but in this

instance, Jim had as much clarity as I have ever heard.
"I'm . . . skip . . . ping!"

Having feared the worst in his absence, I should have been relieved. Instead, I surprised myself by sticking to the standards I have set for all the students in my program.

"You're skipping?! Skipping your computer class?"

Jim rocked violently back and forth in affirmation. Then he stared back up at me with that same defiant stare, his lower jaw protruding and trembling ever so slightly.

"Jim! Why on Earth would you skip your computer class?!"

Again, he struggled to communicate. His head slammed back into his headrest, mouth and eyes wide open, then lunged forward again as if he were trying to escape his chair. Steadying himself, he focused his face, reddened with emotion, on mine. He pushed the words out, past the tears that were welling in his eyes.

"Because . . ." he struggled. "Because . . . I . . . finally . . . could . . ."

His face held the same defiance, chin out and eyes fixed on mine. In those eyes I could see the pride that had waited sixteen years to come spilling out. I suddenly realized how much the independence we had sought for Jim meant to him; I always preached it, but before then I had never *felt* it. It took me a couple of seconds before I could respond.

"Go to the office."

I knew that to avoid hypocrisy, Jim needed the same consequence as any other sophomore caught skipping a class. Jim's defiance didn't lessen much, but without a word, he commandeered his joystick and headed for the elevator. I had the student assistant follow him down as I took the stairs to catch the assistant principal before Jim got there.

"Treat him like anyone else," I told the AP.

As we both sat in the office, Jim receiving his detention repentantly, I couldn't help swelling with pride. At one point, I caught his eye. He couldn't contain a sheepish smile.

"Was it worth it?" I asked him on the way back to the classroom.

He nearly threw himself from his chair, nodding yes. I laughed and mussed his hair.

"Can I trust you to go back to computer?"

He just smiled, grabbed his joystick, and headed for the elevator.

Daniel Wray

Daniel Wray is a significant support needs coordinator for Douglas County schools, Colorado. He received his M.A. in special education in 1992 from the University of Colorado, where he currently teaches education courses. Dan has published two books on church drama and coauthored a third for students with disabilities. E-mail Dan at Daniel.wray@dcsdk12.org. Jim's parents reconciled and are happily living with Jim in Colorado Springs. He continues to exercise his independence and hopes to write an autobiography someday to help others do so as well.

The Class Trip

Whatever creativity is, it is in part a solution to a problem.

Brian Aldiss

It was a typical warm spring day around three in the afternoon when my daughter's school bus pulled up, and she came bouncing down the steps with her dress blowing in the wind. As she excitedly told me all about her day, we waited for her brother's bus to arrive from school. He had to ride a different bus, a short bus. On his bus, no one came bouncing down the steps on their own. They were either assisted by the driver using their hand canes or crutches, or, like my son, they bypassed the steps by riding the wheelchair lift, since a wheelchair was his means of maneuvering around.

His after-school stories usually were not as enthusiastic as hers, but today was different. He rolled to the edge of the lift with papers in hand and a smile on his face, all the while talking a mile a minute and asking me to sign on the dotted line.

As we entered our home, I glanced over those so important papers to find that it was information about a field trip. He eagerly wanted me to sign his permission slip to allow his participation. As I read on, I soon discovered the trip was to a state park about an hour away. The park rests where the ocean meets the bay. The children were going to learn about the habitat of sea life that resided in these areas. Now, you know, where the ocean meets the bay, you are talking about marshlands and beaches and *sand!*

Maneuvering a wheelchair in the sand is a next-to-impossible task, and trying to explore a marshy area would be just plain futile! However, this mom handled the inquiry from her son, Darryl, like every other that had come before by saying, "If you really want to do this, we will find a way." The next day, the slip was returned to school, soon followed by a call from the teacher asking me how this would be possible since Darryl could not walk. I assured him I would handle it.

As most of you know, moms with children with disabilities will not take "no" for an answer when it comes to our children being able to participate as fully as possible in an able-bodied world.

I made a phone call to the state park and spoke to a not-so-friendly park ranger about borrowing a beach wheelchair from a neighboring beach. My mission was to have one available to us when we arrived at the park. After thirty minutes of explaining the situation, I felt sure I had convinced him that I was a responsible parent and would take full responsibility for all actions pertaining to his precious, expensive chair and my son, the occupant.

Before we knew it, the day had arrived. It started out on a good note because the school had made arrangements for a "big bus" with a wheelchair lift to make the trip. My son was actually riding the same bus as his friends! He was ecstatic!

The hour ride was a noisy, bouncy, hot experience. The smell of sunscreen and bug spray germinated the air in the bus so badly that neither sun nor flies would dare to enter.

I will admit I was a bit nervous as to whether or not the park ranger would be there to meet us or if this whole ride was to be in vain for my son.

Fortunately, he was waiting for us as we pulled in. The beach chair with its big yellow rubber tires was an attraction for all. Everyone wanted to push Darryl along the marshy paths and through the sand. On that day, he was everyone's best friend. But, as always, the attraction wore off, and left to work were the same four neighborhood boys who had been by Darryl's side since pre-K, never failing to lend a hand when needed, and never looking at Darryl as a kid with a disability but as a friend.

Three hours into this never-ending educational experience of crab mating and migration, the four boys, my son, and I had fallen behind. Just as the teacher was rounding the bend up ahead with the tour guide and the rest of the class, he looked back and very sternly instructed me to "get those boys away from the water's edge and catch up!" I explained to the four chair-pushers—really, two would have been able to do the job—that the shoreline drops off suddenly, and they needed to come up on the sand a little more because I did not want them falling in and getting wet. They assured me they were fine. I was filled with joy watching them splash around mischievously and wondered how those big yellow rubber tires would float if given the chance.

I soon realized I needed to start acting like a mom and a chaperone and call them in so we could catch up with the rest of the class, but I was caught up in the fact that my son was having so much fun with his friends, and the laughter was as refreshing as the cool ocean breeze.

Just as I came to my senses to reel them in to where they belonged, you guessed it, the shoreline dropped, and down they all went!

Picture this: four healthy fifth-grade boys, all knowing how to swim, were floundering all over themselves as they were now in the bay up to their necks, all the while reaching to save Darryl, who was now floating off the chair! Thanks to the tide, the chair was moving south while Darryl was floating north! I came out of my shoes as fast as I could and headed to the water to save all five souls that I was responsible for—and, yes, that precious chair, too!

What could have been a stressful and dangerous situation was nothing short of a hilarious, wet mess! All you could hear was laughter and five fifth-grade boys gasping for air from laughing so hard, and thankfully not from water intake. As I was hauling them to shore after catching my son and fastening him back into that expensive state-owned chair that almost ended up in the middle of the Atlantic, we were greeted by the teacher, who came out of the middle of nowhere. As he glared at me for an explanation, the kids hung their heads and wouldn't even make eye contact with him. I finally smiled and said, "Sorry, but my son was having fun, real fun, with his peers, and that is not an everyday occurrence for us." He looked at me with a half-smile and walked away.

The ride home was just as noisy as the ride down. Six of us were soaking wet and uncomfortable. Six of us learned nothing about mating crabs or their migration skills. And one of us, the teacher, thanked me for teaching him something that day.

It took that mishap for a very good teacher to see that sometimes the best-laid lesson plans are not prewritten the week before in a lesson plan book.

The lesson of friendship, camaraderie, and laughter was learned that day where the ocean meets the bay.

Debra Behnke

Debra S. Behnke's passion for being an advocate for individuals with disabilities runs deep in her soul. Mother of two grown children, she enjoys delivering speeches about the joys of raising a child with a disability, sibling issues, and being left a widow at a very young age. She works full-time for the local government and can be reached at missdebbie@hotmail.com. Darryl is now twenty-six years old and lives independently in his own apartment with outside services to help him with his daily needs.

Good Night, Faith

Bloom where you're planted.

Author unknown

It was just a slumber party. In the life of most little girls, what's another slumber party? In the life of our little girl, it was a milestone—for her and for us.

When Faith was born eight years ago with Down syndrome, weighing only three pounds and struggling for life, we wondered what kind of future she would have. Our oldest daughter, Joy, was fourteen at the time, so we were well versed in the activities of a typical little girl. But Faith was, by no means, typical. One thing we were sure about—to the best of our ability, and hers, Faith would be treated as "normally" as possible. Preschool, Brownies, kindergarten, Sunday school, elementary school—in every area, whether at home or away, we wanted her to be treated just like any other little girl.

Of course, not everyone was as convinced as we were. We received advice to segregate her in special-education classes. But we wanted something different for our Faith. And so we entered the bureaucratic world of school

readiness, mainstreaming, inclusion barriers, accommoda-
tions, modifications, and revised expectations. We've
found that, frequently, school officials' expectations for
her are lower than ours. It is a worthwhile challenge to
keep her included with her typical peers in the general
education classroom as much as possible. One of our
biggest issues is educating the educators!

*But how would Faith handle everyday little girl things, like
sleepovers?* We received our answer last weekend. Faith was
invited to her first sleepover—a birthday party. Of the ten
girls who would attend, six were in her Brownie troop.
The others were new to her. Faith's Brownie "sisters" have
always been helpful and supportive of her. Some have
been together since attending church preschool. The
sleepover mom and her daughter were new to our area, so
Faith didn't know them as well as the others. Saturday
afternoon arrived soon enough.

We dropped her off with the other eight-year-old girls at
four o'clock. Faith ran into the house and upstairs to greet
the other girls. At the top of the stairs, she turned and said,
"Bye, Mom." I stayed downstairs awhile, then went up to
tell her I was leaving. She was surprised I was still there
and dismissed me with another, "Good-bye, Mom!" The
sleepover mom took it all in stride, assuring me that Faith
would be no problem. I couldn't decide if she was being
optimistic or naive.

I came home and waited by the telephone. Silence. They
say, "No news is good news." I wasn't so sure. I stayed up
imagining . . . the worst. *Was she scared? Would she fit in?
Would she fall off the top bunk? Was it a mistake to send her? Was
the party ruined because of my daughter?* And still I waited. By
9:00 PM, I couldn't take it any longer. I told myself, *One call.
Just one call . . . in case Faith needs me, or perhaps the sleepover
mom needs some help or . . . or . . . or . . .* So I called. Sleepover
mom said Faith was doing fine, and would it be okay for

her to have another piece of cake? I hung up the phone with a sigh of relief and a smile.

We picked Faith up the next morning at ten o'clock. We were excited about her accomplishment. She was excited about her adventure and did not want to come home. Sleepover mom filled us in on the details. Faith had slept in a top bunk (another new accomplishment) and went to sleep at midnight, neither first nor last of the girls to sleep. I was so happy to hear her say that Faith would be welcomed back anytime. She had assured me, the day before, that Faith would be no problem. Lo and behold, Faith was no problem! We had wondered how Faith would handle little girl things like sleepovers. Now we had our answer: she would handle them just like any other little girl.

Paulette Beurrier

Paulette Beurrier is a career mom. She lives in south Florida with her husband and nine-year-old daughter, Faith, who recently began playing on the Little League Challenger League. Her first time out, she knew just what to do as she tapped the bat on the ground before batting. While practicing her catching, she repeatedly hit her fist into her mitt. She looked like she'd been playing for years! Paulette's two grown and married children live nearby. Paulette advocates for Faith and studies Down syndrome. Her hobbies, besides writing, are sewing, reading, and playing with her grandchildren. She can be reached at LifewithDS@yahoo.com.

My Dad Made the Difference

All about me may be silence and darkness, yet within me, in the spirit, is music and brightness, and color flashes through all my thoughts.

                                                    Helen Keller

"There's nothing I can do," the eye doctor told my parents. "Take your baby home. She's blind." Mom and Dad clung to each other and wept freely. "All I can do is give her a full, happy life," Dad vowed. "I don't know how else to treat her except as I would any other child."

As I grew, my parents realized I could see partially. The greatest gift Dad gave me was expecting me to meet my potential and to persevere, even with my sight limitation. One day after school, my dad came home from work early and saw me holding *Dick and Jane* close to my eyes, struggling to read the letters. "Dad, I can't do this. It's too hard," I told him.

"Honey, you're not a quitter. I'll help you."

My brother banged through the door and blurted, "The kids are saying my sister is stupid because she can't read. Is that true?"

My voice quavered. "My eyes are bad, Dad. Does that mean I'm stupid? Will I ever be able to read?"

Dad squeezed my hand. "You can't see well, but that doesn't mean you're stupid. We'll work together, and you will read."

Dad made me want to try. He took out markers and paper. While I lay on my stomach, he painstakingly drew letters big enough for me to see. It took hours. I also have some hearing loss. He pronounced the phonics slowly and distinctly so I could hear them. I learned to read and proudly read *Dick and Jane* with the rest of my first-grade class. Because of my dad, I had confidence in myself as a reader—until middle school.

One afternoon at the end of class, the teacher stepped out of the room, and a student taunted me. "You blind bat. If you get your face any nearer to that page, your eyes will fall out of your head!" I ran out of the school, tears glistening on my cheeks.

Dad was home when I burst into the house. "I thought I was a good reader, but I guess I'm not. The kids are making fun of me." I told him what my classmate had said.

Dad hugged me. "I'm sorry, Pam. Kids can be cruel, but that doesn't change the truth. You can read, right?" I nodded, unable to speak. "You can read. Your classmate can't take that away from you."

The knot in my stomach went away after Dad's encouragement. I walked over to the picture window and looked out. I saw our old sycamore tree blowing in the breeze against the blue sky. I noticed the plush green grass, Dad's enormous red roses on the hedge by the house, and how the amber sun shimmered as it began to set in the distance. "Dad, I see—how can I be blind?"

"From what you've described, you see big items, not detail. Others don't know how much you can or can't see. It's up to you to show them how capable you are," Dad said.

I had a chance to prove this to myself soon after. At a fast-food court, the waitress asked my dad, "What does she want to order?"

"Excuse me," I spoke up and smiled. "I can decide for myself what I want." Dad nudged me and said, "That's my girl."

I used the sight I had and knew I was independent even as a blind person. Dad advised, "Take your cane in places like the grocery store so people will know you're blind. It's okay to let someone assist you because you do all you can on your own."

Dad taught me to laugh at myself. He reminded me of the time I tried to pick up a sign that was painted to the floor. Another time, we ate in the deli, and I attempted to eat flowers off an empty plate. When I was ten, I wanted to ride a two-wheeler bike. I heard Dad say to Mom, "I'm not going to hold Pam back from the adventures any kid has." On my first attempt, I said, "Dad, what if I fall off?" He replied, "You'll get on and try again."

I recall summers outdoors roaming with my friends. We crossed streets, played in the creek, and swung on a tire swing. In order to roller-skate, I used big landmarks: carport poles, garbage cans, a sidewalk contrasting with the grass, and the dark shadow of the house. Once, however, I smacked into a pole anyway. While the dentist capped my tooth, he objected, "Why are you letting her skate?"

"Don't sighted children smash into poles?" Dad asked.

The dentist seemed appalled. He left for a minute, and I remarked, "Dad, don't tell him yesterday I climbed a tree."

"I won't. It will be our secret."

In the car, I exclaimed, "Dad, why do people think I can't do stuff?"

"They can't comprehend how they would do it if they couldn't see."

Dad continued to mentor and sustain me until all seven

of my children were grown, and I became a grandmother. The legacy he gave me—unconditional love and determination—lives on within me and through them. I wouldn't be who I am today if it weren't for my dad. He made the difference for me to believe in myself.

Though my dad has died, I still feel him spurring me on, like that day I went on a field trip to Astoria, Oregon, where a column overlooks the surrounding beach area. "You can't climb that tower. You'll get hurt," a teacher informed me.

"Watch me," I replied. "Nobody tells me I can't do something." I started toward the column.

"She's spunky. I like that," another teacher said, following me, cheering all the way, just as Dad would have.

Pam Johnson

Pam Johnson is a freelance writer, published in numerous magazines. Although she is legally blind and hearing impaired, she enjoys life. She loves exercising, going to the beach, playing guitar, and is a volunteer counselor. She has seven children and eight grandchildren. Pam recently married and currently goes by the name Pam Bostwick. Contact her at pamjohnson7721@netzero.net.

The Most Important Words

Wise sayings often fall on barren ground, but a kind word is never thrown away.

Arthur Helps

"There's nothing wrong with you!" These were the words that my Nana would gruffly say whenever the topic of my autism would come up, and probably the most important words I would ever hear as a child and then as a teenager. Out of all the members of my family, and every adult, teenager, and child I would ever come across, I was closest to my grandmother because she understood something that the others did not: There was nothing "wrong" with me. I was different, and that was all. She did not treat me any differently from my brother or cousins. She did not focus on what was so "terribly wrong" with me. And she was never any more impressed with my accomplishments than she would have been if my brother, cousins, or anyone else had accomplished them. Nana had faith in me and what I could do.

Of course, Nana knew that I had painful digestive problems, headaches, and extreme sensitivity to smell, touch, and hearing. When I got overloaded with any of that, I would act strangely to try and calm myself. However, she had high blood pressure, and had had a heart attack and two strokes in the past, so she just saw my problems as medical things that I would have to deal with just like she dealt with hers.

I am now thirty years old. I am married, work in a high-paying job in the information technology (IT) industry, and am an area governor in Toastmasters. I graduated from college with a 4.0 GPA, I went to a regular school, and I never had special education (although it was hard for me). I drive a new car and conduct public speeches to professionals and parents about autism from a different perspective. Of course, I still have my medical problems, get overloaded easily, have digestive problems, and really don't like going to large social events. That will never change.

I truly believe that the messages we hear as children really shape who we become as adults. Many of us spend so much of our lives hearing what is so terribly wrong with us that we start to believe that we *are* terribly wrong! The words of trusted adults have incredible power over children . . . even those who have autism. The negative messages drive many teens and adults with autism to depression, suicidal thoughts, and so on. The positive ones help them grow up to become productive and happy adults. I am a productive and mostly happy adult because an important person in my life had faith in me and gave me the right message while I was growing up . . . even if it was said in a gruff tone. To my dying day, I will be grateful to my late grandmother for telling me that there is nothing "wrong" with me!

Daria J. Skibington-Roffel

Daria J. Skibington-Roffel is a writer, public speaker, artist, and activist focusing on respect, understanding, and acceptance for children and adults with autism. She works as an IT professional and is pursuing a bachelor's degree in psychology. Daria was diagnosed with autism at the age of two. Please e-mail her at djsroffel@yahoo.com.

Something in Football

For life to be a dream come true, it is critical to know who is dreaming.

Jay Robb

"Hey, Seth! Gimme five!" The huge hulk of a man clothed in bright shades of yellow and grass-colored green, complete with helmet, shoulder pads, and leg pads, hollers to another, much smaller, young man, and hands slap together as they pass. Smiles flash, and it's obvious these two like each other.

The University of Oregon football team, coached by Mike Bellotti, is getting ready for the upcoming "Civil War" game played each year against neighboring Oregon State University's Beavers team.

This year, like every other year, the intensity of competition will be palpable as the two teams vie for position as Oregon's number-one winning team. And Seth will be right there as always—constant supporter, loyal fan, and much-loved colleague. Probably no one would look at Seth and say, "Now there's a kid who's born to play football."

Not quite as tall as his brother or sister, Seth's Down

syndrome, a genetic disorder that affects approximately one in every eight hundred to one thousand births, may have played a role in his shorter stature.

As a child, the tow-headed boy with sparkling blue eyes knew how to attract friends with his great sense of humor. He knew how to dance and wasn't shy about joining in wherever there was music and a beat. But more than that, Seth knew a lot about football. Being part of a family that attended every one of the Oregon Duck games, Seth's knowledge of football grew along with his interest.

Challenges would come, as they do for everyone, but never was he deterred when it came to learning everything he could about his favorite sport. After high-school graduation, Seth enrolled in the Community Living Program, where life skills are taught and practiced before young adults actually move out on their own. "Do you have an idea what he might have an interest in doing, like something he might be good at?" an instructor asked Seth's mom one afternoon.

"Yes," she answered without hesitation. "Something in football."

Her quick smile hinted at the reality that that might not be the easiest thing to bring to fruition. But her son had his dreams. She knew her oldest son's life passion. He longed to be a part of football. While attending one of his sister's basketball games with his family, Seth walked over and introduced himself to one of the parents who was watching the game as well. It was Mike Bellotti, the head coach for the Oregon Ducks football team.

Days later, Mr. Bellotti would ask Seth's parents if they thought he might like to assist the Ducks. Neither would have to wonder about the answer. It has been six years since Seth started helping with the University of Oregon Ducks as assistant to the equipment manager. Beginning in August, when the team practices twice a day, Seth is right there, and he knows every teammate's name and position. He knows the rules of the game and all the signals, easily keeping up with the referee in making the calls. Though running with the ball to score a touchdown or jumping out to block the opposition may never be in his future, Seth is as much a part of the Ducks as his dreams had anticipated—and more.

"Have good offense, good defense, protect the quarterback. Right here! Right now!" Seth regularly speaks to the team with words of encouragement. They are as blessed to have him on their team as he is to be there. Though it may have turned out very differently for this persevering young man, his quiet confidence proved him a winner, far exceeding the expectations of those who might have imagined a limit to his abilities.

Seth is living his dream. He loves his work and his life, and when he returns to his well-kept one-bedroom apartment, he enjoys the satisfaction of being on his own and the pride of accomplishment. Seth's parents are empty nesters now, and his siblings are also grown and out on their own. Joel is away at college, and Paige is at the University of Oregon. And, of course, so is Seth. During the season, he can be found where he is most at home, where he thrives, doing what he was born to do—"something in football."

Lauri Khodabandehloo

Lauri Khodabandehloo just completed her book, *Sunshine in My Soul,* about the trials, heartache, joys, and blessings of raising a child with autism. She has a passion for speaking on autism and God's grace, and is a member of SAIL Housing, a parent-driven organization that supports independent living for those with developmental disabilities. She can be reached at laurikhoda@comcast.net. Seth continues to work with the team at the University of Oregon and has been living on his own in his loft apartment since graduation from the Life Skills Community Living Program. He is busy with the routine of life but makes time to spend with friends and family, and keeps them updated and informed with his awesome knowledge of the game of football.

A Revelation

Life's under no obligation to give us what we expect.

Margaret Mitchell

"There's an arrow in your butt," he exclaimed to the afternoon sun. Brushing the damp brown hair out of my eyes, I was sure I was going to die soon if I didn't get to my emergency inhaler. Maybe I had already died and gone to hell. The raging Kentucky summer glared at me from the blacktop of our uphill driveway. The 95-degree heat was nearly matched by the humidity, which made the air thick enough to slice. I panted, jogging beside him as the knobby tires of Zayne's bicycle murmured encouragement to my well-worn sneakers. I groaned to myself, *Why did I choose the end of June to teach Zayne to ride a bicycle without training wheels?*

From the moment he was born, I knew Zayne was different. At first I thought he was rocket scientist different. You know, the kind of different that helps a person change the whole world at the blink of an eye. After all, Zayne immediately memorized almost everything he saw and heard, and besides, he was my son. But sometime after the eighteen-month mark, Zayne began to speak less and less. Every day he traveled a little further into his own mind, until eventually he communicated only in basic sign language and certain random echolalic phrases from his favorite television shows and movies. It was during this time that I slowly began to realize that the kind of difference Zayne possessed was the kind that changed the world one person at a time.

This realization blanketed my being even before Zayne was diagnosed with PDD-NOS, an autism spectrum disorder that affects Zayne's ability to reason, communicate, and understand the world at large. As Zayne grew older, he began to have emotionally devastating meltdowns. This made even the simple things like getting him out of bed difficult, and making Zayne do things for himself was sometimes more than I could handle. *How do you make a child pick out his school clothes when he is screaming obscenities and flailing his limbs wildly at an invisible offender?* It was just easier to do things for Zayne. I was only dimly aware at the time that as he retreated from everyday life, I advanced, and my advancement was smothering him. I became like kudzu, growing, reaching, tightening my hold on Zayne's life. Success for me became simple: survival. But I later learned that while a good grip does lend support, it also restricts movement and growth.

Sweat dripped from my neck, arms, back, and legs. With every exhalation, I expelled a wheeze, but still I continued to jog beside him with one hand on the right side of the handlebars and one hand on the back of the black bicycle seat. I couldn't give up now. If he could learn to do this, there was still hope. *Other kids learn to do this when they're six. Zayne's nine. He has to do this*, I thought. All of my dreams for him—learning to drive, having a job, making a friend—materialized in my mind. If he could learn to ride, he could learn to live. He could learn to love. I could learn to let go.

Eight laps we ran around the course devised for safety rather than ease of use. Down the grassy hill, wide left turn around the pear tree near the road, up the paved driveway hill, wide left turn into the grass. We were like an awkward comet revolving our way in and out of the solar system. Nine, ten, eleven. Zayne, in his huge red and white striped riding helmet still wobbled, but he grew steadier with each lap. Sweat ran down my arm, causing my hand to slip off the lime green handlebar. I let go. The gleaming silver and green bike was a knife that sliced a new clean line through the grass, dragging me behind as I clutched at the seat with my left hand. In the confusion I had to remind my legs to keep running.

"There's an arrow in your butt," Zayne crowed again with delight. I wished that he would say more than just lines from the movie Shrek. I wished he could tell me his fears, his thoughts, his dreams. He was so close. He needed this, and what was more, I needed to know he could do this. We greeted the sweltering pavement again, and this time Zayne surprised me with a line from Finding Nemo that he had not said in a while: "It's time to let go." Obediently, I loosened my grip on the back of the seat. When he pedaled up the driveway, I was three inches off the ground. All of my sweat, heartache, and uncertainties melted into a reflection pool at my feet. I realized that, just like anyone else, Zayne really is the master of his fate, and although I will doggedly jog beside him for as long as he needs me, the day eventually will come when he will choose to pedal on, leaving me behind to rejoice in his wake.

Lisa Logsdon

Lisa Logsdon received her master's degree in education from Western Kentucky University in 2005 and her bachelor of science from the University of the Cumberlands in 1995. She teaches English and media to high-school students in Southern Kentucky. Zayne continues to make remarkable progress, both at school and at home. His hobbies include therapeutic horseback riding, drawing, and collecting toy cars. He rides his bike, without assistance, often.

"You made this on February 21, and I really hated it."

Bearing Gifts

Success is almost totally dependent upon drive and persistence. The extra energy required to make another effort or try another approach is the secret of winning.

Denis Waitley

Christmas with my brother Ken was always a magical time. He never got "too cool" to be excited over the holidays the way the rest of us did. Ken was born smack in the middle of my parents' twelve kids. He was born a month early in an era when pediatric intensive care units weren't what they are today. Halfway through the delivery, the doctors realized the umbilical cord was wrapped around Ken's throat, cutting off the oxygen to his brain. By the time he was in the doctor's hands, it had been cut off long enough to leave him with cerebral palsy, mild retardation, and profound deafness. But God is good, and he more than compensated for Ken's disabilities by lavishing on him a sparkling personality, a gusto for life, a childlike faith, and a magnetic smile that drew people to him.

Because my brother Mark was born less than a year

after Ken, and my sister, Gail, had been born ten months before, babying Ken was not an option. He was part of the gang from day one, and although he didn't walk until he was twelve, he never had trouble keeping up with the rest of us, or the passel of neighborhood kids and cousins who hung around our house.

In the hospital, the doctors had advised my parents not to see Ken, to put him in a "special home" and forget they'd had him. They predicted he'd never walk or talk, never feed himself, and wouldn't live past his tenth birthday. Ken was seven by the time I was born, and I'm glad the doctors never told him any of the above. The Ken I knew was lean and taut, feisty and impish, and ate anything that didn't eat him first. He loved a party, being the center of attention, and everything to do with Christmas.

One of my favorite Christmas memories was a year when our grandparents sent us a new swing set. From first glance, Ken was fascinated with the slide. He spent the holidays on the ground offering a blow-by-blow commentary as the rest of us slid down. He'd squeal with delight as we started down the slide, throw his head back, and laugh when we landed with a splat at his feet, then chase us on all fours trying to grab us and tickle us before we could crawl back up the ladder again. He never tried to traverse the ladder himself, though. His scrawny, twisted legs just didn't work like that.

The day the rest of us started back to school, Mama knew what she had to do. She bundled up Ken, took him out to the backyard, pointed him toward the ladder, and began to pray, "Okay, Lord, Ken wants to go down the slide. I'm gonna need all the help I can get to let him try." Years later, she told me how hard it was watching him climb and fall, climb and fall again and again. He tore both knees out of his pants, cut one elbow, and bloodied his forehead, and one particularly bad tumble left him rocking on the lawn crying and holding a knot on the back of his head.

The neighbor to the back of us came to the fence and yelled at my mama. "What kind of woman are you? Get that baby off that ladder!" Mama told her as nicely as she could that if it bothered her, she'd have to close her curtains and stop watching. Ken had decided he was going down the slide, and down the slide he would go, no matter how long it took him.

By the time the rest of us got home from school, Ken was black and blue and smiling from ear to ear. Not only could he get up and down the slide with lightning speed, but heaven help any kid who got in his way.

That was a generous gift my grandparents sent us that year. I'm sure it set them back a bit. But the real gift came from my mom, who loved my brother Ken enough to watch him struggle, to pray for the courage not to interfere, knowing how important it was for Ken to do things on his own.

That was almost fifty years ago. I wish I knew where those doctors are now. They were so ready to tell us all my brother would never do. Obviously, they didn't know the God we knew. What would they say if they could see Ken now at age fifty-five, living independently and holding down a job? They didn't know back then that God had a much bigger plan for my brother, and they didn't know the mama who loved him enough and trusted God enough to give him the best Christmas present he'd ever receive.

Mimi Greenwood Knight

Mimi Greenwood Knight is a freelance writer and artist-in-residence living in Folsom, Louisiana, with her husband, four kids, four dogs, four cats, and one knuckleheaded bird. Her essays and articles on parenting have appeared in *Parents, Working Mother, American Baby, Christian Parenting Today, Campus Life, Today's Christian Woman, At-Home Mother,* on various websites, and in anthologies, including seven Chicken Soup books. See more of her work at www.writergazette.com/mimi greenwoodknight.shtml or contact her at djknight@airmail.net.

"Only 364½ days until Christmas!"

The Freed Bird

Come to the edge. No we'll fall. Come to the edge. No we can't. Come to the edge. No we're afraid. And they came. And he pushed them. And they flew. . . .

Guillaume Apollinaire

The teenage years are ones of blossoming independence for most. However, being a teenager with a disability is often painful. I watch other kids gain automatic freedoms, while I have to fight the whole way, grasping for my independence like a mountain climber heading for the summit with only dental floss as a climbing rope. The people at the top of the mountain, helping me through the sweaty climb, cheer me on as I wallow in this insurmountable challenge. Sometimes, I hate them for cheering. I hate them for making my life feel like the contrast between achievement and failure. This was how I saw Shawn during those early teen years.

Shawn was my school aide, and she cheered me through the fight and threw me a thicker rope. The only thanks she got at times was a grumble and an argument from me, who couldn't accept her help. *I should be able to do this on my own,* I thought. She knew this about me, and never wavered in her support. She never got bored sitting on those inviting rocks, waiting for me to ascend and sit with her to enjoy the view from the vantage of success. I hated feeling like I needed help and, sometimes, seeing her was a painful reminder of my incompetence.

All of this changed one sunny school day when the blossoms were emerging from the long-dormant fruit trees. Shawn and I were walking to the library, and I wished that I never needed her. I wished that she would go away, and hoped that she would take my problems with her. As we approached the door to the library, we both looked down at the crumbling wood flooring, puzzled by the sight of a tiny mound of birdseed that clearly blocked our path. As we walked into the library, I felt distraction flowing from every crevice in the room.

"What's going on?" Shawn asked the distraught librarian.

"A bird flew into the library, and we have been trying to get him to fly out of here all day," explained the exhausted librarian.

Shawn, unshaken, saw us to an empty table so I could finish a very arduous history assignment. The small bird seemed to be lost in the building, mistaking windowpanes for exits, fluttering against the invisible opposition.

The bird dived over our heads in several dry runs to freedom. I ducked, but Shawn's eyes followed the frightened bird. The bird fluttered closer and closer to us each time he dived. Rather than fight the impossible distraction, we watched the bird, hoping that it would soon find the freedom it desperately sought. Finally, the bird was momentarily trapped behind a book that was propped up against the window. Shawn leaped up, brought my history book to the window, and covered the deceptive opening to freedom, trapping the bird. She commanded the librarian, "Get me a towel. I will take care of this." The librarian, scattered by the surprise capture, scurried through her office and finally produced a tattered, old yellow terry-cloth rag. I sat at the table, motionless, suspensefully watching the bird as Shawn delicately scooped it up, wings, beak, and all, in the first attempt. Her calm seeped into the bird, who moments ago was frantically flitting about. She held the bird securely as she walked with sound footsteps out the door, leaving a large footprint in the useless pile of millet and seeds. I ran to the door to witness the event that I so longed for: freedom. She brought the bird to the far corner of the library, pointing its head in the direction of the best course away from captivity. Shawn placed the bird, still wrapped in the yellow rag, on the ground and walked away, leaving the bird to find his way to freedom. The bird crept slowly beyond the rag, and quickly flew off into the wide and beautiful spring sky.

Suddenly, I realized that I was just like this tiny, frightened bird. Shawn was not my captor. She was gently holding me on my way to freedom. I was fighting my disability and my obstacles, but no longer would I fight her as my enemy, but celebrate her husbandry of my life. Soon, I would sit on the top of that mountain, and fly off of it, free.

Dillon York

Dillon York is a sixteen-year-old who has autism and cannot speak. He uses adaptive communication technology to expose his thoughts. Without this technology, he could not write, and would remain silent. He is an advocate for greater understanding of autism and for communication for all. He is working on a poetry anthology and a novel. Please visit his website at www.dillonsbuzz.com.

Who Is Jack Canfield?

Jack Canfield is the cocreator and editor of the Chicken Soup for the Soul series, which *Time* magazine has called "the publishing phenomenon of the decade." The series now has more than 140 titles with over 100 million copies in print in forty-seven languages. Jack is also the coauthor of eight other bestselling books, including *The Success Principle: How to Get from Where You Are to Where You Want to Be, Dare to Win, The Aladdin Factor, You've Got to Read This Book,* and *The Power of Focus: How to Hit Your Business, Personal and Financial Targets with Absolute Certainty.*

Jack has recently developed a telephone coaching program and an online coaching program based on his most recent book, *The Success Principles.* He also offers a seven-day Breakthrough to Success seminar every summer that attracts 400 people from about fifteen countries around the world.

Jack is the CEO of Chicken Soup for the Soul Enterprises and the Canfield Training Group in Santa Barbara, California, and founder of the Foundation for Self-Esteem in Culver City, California. He has conducted intensive personal and professional development seminars on the principles of success for more than a million people in twenty-nine countries around the world. Jack is a dynamic keynote speaker and he has spoken to hundreds of thousands of others at more than 1,000 corporations, universities, professional conferences, and conventions, and has been seen by millions more on national television shows such as *Oprah, Montel, The Today Show, Larry King Live, Fox and Friends, Inside Edition, Hard Copy,* CNN's *Talk Back Live, 20/20, Eye to Eye,* the *NBC Nightly News,* and the *CBS Evening News.* Jack was also a featured teacher on the hit movie *The Secret.*

Jack is the recipient of many awards and honors, including three honorary doctorates and a Guinness World Records Certificate for having seven books from the Chicken Soup for the Soul series appearing on the *New York Times* bestseller list on May 24, 1998.

To write to Jack, or for inquiries about Jack as a speaker, his coaching programs, trainings, or seminars, use the following contact information:

Jack Canfield
The Canfield Companies
P.O. Box 30880 • Santa Barbara, CA 93130
phone: 805-563-2935 • fax: 805-563-2945
E-mail: info4jack@jackcanfield.com
www.jackcanfield.com

Who Is Mark Victor Hansen?

In the area of human potential, no one is more respected than Mark Victor Hansen. For more than thirty years, Mark has focused solely on helping people from all walks of life reshape their personal vision of what's possible. His powerful messages of possibility, opportunity, and action have created powerful change in thousands of organizations and millions of individuals worldwide.

He is a sought-after keynote speaker, bestselling author, and marketing maven. Mark's credentials include a lifetime of entrepreneurial success and an extensive academic background. He is a prolific writer with many bestselling books, such as *The One Minute Millionaire, Cracking the Millionaire Code, How to Make the Rest of Your Life the Best of Your Life, The Power of Focus, The Aladdin Factor,* and *Dare to Win,* in addition to the Chicken Soup for the Soul series. Mark has had a profound influence on many people through his library of audios, videos, and articles in the areas of big thinking, sales achievement, wealth building, publishing success, and personal and professional development.

Mark is the founder of the MEGA Seminar Series. MEGA Book Marketing University and Building Your MEGA Speaking Empire are annual conferences where Mark coaches and teaches new and aspiring authors, speakers, and experts on building lucrative publishing and speaking careers. Other MEGA events include MEGA Info-Marketing and My MEGA Life.

He has appeared on *Oprah,* CNN, and *The Today Show.* He has been quoted in *Time, U.S. News & World Report, USA Today, New York Times,* and *Entrepreneur.* In countless radio interviews, he has assured our planet's people that "you can easily create the life you deserve."

As a philanthropist and humanitarian, Mark works tirelessly for organizations such as Habitat for Humanity, American Red Cross, March of Dimes, Childhelp USA, and many others. He is the recipient of numerous awards that honor his entrepreneurial spirit, philanthropic heart, and business acumen. He is a lifetime member of the Horatio Alger Association of Distinguished Americans, an organization that honored Mark with the prestigious Horatio Alger Award for his extraordinary life achievements.

Mark Victor Hansen is an enthusiastic crusader of what's possible and is driven to make the world a better place.

Mark Victor Hansen & Associates, Inc.
P.O. Box 7665 • Newport Beach, CA 92658
phone: 949-764-2640 • fax: 949-722-6912
website: www.markvictorhansen.com

Who Is Heather McNamara?

Heather joined the Chicken Soup family in 1996. After ten years she left her role as senior editor but has continued to "coauthor" many titles in the Chicken Soup series.

Today Heather lives in a rural outpost of the San Fernando Valley, where she shares her life with her husband, Rick, and daughter, Kyla. They enjoy the panoramic view of the valley, her garden, and two dogs—both adopted strays. This year has been especially exciting with the addition of two nephews and one niece.

Heather felt sheer joy by being part of such a rewarding experience. The website www.soulsupporter.com, was dreamed of one night after reading so many of the stories that were submitted for this book. Heather noted that many of the parents of children with disabilities lamented that their child had never been invited to a birthday party, and so an idea was born to help these families connect both universally or locally.

Heather coauthored *Chicken Soup for the Unsinkable Soul*, *Chicken Soup for Every Mom's Soul*, and *Chicken Soup for the Sister's Soul*, and is currently working on a book for adults with disabilities.

While enjoying her role as full-time mom to Kyla and working on her next Chicken Soup title, she is also a partner in Balance Day Spa in Santa Monica along with her sister Katy.

You can reach Heather at: hmcnamara@verizon.net. Or visit her website at www.soulsupporter.com.

Who Is Karen Simmons?

Karen Simmons is the founder and CEO of Autism Today, a world leader in autism information and resources featuring experts like Dr. Temple Grandin and more. Autism Today also integrates theories and practices that benefit the autism spectrum into other special needs communities, such as Down syndrome, attention deficit hyperactivity disorder, non verbal learning disorder, Tourette syndrome, and fetal alcohol syndrome.

The Autism Today website provides online support to millions of parents, caregivers, therapists, educators, para-professionals, community members, and those living on the autism and special-needs spectrum. Resources include books, CDs, audio seminars, tele-seminars, and webinars, as well as access to worldwide conferences and workshops. It also hosts a membership-based community for blogs, podcasts, and forums.

Karen's book, *The Official Autism 101 Manual*, is winner of the 2007 Independent Publisher Book Gold Medal Award (IPPY) in the health, medicine, and nutrition category. Her other books include *Little Rainman, The Autism Experience, Artism,* and *Surrounded by Miracles.* Her CDs include *Peace of Mind for Autism* and *Autism from the Soul.*

Karen presents internationally to universities, schools, nonprofit organizations, hospitals, and parent groups. She is the founder of the nonprofit KEEN Education Foundation designed to enhance education for children.

Karen's passion for those with autism and special needs comes from her own experience as the parent of six children, two with special needs. She makes her home in Alberta, Canada, with her husband, Jim Sicoli, and their six children, Kimberly, Matthew, Christina, Jonathan, Stephen, and Alexander.

Visit Karen's websites to receive gifts and your free membership package.

Presenting Today Seminars: *Making the World a Better Place*
phone: 780-482-1555 • fax: 780-452-1098
www.karensimmons.com and www.autismtoday.com

Permissions

We would like to acknowledge the following publishers and individuals for permission to reprint the following material. (Note: The stories that were written by Jack Canfield, Mark Victor Hansen, Heather McNamara or Karen Simmons are not included in this listing.)

See Me. Reprinted by permission of Melissa Riggio with Rachel Buchholz/National Geographic Image Collection. ©2006 Melissa Riggio with Rachel Buchholz/National Geographic Image Collection.

Welcome to Holland. Reprinted by permission of Emily Perl Kingsley. ©1987 Emily Perl Kingsley.

In the Game. Reprinted by permission of Stephanie D. Thompson. ©2005 Stephanie D. Thompson.

A Message from John. Reprinted by permission of Joanne Elizabeth Clancy. ©2000 Joanne Elizabeth Clancy.

The Miracle of Jay-Jay. Reprinted by permission of Louise Tucker Jones. ©1985 Louise Tucker Jones.

Out of the Mouths of Babes. Reprinted by permission of Sarah Elizabeth Smigal. ©2006 Sarah Elizabeth Smigal.

Tomorrow. Reprinted by permission of Jill Ann Presson. ©2006 Jill Ann Presson.

No Words. Reprinted by permission of Stacey Marie Flood. ©2000 Stacey Marie Flood.

Seeing Through Josh's Eyes. Reprinted by permission of Deborah Colleen Rose. ©2006 Deborah Colleen Rose.

The Voice of Reason Wears SpongeBob Underpants. Reprinted by permission of Shari Madonna Youngblood. ©2006 Shari Madonna Youngblood.

One Mother to Another. Reprinted by permission of Donna Marie Turenne. ©1999 Donna Marie Turenne.

Reaching Back. Reprinted by permission of Pamela Marie Wilson. ©1991 Pamela Marie Wilson.

A Reason to Celebrate. Reprinted by permission of Janet Lynn Mitchell. ©2002 Janet Lynn Mitchell.

My Finest Teachers. Reprinted by permission of Virginia Katherine Johnson. ©2000 Virginia Katherine Johnson.

Out of the Mouths of Babes. Reprinted by permission of Cheryl Marie Kremer. ©2000 Cheryl Marie Kremer.

The Vacation. Reprinted by permission of Michelle M. Guppy. ©2003 Michelle M. Guppy.

What They Forgot to Mention. Reprinted by permission of Sandra Beth Sotzen. ©2006 Sandra Beth Sotzen.

Is That All? Reprinted by permission of PeggySue Wells. ©2005 PeggySue Wells.

The Little Boy Who Waves. Reprinted by permission of Michelle M. Guppy. ©2004 Michelle M. Guppy.

All She Has. Reprinted by permission of Connie C. Ellison. ©2005 Connie C. Ellison.

One Brief Hour. Reprinted by permission of Suzanne Woods Fisher. ©2006 Suzanne Woods Fisher.

The Gift. Reprinted by permission of Jeffrey J. Cain and the Society of Teachers of Family Medicine, www.stfm.org. ©2004 Jeffrey J. Cain.

I Won't Do It. Reprinted by permission of Nanette Whitman-Holmes. ©2006 Nanette Whitman-Holmes.

Out of the Mouths of Babes. Reprinted by permission of Jimmy Ernest Hinkley, Jr. ©2005 Jimmy Ernest Hinkley, Jr.

McBuns! Reprinted by permission of Trisha Kay Kayden. ©2005 Trisha Kay Kayden.

Challenges. Reprinted by permission of Mary Sue Mooney. ©2006. Mary Sue Mooney.

What's the Truth About Thomas? Reprinted by permission of Jeanne Pallos. ©2007 Jeanne Pallos.

Kids Amaze Me. Reprinted by permission of Chynna Tamara Arlene Mae Laird. ©2006 Chynna Tamara Arlene Mae Laird.

A Whale of a Time. Reprinted by permission of Michelle Marie Kelly Ward. ©2006 Michelle Marie Kelly Ward.

Talking to Strangers. Reprinted by permission of Jennifer Lawler. ©2006 Jennifer Lawler.

On the Inside. Reprinted by permission of Susan Fahncke. ©2003 Susan Fahncke.

Broken-Down Signs. Reprinted by permission of Scott Harrison Newport. ©2006 Scott Harrison Newport.

Broken Shells. Reprinted by permission of Deborah Hickey Jaskot. ©2006 Deborah Hickey Jaskot.

Dancing with Myself. Reprinted by permission of Stephanie D. Thompson. ©2007 Stephanie D. Thompson.

Sunday Morning. Reprinted by permission of Hillary Mims Key. ©2006 Hillary Mims Key.

Speech Therapy. Reprinted by permission of Karen M. Brill. ©1998 Karen M. Brill.

Toss of a Coin. Reprinted by permission of Theodore Kuntz. ©2005 Theodore Kuntz.

Miniature Angels. Reprinted by permission of Susan Fahncke. ©2003 Susan Fahncke.

Milestones. Reprinted by permission of Gina Eileen Morgan. ©2002 Gina Eileen Morgan.

Baby Steps Came in Her Own Time. Reprinted by permission of Beverly Beckham. ©2006 Beverly Beckham.

The Race. Reprinted by permission of Lisa Jean Schlitt. ©2004 Lisa Jean Schlitt.

Perspectives. Reprinted by permission of Richard Joseph Sobsey. ©2001 Richard Joseph Sobsey.

In Life and in Death, Always Faithful. Reprinted by permission of Sarah Rutherford Smiley. ©2005 Sarah Rutherford Smiley.

A *Revelation*. Reprinted by permission of Lisa Logsdon. ©2006 Lisa Logsdon.   331

Bearing Gifts. Reprinted by permission of Meredith G. Knight. ©2007 Meredith G. Knight.

The Freed Bird. Reprinted by permission of Dillon Matthew York and Julia York. ©2006 Dillon Matthew York.

Improving Your Life Every Day

Real people sharing real stories — for nineteen years. Now, Chicken Soup for the Soul has gone beyond the bookstore to become a world leader in life improvement. Through books, movies, DVDs, online resources and other partnerships, we bring hope, courage, inspiration and love to hundreds of millions of people around the world. Chicken Soup for the Soul's writers and readers belong to a one-of-a-kind global community, sharing advice, support, guidance, comfort, and knowledge.

Chicken Soup for the Soul stories have been translated into more than 40 languages and can be found in more than one hundred countries. Every day, millions of people experience a Chicken Soup for the Soul story in a book, magazine, newspaper or online. As we share our life experiences through these stories, we offer hope, comfort and inspiration to one another. The stories travel from person to person, and from country to country, helping to improve lives everywhere.

Share with Us

We all have had Chicken Soup for the Soul moments in our lives. If you would like to share your story or poem with millions of people around the world, go to chickensoup.com and click on "Submit Your Story." You may be able to help another reader, and become a published author at the same time. Some of our past contributors have launched writing and speaking careers from the publication of their stories in our books!

Our submission volume has been increasing steadily — the quality and quantity of your submissions has been fabulous. We only accept story submissions via our website. They are no longer accepted via mail or fax.

To contact us regarding other matters, please send us an e-mail through webmaster@chickensoupforthesoul.com, or fax or write us at:

Chicken Soup for the Soul
P.O. Box 700
Cos Cob, CT 06807-0700
Fax: 203-861-7194

One more note from your friends at Chicken Soup for the Soul: Occasionally, we receive an unsolicited book manuscript from one of our readers, and we would like to respectfully inform you that we do not accept unsolicited manuscripts and we must discard the ones that appear.

Chicken Soup for the Soul.

Our 101 BEST STORIES

On Being a Parent

Inspirational, Humorous, and Heartwarming Stories about Parenthood

Jack Canfield & Mark Victor Hansen
edited by Amy Newmark

Parenting is the hardest and most rewarding job in the world. This upbeat book includes the best selections on parenting from Chicken Soup for the Soul's rich history, with 101 stories carefully selected to appeal to both mothers and fathers. This is a great book for couples to share, whether they are embarking on a new adventure as parents or reflecting on their lifetime experience, with stories written by parents about children and by children about their parents.

978-1-935096-20-7